Peak Bloom

First Edition Printed April 2001

ISBN 0-9642423-8-9

Peak Bloom

by
Marilyn Quinn

Illustrations by
Rebecca Woods Bloom
and Marilyn Quinn

White Willow Publishing
Jackson, Wyoming

To my son Cooper,
who has spent more time beside me
in my gardens than he probably ever
wanted to!

Special thanks to Becky Woods
for the extra time she spent
putting this book together.

Acknowledgments and Credits

Cover photos by Mary Gerty. Cover and book design by Rebecca Woods Bloom. Illustrations on pages 48-51 from *Weeds of Wyoming*, University of Wyoming Extension Bulletin 498, June 1969. Illustrations on pages 2, 6, 176, and 182 copyright free clipart. Illustration on pages 184, 192, 196, 198 and 200 from *Wyoming Trees*, University of Wyoming Extension Service Circular 164R, November 1964. Illustrations on pages 14, 16, 34, 60, 62, 80, 87, 94, 208, 215 and 216 by Marilyn Quinn. All other illustrations by Rebecca Woods Bloom. Every effort was made to attribute quotes and sayings. Unattributed quotes that are identified with release of this publication will be credited in future editions.

Table of Contents

The Basics

The Gardens

Lawn, Trees & Shrubs

A Gardener's Ready Reference

Introduction

B ecause I've written a weekly gardening column for the *Jackson Hole News* for the past 16 years and have been contracted to plant all of the town's public parks each summer, I've come to be known as Jackson Hole's "flower lady." I'm often stopped on the street and asked gardening questions: "Is it safe to plant yet?" "Why don't my tomatoes produce more fruit?" Or, told of successes: "My delphinium is six feet tall!" "I've never had such big pansies—three inches across!"

When I give out advice, I try to be honest. The high, dry climate of Wyoming has limitations that must be accepted to be successful at any type of gardening. It is, however, hard to be realistic with northern and high elevation gardeners. They don't really want the hard facts, only words of encouragement. They want to grow peaches, have roses climbing up the sides of their houses, and pick succulent sweet corn in their backyards. All rather unlikely in Jackson Hole and most corners of the northern Rockies.

But it is certainly possible to grow a wide variety of plants in a mountain climate and to grow them well, in spite of a short, weather-challenged season. I've written this book to share what I've learned gardening in the mountains for the past 25 years. Gardening here is not easy, but I can think of few pursuits as worthwhile.

I can't guarantee success—gardening is still full of mystery and magic even to me—but I hope the information and advice offered in *Peak Bloom* will be of use to mountain and northern gardeners.

Marilyn Quinn

The Basics

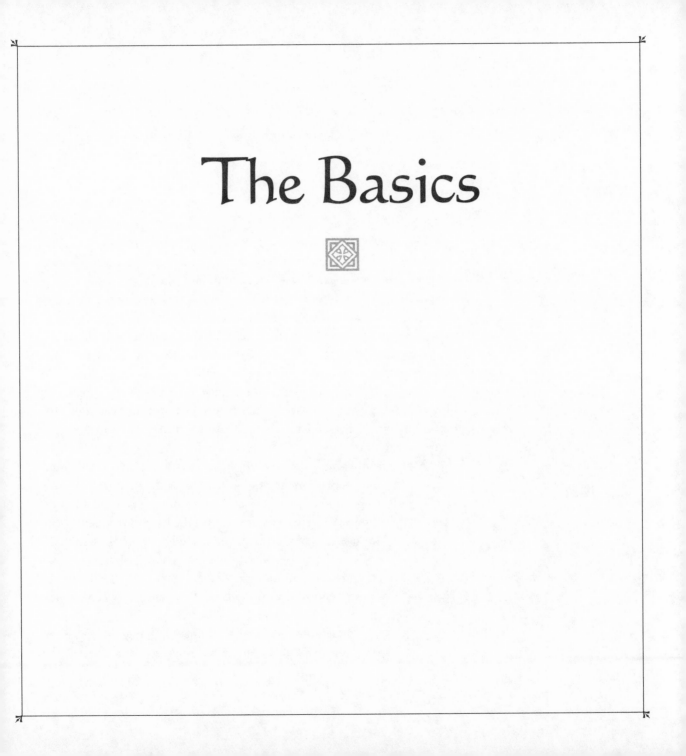

Getting Started

Spring revives the garden one breath at a time. Nowhere does this seem truer than at gardens at altitude. I live up high and am still buried in deep snow when gardeners in the valley enjoy green grass and emerging daffodils. Nothing fills me with more joy than seeing the soft hazy green of fresh aspen leaves creep up the hillsides.

Creep is the correct word: Each 100-foot gain in altitude delays spring's arrival by a day. According to local horticulturists, there is also a formula that evaluates the impact of latitude: one degree difference in latitude south or north equals 300 feet difference in elevation higher or lower. The growing climate at 6,200 feet in northern Wyoming, for example, would be similar to 7,400 feet in central Colorado, four degrees to the south.

March is obviously the start of many wonderful changes. Nature has an uncanny way of making things happen at the right time. Clever gardeners take note and put their observations to good use. Waiting to plant seeds till the leaves are green on the local ski hill or onions when the violets bloom is useful folklore. When these events occur the temperature is warm enough for germination and growth. We gardeners call this common sense; scientists who study the relationship between climate and biologic phenomenon call it phenology.

Right now I'm filled with crazy longings—to go barefoot across new grass, to watch bright flowers sway in the wind and listen to my honeybees buzz on a hot, sunny day. Last week I noticed that the buds on the trees in town are swelling, the blackbirds were singing and the vegetable seeds are on sale at Albertsons. Common sense or phenology, it won't be long now. I'll be ready!

Gardenspeak

Gardening, like many pursuits, has its own jargon. While veteran gardeners wield these terms easily, each new growing season sprouts a new crop of gardeners to whom terms like "dampening off," "soil pH" and "biennial" might be puzzling. Below is an abbreviated 101 course on "Gardenspeak," useful to both novices and old-time gardeners like myself who think we know it all...but can't remember squat.

Annual
> Plants that go through their entire life cycle—growing, blooming, setting seed and dying—within a single season.

Bedding plant
> Plants suitable for planting in masses. Typically, bedding plants are short, colorful annuals such as marigolds, petunias and pansies. Bedding plants are often used in container plantings as well.

Biennials
> Plants that require two years to complete their life cycle. They produce foliage and good roots in their first year, then flower and set seed in their second season.

Compost
> Organic matter that has broken down over time to form a crumbly substance with which soil is enriched and plants are fed.

Deadhead
> Removing old, spent flowers to prevent seed pods from forming and to improve the plant's appearance. A.K.A Jerry Garcia fan.

*Inch by inch
Row by row
Gonna make this garden grow*

—

Pete Seeger

Dormant period
> A time of no apparent growth. Cold, heat or drought can cause dormancy. In mountain climates, plants are dormant in winter.

Direct seeding
> Seed is planted directly into the garden as seed, and not as a transplant.

Ground cover
> Low growing plants that, when grouped together in numbers, spread to fill a given space like a carpet.

Hardening off
> The process of acclimating seedlings that have been started indoors before planting outside. Cut back on water and fertilizer and set them outside for a few hours a day.

Heirloom seeds
> Varieties that have been handed down to generations of gardeners. These varieties have not been grown by breeders with commercial needs in mind.

Hybrid
> Plants that result from cross-breeding varieties. Hybrids do not breed true, so do not save their seed.

Humus
> Decayed plant or animal material in the soil.

Open-pollinated
> Any non-hybrid variety of plant that is pollinated via wind or insects.

Perennial
> Any plant that lives more than two years (some may live for decades). Perennials reappear year after year from their roots. Some plants classified as perennials elsewhere are short lived in mountain climates.

Set out
> Plant a seedling in the garden.

Soil pH

>A measure of the acidity or alkalinity of the soil. Soils are clas-
sified as acidic if their pH is below 7 or alkaline if above 7. A
pH of 7 is neutral.

Thin

>Pull up or pinch out young plants so remaining plants have room
to grow and mature.

Topdressing

>Applying fertilizer, compost, manure or other nourishment to
soil without digging or mixing it in.

Latin Names

In the past people using long scientific names for plants in their
gardens have put me off. They sounded boring and pretentious—and
reasoning "a rose by any other name would smell as sweet"—I didn't
think it much mattered.

But recently, I've realized correct plant names can be useful as well
as important. Names enable us to order unusual plants from a catalogue, describe a plant form to an interested friend, and look up information and advice in books. Although I doubt I'll learn all the Latin
binomials, many of the names have sunk in by a mysterious sort of os-
mosis that allows me to decipher formerly foreign words.

Latin names have two parts. The first word indicates genus, the
group to which the plant belongs. The second identifies the species and
is usually descriptive, telling us something about the plant. If you want a
plant with yellow flowers or leaves, watch for species names that include *aureua*, (golden yellow), *luteus* (yellow), or *sulphureus* (sulfur colored yellow).

Macculataus means spotted, *variegatus* is variegated and *pubescans*
means covered with soft hairs. A plant that grows low or creeps has
repens in its name, while tall back-of-the-bed border plants are *giganteus*.

*A perennial
is a plant
that would
have come
back next
year
if it had
survived.*

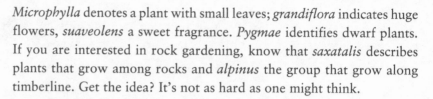

Tip

Buy only good quality, weather resistant hoses. They cost more but last longer and don't kink and leak like their cheaper counterparts.

Microphylla denotes a plant with small leaves; *grandiflora* indicates huge flowers, *suaveolens* a sweet fragrance. *Pygmae* identifies dwarf plants. If you are interested in rock gardening, know that *saxatalis* describes plants that grow among rocks and *alpinus* the group that grow along timberline. Get the idea? It's not as hard as one might think.

Below is a list of other common Latin words that will help you identify plants by color and other characteristics:

Color
Alba: white
Caerula: blue flowers
Nigra: dark
Purpurea: purple
Roseas: rose-colored, pink
Ruber: red
Viridis: green
Argenteus: silver

Characteristics
Controta: contorted
Edulis: edible
Montana: of the mountains
Odorata: scented flowers
Scandens: climbing
Sempervirens: evergreen
Stricta: upright
Sylvestris: of the woods—a clue that the plant may be good in shade.

All this is not to say you shouldn't call plants by their common names. Love lies bleeding, baby's breath, cupids dart and hen and chicks are descriptive as well as delightful folk names. Use names to communicate clearly and leave it at that. Learning the correct name does not make you a gardener. You must know the plants, and that takes years of acquaintance.

Tools of the Trade

Most veteran gardeners agree there are only half a dozen tools that are essential. But which ones are they? Listed below are my picks; I imagine many other gardeners also find these tools the most useful.

Trowel

It is trite but true: You get what you pay for, especially when it comes to these hand tools. Trowels are meant to dig holes—over and over and over again. Invest in a high quality trowel that is a single piece of forged stainless steel with a wooden handle. With proper care, it will last a lifetime.

Garden fork

Next to a trowel, a stout-pronged garden (or manure) fork is the most useful tool in my possession. Garden forks can be used to loosen soil, break clods, turn and mix compost, dig potatoes, divide large clumps of perennial flowers, and perform countless other tasks. Don't leave home without one.

Garden rake

Garden rakes push loose dirt around. Relatively heavy, these steel, short-toothed, flat-headed rakes resemble a gap-toothed comb. (Leaf rakes are fan shaped and lightweight). I use mine to level soil, especially before planting.

Shovel

The flat cutting edge is sometimes useful for slicing but mostly these tools are for plain old digging. Look for a sharp-edged rounded point on the cutting edge when you buy.

Wheelbarrow

A wheelbarrow is your garden U-haul, and most likely your costliest investment. Once you get one you'll find many uses for this multipurpose garden tool, including lugging compost, handling weeds and hauling mulch.

Hoses

For years I bought cheap, poor quality hoses. Their kinky, joint spraying, sun-cracking tendencies aggravated me so much I finally spent the money on a high quality hose. Thicker and better made, the difference amazed me. Save yourself garden headaches and buy a good hose.

It is curious, pathetic almost, how deeply seated in the human heart is the liking for gardens and gardening.

Alexander Smith 1863

Tip

It is ridiculously easy to misplace garden tools as you work. (I, myself, am a master at this I shudder to think of the lost hours spent searching for a pair of clippers.) Buy tools with bright colored handles or paint a red or orange stripe on them so you can easily spot them if you set them down.

Although I could garden without them, I also use a pair of pruning shears (particularly useful in my flower garden) and a handy galvanized bucket. There are dozens of other garden aids and implements on the market today, but I rarely succumb to buying them. The tools listed above are enough to get started and if you buy wisely, they will endure and even improve with age. I have had some of my tools for many years. They've become faithful companions and I'm as loyal to them as one can be to inanimate objects. I love their feel, utility and the way they look, and can't imagine replacing them with a new-fangled gadget.

Selecting a Site

Gardening successfully in mountain and northern climates is not easy. The right plants must be chosen and planted in the right places for any measure of success. Sun and shade requirements, the location of a potential garden site in relation to your home, soil, and the effects of snow should all be considered.

Light requirements

Light has a big effect on the appearance and health of plants. In gardening books, seed catalogues and even on the tags stuck into nursery pots, light is always discussed. A plant may need shade, partial shade or full sun. So what do these terms mean?

"Full sun" means a minimum of six hours of direct sun each day, between 9 a.m. and 4 p.m. when the sun is strongest. Morning and late afternoon the sun is low on the horizon. The light is filtered and diffused through more of the atmosphere, making it relatively weak.

"Deep shade" is an area where sunlight is blocked. Beneath a large spruce tree or the overhang on the north side of the house are examples. Too much shade creates real problems for plantings at higher altitudes because of relatively cold climates.

"Partial shade" means just what it says: full sun for part of the day and shade for part of the day. Plantings in partial shade may be affected by reflected light from adjacent buildings. Walls reflect sunlight and also store heat, so plants may grow really well next to them.

"Dappled" or "filtered shade" is a mix of sun and shade that occurs under aspens or through an overhead lattice. Most plants that grow well in full sun could also be grown in this situation. You may want to try some shade plants in this light. They'll probably benefit from the extra warmth that sunlight provides.

If your plant's branches are elongated with few flowers, it may need more light. Plants that receive too much light (usually not a problem) may look stunted with smallish, bleached leaves. If a plant is receiving light from just one side, it will stretch towards that side.

Variations imposed by geographical location are rarely taken into account when plants and their light needs are discussed. Latitude and the attendant sun's angle, elevation, and the amount of cloud cover can affect how much light a plant gets. In the southern states, the summer sun is stronger than in the northern states. Plants that do well in full sun in northern states may require some shade in the South.

Before you decide which plants to purchase, take notes on how much light various areas of your yard receive. Talk to your gardening neighbors and find out what has worked for them. It can make a big difference.

While the "right" place for planting flowers varies with the species, growing vegetables is a different story. They need sun, period. I can't overemphasize the need for a sunny spot in a cold climate. Although root crops and leafy vegetables may get by on six, eight hours of direct sun a day is the minimum needed by most vegetables for optimum growth.

Sun requirements mean that vegetable gardens should be situated where trees, shrubs and buildings don't block part of the day's sun. Light is critical: it has to have priority when you choose a site for your garden. A gentle slope to the south is ideal. The soil warms up faster in the

All gardeners know better than other gardeners

Chinese proverb

9

Tip

Plan to run vegetable rows north to south to avoid having your vegetables shade each other. Taller plants and trellis grown crops such as peas should be planted on northern and western sides of the plot.

spring and cold air will move downhill and settle below the garden, not in it.

Proximity to your residence

Siting your garden close to your residence increases the chances you'll give it the time and attention it requires to thrive. (The exception, of course, is community gardens that offer plots for those who lack space at home). Don't plan on growing a vegetable garden in the back 40 acres, or you'll need a mighty long hose: gardens in much of the Rockies require supplemental watering. Consider as well how hard it could be to haul compost, manure or mulch to a distant garden.

When you choose a spot for a garden, try to find an area graced with a degree of good soil. If everything else tells you that this is the spot your garden should be in—and the soil is horrible—put it there anyway. Soil can be improved over time. You'll have to work and work and work to get the ground in the best condition for growing good flowers and vegetables, but it can be done.

Snow considerations

Few of us take snow into consideration when we plant. Who thinks of winter ice and snow when they are merrily digging away on a sunny day in June? But heavy snow and snow removal can cause damage.

Think back to winters past. The perennial flowers you planted under the wide overhang became winter killed. The juniper bushes around the house get crushed each year when the ice and snow slide off the roof. The snowplow battered the beautiful trees and shrubs bordering your driveway.

A little planning goes a long way to remedy these seasonal problems. Make notes during the winter. Write down what the problems in your landscaping might be and what might correct them.

Common cold climate landscape considerations include:

Overhangs

If your winter brings little snow and very cold temperatures, perennial flowers and bushes planted under overhangs will do poorly. They miss most of the snow and consequent insulation and moisture. If you have such a troublesome area, consider shoveling snow into it occasionally during the winter, or re-plant it with a hardy ground cover that can withstand difficult conditions.

Sliding snow

If your woody foundation plantings suffer from hundreds of pounds of snow sliding off the roof on top of them, move them next spring. Note the width of the piles of fallen snow this winter. Plant bushes and shrubs far enough away from the house to be out of the way of snowslides. Similarly, don't plant in "dump zones" below a shoveled upper story deck.

Snowplow damage

Expensive trees and bushes are often damaged by plows if they are planted too close to a driveway or road. Make life easier for the snowplow driver and yourself by leaving an open area where the snow can be piled up. Or, utilize a snowblower instead of a plow to gently disperse the snow.

Roadway/walkway salt

Although roads aren't salted where I live, accumulated salt will damage plants and bushes. Use kitty litter or sand on your walk-ways to limit damage.

It may be a lot to ask: a spot with lots of sun, with rich well-drained soil shielded from the elements, that is also close to the house and a water faucet. Don't be discouraged if you lack the ideal spot. Few gardeners have it. Do the best you can with what you've got and plan a garden to fit your needs. Some of the most inspiring flower and vegetable gardens I've seen have not been in optimum places.

Nothing will ever be attempted if all possible objections must be first overcome.

Samuel Johnson

11

Tip

Old wives' tale are superstition mingled with good sense. One recommends sowing and transplanting seed only with a waxing, never a waning, moon. Scientifically, it has been proven that lunar rhythm effects growth. We are also advised not to sow naked. Good advice. Seed shouldn't be sown when soil is cold. We are less likely to plant at these times if we must be in the buff when we do it.

Landscape Architects

If you are building a new house or have recently moved into a house with a yard that needs improvement, consider hiring a landscape architect. Landscape architects have studied design and usually have a good grasp of what plants grow in the area they practice. To be licensed they must possess a college degree in the subject and pass required tests. A "landscape designer" may have artistic ability but does not possess these credentials.

A landscape architect studies your property to develop a master plan. People are often dissatisfied with their landscape because their gardens and yard have been placed piecemeal without considering the property in its entirety. Harmony stems from repetition of line, shape, color and texture. This is what makes your property beautiful and what a landscape architect has to offer. "Integrated whole" are words I often hear when talking to landscape architects: no misplaced flowerbeds, no hodgepodge bushes and shrubs added on impulse.

A landscape architect plans the design but may not execute the digging and planting: You are paying for expertise, not elbow grease. These chores as well as installation of irrigation systems and rock and concrete work, are often contracted out under the architect's supervision. Property owners can also undertake them by following the master plan blueprints.

When selecting a landscape architect, ask local garden centers and friends for recommendations. Next, interview your candidate and get to know his or her work. Don't just look at project plans; visit the sites themselves. It is acceptable to request client references and call them to see if the work was performed professionally, on time and on budget.

Try to find a professional whose style is compatible with yours. Some take a natural approach. Others may like bridges, walls and walkways. Your architect should be respectful of what you want and like, while helping you define your needs. Finally, make sure the person you hire will give your project the attention it deserves. If he or she is already working on a large, time-consuming project, yours may not be a high priority if it is small and low budget.

The services of a landscape architect aren't cheap. Think of the cost as a long-term investment. After all, you will be living with the results for a long time. If the master plan is too pricey for your modest budget, the work can be done in phases over several seasons: the sprinkler system and sod the first year, trees the next, and the perennial flower beds after that. A good plan will always be there to follow.

Garden Design

Beautiful gardens don't grow by accident: they are designed. You will be disappointed if your flowerbed is done blooming in July, or the tulips hide the crocuses. When mapping out your garden, pay attention to the length and time of blooming season, the size of plants in relation to each other, and space limitations. It is helpful to sketch your proposed flower and vegetable gardens on a piece of graph paper so you can visualize heights, color and how many plants/seeds you'll need.

Pencil gardening doesn't stop there. Like most things in life, gardens evolve. Hand in hand with the urge to create a garden comes the urge to keep track of it in writing; to note what you do in your garden, when you do it and what happens—a lasting record of what worked and what didn't each season. This is especially valuable when gardening in the less-forgiving Rockies. When was the first frost? When was the last? When did I plant those daisies that did so well? My memory hasn't told the truth in years. A written record saves me money and grief.

Few of us write down everything from soil temperature to the number of potatoes we raised, but once started garden journaling becomes a habit difficult to break. If you received a pretty journal as a present and are not intimidated by actually taking it outside and thumbing through

For me, gardens are made to nap in.

Bennett Cerif

13

it with dirty hands, then by all means use it. I've found my best garden journals are inexpensive, wide-ruled spiral bound composition notebooks purchased at the grocery store. They soon become messy and mud-streaked and somewhat indispensable.

Write when you have time and keep your records simple. Apart from a constant litany about the weather, tracking data such as planting times, first harvests, first flowers, fertilizers and the flavor and quality of crops is helpful. Almost anything may be useful information the following season. I know a couple who faithfully recorded their arguments over varieties one liked and the other hated. (Hopefully, this cut future spats in the bud. So to speak.) The notes I most often refer to are:

Bloom Time

Since I design and maintain gardens for part-time residents in Jackson Hole, my most important record is the bloom time of many flower varieties. I don't want flowers under my care to be finished when my clients arrive for a summertime vacation! Bloom times in mountain and northern climates seldom follow the norm. The spring flowers of other regions tend to be summer flowers here. My notes remind me of the cool summer we had in 1995, when the nights remained chilly and Fourth of July was celebrated between snow flurries. My late blooming asters and coneflowers were so slow that they had just begun to show color when the first frost slammed them. I won't take a chance and plant them in prominent places again.

Effective Combinations

My jottings help me remember what combinations were effective and harmonious, and what fell flat. Reading a July 1998 entry, for example, I recalled that although the ladies mantle was gorgeous with its masses of foamy, chartreuse flowers, it overwhelmed the sweet William planted behind it.

Wildlife Signals

It is helpful to note wildlife behavior and signals. I know by reading my journal that our 6,800-foot elevation home won't hear the cheery call of the olive-sided flycatcher until the weather warms enough for their main food, insects, to be out. When insects arrive, sustained warm weather is not far behind.

Ordering Guides

Records are useful as ordering guides. Tuck or tape copies of past orders in your notebooks and note the planting outcome so you won't make the same mistakes over and over. It is ridiculously easy to order too much or too little or the wrong varieties. As I said before—I think—memory is an unreliable informant. It is better to have a record.

If you faithfully record how your garden grew over one full season, you'll make two discoveries: Keeping it was a bother. And it produced one of the most helpful garden aids you'll ever have.

Garden Paths

A few years ago I was hired to care for a large flower garden. I quickly realized it needed a pathway winding through it: tiptoeing through the tulips without wet feet required something to walk upon.

A walkway does many things. It is, of course, functional. It can get you from here to there, keep your shoes from caking with mud, and provide firm footing without fear of compacting the soil or crushing something when it is time to divide or trim. While a garden path's primary function should be access, it can definitely rise above the level of utilitarian use. A path can and should be downright pretty, adding organization and inspiration to a planted area.

Summer gardens bloom glorious in winter dreams

Garden paths can be made of crushed gravel or bark. Though economical, neither is my favorite choice because they must be contained and occasionally replenished. I prefer flat stones, concrete pavers or bricks: durable materials that offer more permanence and withstand heavy traffic. Make your path wide enough to navigate easily (never less than two feet across), more spacious if you plan to let foliage spill over the walkway.

I chose flagstones from a local rock company for the flower garden pathway I installed, selecting the largest pieces I could easily handle; bigger pieces seem to amplify both color and texture. After laying the stones on top of the ground, I planted low-growing thyme around them. I recommend planting creeping, ground-hugging vegetation between and around the stones. The foliage usually appreciates the quick drainage and radiant heat, and easily fills out and softens bare walkway space. It also helps stabilize the path by keeping the stones in place. Low-growing thyme is an excellent walkway choice. Durable and fragrant, it can withstand an accidental footstep. Other plants that quickly fill up space include Corsican mint, creeping veronica, some of the saxifrages and ajuga, a shade loving creeper. Short mat plants also add interest to pathways.

Plan the course of your path carefully. A garden may need more than a single path, but too many spells chaos, just as letting people take their course without direction can do. And although a curving path usually looks enticing, forcing an arc can feel pointless or fussy. If a straight path is what you need, then by all means, follow the straight and narrow.

A well placed garden path should make your work more efficient and give you the opportunity to "take time to smell the roses."

Stepping Stones

Some of the most appealing pathways are made from individual stepping stones. Stepping stones may be purchased at lumberyards, but designing your own is a gratifying project the whole family can do. My son Cooper and I made concrete stones last season because I sorely needed a good pathway to my vegetable garden, and I liked the idea of making my own. As we experimented we became quite imaginative, utilizing nature items we had gathered on vacations and mountain hikes.

Except for bagged fast-drying concrete mix, most of the materials you'll need can be found around the house. Start by gathering together the necessary supplies: a plastic dishpan or bucket for mixing, a trowel, a bag of masonry mix, decorations and forms. I use whatever is handy. Old aluminum lasagna pans, plastic pans from the second hand store greased with Vaseline, or corrugated cardboard boxes dusted with sand are all options. A strip of lath bent in a circle could be set right in the garden so that the form, like a cookie cutter, doesn't need a solid bottom. Your form should be a minimum of two inches thick to make the stepping stone deep enough to bear weight without cracking. Different forms can be used if care is taken to keep the stones the same depth for an even pathway. Stones are typically 12-18" wide.

Make your stones on a dry day when the temperature is between 60-70 degrees Fahrenheit. Cooler temperatures slow drying; hot air speeds it up and may cause cracking. Mix the concrete to the consistency of cookie dough, firm but not too runny. Scoop the mix into waiting forms, then trowel smooth and level. If you want to decorate your stones, now is the time to press distinctively shaped leaves and flowers (upside down daisies work well) into the mix. Remove the foliage and blossoms when the concrete begins to set up, usually two to three hours. Wash your tools as soon as you finish so concrete doesn't harden on them.

We embedded a border of seashells, old marbles, colored sea glass

What a man needs in gardening is a cast iron back, with a hinge in it.

Charles Warner

17

and pieces of petrified wood. Pretty shards of broken pottery, stained glass and other materials durable enough to withstand the weather and occasional footstep could also be used. Impressions should be deep enough to see, but shallow enough so water collected during a rain will dry quickly. Deep impressions foster chipping and cracking, especially in cold winter climates.

When the concrete has completely set, carefully remove your form and place your stone.

I delight in seeing one-of-a-kind stepping stones beneath my feet. I think of them as very personal works of art...my gallery in the grass waiting to be discovered.

Garden Art

Gardening is by definition an artful pursuit. Gardeners delight in decorating the great outdoors—not only with beautiful plants, but also with interesting man-made objects that go beyond garden design into the realm of art.

Some objects may once have been useful, like the leaky canoe being used as a petunia planter in Pinedale, Wyoming, or the weary old wheelbarrow filled with vibrant nasturtiums on my Midwest friends' deck. Other "art" placed in the landscape has no use other than to make us giggle. We've all seen wooden cutouts of a gardener's behind and flocks of pink plastic flamingoes pecking at the marigolds. I've spied a six-foot cement mouse living in Boise, Idaho. A huge concrete pigeon cooing among the canna lilies in Alabama. A yellow brick road through the melon patch that made me long for ruby slippers.

While some gardeners inexplicably love tacky yard ornaments loitering in front of their house (you know who you are), I lust after the pricey objects living on the glossy pages of mail order catalogues. Yes indeed, if I had a spot for a Grecian urn, a beautiful sundial, teak benches or elegant statuary and fountains, I might be tempted to take out a bank loan and buy them. I would love to have a well-placed gargoyle protect my garden from gremlins, or trendy granite stones engraved with inspirational words like "dream" or "imagine" to place in strategic places throughout the garden. My unmoved husband "dreams" and "imagines" paying for college tuition.

There has recently been a revival of Victorian gazing globes, truly my favorite garden art. These great glass globes with mirror coatings are placed on pedestals to reflect the garden and sky in their shimmering surface. I first came across gazing globes in a spectacular rose garden in Canada and have never forgotten their beauty. When an Internet gardener recounted her success creating an inexpensive gazing globe by spray painting a bowling ball with metallic paint, thrift shops across the country were relieved of this particular sporting item. Apparently, gazing globes are on other's wish lists, too.

Art and gardening both offer people a creative outlet in their lives. Gardening need not be restricted to straight rows of carrots and marigolds. And just about anything goes in the world of art. So let your imagination flow. There is room for art in everyone's yard.

A Gardener's Ode to Shel Silverstein

I'm lying here holding the grass in its place
Pressing a leaf with the side of my face
Tasting the berries to see if they're sweet
Counting the toes on a centipede's feet
Memorizing the shape of a cloud
Warning the robin to not chirp so loud
Shooing the butterflies off the tomatoes
Scanning the sky for pesky tornadoes
Supervising the work of the ants
Thinking of pruning the cantaloupe plants
Timing the sun to see when it sets
Talking to ladybugs I've adopted as pets
I've planted a garden, and now
I can't shirk...
But nobody told me it would be this
much work!

Tip

Eggshells are a source of calcium for plants. Dry the shells well in the microwave and crush them as fine as possible to add to the soil or planter mix.

The Soil

Before all else in gardening is the soil. I've heard farmers say they can taste the difference between sour (acid) or sweet (alkaline) soil. Rather than eat dirt, I send in soil samples to be tested—for a small fee—to my county extension office if I'm starting a new garden. Home test kits are available for people who enjoy doing things themselves.

Whether you taste it or test it, gardeners should be concerned with the acidity or alkalinity of soil as measured on the pH scale. The 'pH' measures the concentration of hydrogen ions in a soil or water solution. Ions are formed when water molecules and certain chemical compounds break apart. If the number of hydrogen and hydroxyl ions is the same, the soil is neutral. The pH scale runs from 0 to 14. At pH 7, soil is neutral. Below 7, it becomes increasingly acidic; above 7, it becomes alkaline.

What does all this technical stuff mean to gardeners? And why do we even need to know it? If your soil is too acidic or too alkaline plants are unable to fully absorb nutrients from the soil, even if you add fertilizer. Vegetables and most flowers grow best in neutral soil with a pH of 6.5-7. Neutral soil also offers the most favorable environment for microorganisms vital to soil fertility. Bacteria, fungi, mites, ants, millipedes and earthworms release nitrogen as they break down organic matter, transforming it into enriching humus.

Alas, marvelous, neutral dirt is often scarce at high altitudes. To come close to an ideal soil you have to work hard to make up the deficits. Arid western soils tend to be alkaline, composed of eroded rock with very little humus. Adding lots of manure, compost and peat moss—really, any organic matter—reduces alkalinity. Dig these amendments deeply into your garden plot annually to help neutralize your soil. If your soil pH test reveals extremely alkaline soil, you may need to add sulfur as well.

Adding dolomitic limestone neutralizes acidic soil. Talk to your extension office representative about appropriate amounts.

Clay Soil

At least once each spring I take on a job that involves digging a new flower or vegetable bed in soil the consistency of library paste. Digging creates gooey clods and walking on it feels like you have balled-up socks inside your shoes. The only footwear that doesn't die under the onslaught is rubber boots that can be cleaned off with a hose.

This darned stuff is, of course, clay.

Why is clay so obstinate? The finely ground, microscopic particles that make up clay stick together. Air cannot freely circulate amongst the goo, and the compacted particles inhibit drainage: There is just no place for the water to go. The result is a solid and impervious, lumpy and hard-to-manage soil. Roots don't have a chance.

Enter our hero: Compost (or any organic amendment incorporated into the soil). The more organic material we work into clay, the easier our plants can send out roots to feed. The richer soil invites more earthworms, which help aerate the soil, and allows water to drain by breaking up the mass of clay particles.

If clay is particularly prevalent, consider adding sand as well. Fine sand is usually available at local cement companies. Or, buy play sand bagged at nurseries and lumberyards for kid's sandboxes. Be sure to ask before you buy if the sand contains salt. Salt makes sand unsuitable for horticultural use.

You can bury a lot of troubles, digging in the dirt.

Tip

If your compost heap is located at a spot that is difficult to reach when the snow gets deep, save your kitchen scraps in garbage cans with lids. The compost will stay frozen all winter. Add it to your pile in the spring.

Clay soil is called "strong land" by farmers and others who till the ground. Though usually rich in potential, this stubborn soil involves extra labor and elbow grease to turn it into workable and fertile loam.

Organic Matter

Organic matter is anything that was once alive: manure, peat moss, eggshells, grass clippings, straw, kitchen scraps. To gardeners, it's magic stuff. Organic matter balances soil nutrients and improves the texture of all soil types. It opens heavy soils, making them more easily workable, and binds sandy soil, improving its water retention. And, it's readily available. Compost, peat, manure and manure tea are all effective organic amendments.

Compost

The best gardeners I know have one thing in common: A compost heap. Here they transform grass clippings, leaves and yesterday's leftover salad into a nutrient rich, no cost soil amendment. Dedicated composters get excited when someone offers to bring them a bag of melon rinds, burnt toast, eggshells or coffee grounds.

They also know all trash is not future compost. Although there are many items that can be tossed on the heap, some ingredients should not be added. These include:

➔ Meat scraps, bones or stale bologna sandwiches. This stuff will decompose, but in the meantime you'll have every stray dog (or bear or skunk or porcupine) in the neighborhood dropping by for a visit.

➔ Cat feces: a big no-no. It presents odor and disease problems.

➔ Sawdust from treated wood. Chemicals used in treatment processes might get into your food chain.

22

- → Garden thugs such as mint and dandelions, or weeds gone to seed. You don't want to cultivate the very plants you are trying to get rid of.

- → Wood chips and pine cones. These take an inordinately long time to break down.

- → Overly bulky materials, such as whole sunflower heads and broccoli stalks. Chop them into small pieces before you toss them in.

- → Polyester, plastics and other synthetics. They don't rot.

- → Barbecue briquettes and wood ash. The first have a high amount of sulfur; the second increases soil alkalinity.

- → Maraschino cherries. These bright red, preserved cherries were still recognizable and intact after three years in a friend's heap. No kidding.

If you don't have a compost pile, get one started. You'll have a place to dump pea pods, radish tops and weeds as you work. And if you set up a compost bin now, you'll have a place to put all those leaves you rake up in the fall.

You may never be one of those unique individuals who become joyful about their compost, but I'll bet that, like me, you'll feel virtuous about all the great recycling you do.

Peat

Peat is organic matter that has naturally accumulated over time, slowly decomposing under moist, wet conditions. Highly valued as an organic soil amendment, it lightens and aerates clay soils and helps sandy

Compost. A rind is a terrible thing to waste.

23

Tip

Earthworms are a sign of healthy soil. Fish with dough balls.

—

soils retain water. I use this wonderful resource in all my gardens.

Peat moss is widely available and readily portable in compressed bales. Make your price comparisons by weight rather than volume: a bale of peat can yield up to twice its volume when broken loose.

Most peat moss bales sold in the US are shipped from Canada, where peat is harvested from bogs. Be aware that what took centuries to form can be harvested in hours. I can't help but feel guilty every time I use a bale. As with so many things today, we're aware of the environmental cost but use the product anyway. I make sure I don't waste it and console myself knowing beautiful plants, trees and bushes are given back to Mother Nature.

Manure

There is no soil amendment better than manure. It dramatically improves the tilth of soil by adding all-important humus, something no chemical fertilizer can do. It contains plant nutrients that are released both immediately and throughout the growing season. It creates a healthy environment for earthworms, which in turn help improve soil by keeping it loose and aerated. It stimulates microbial life.

Bottom line: Nothing matches manure. Wheelbarrows full of this ugly brown stuff are one of the main standbys in my gardens. Although I'll take whatever I can get—cow, chicken, horse or rabbit—it is important to note that only the excreta of herbivorous animals should be added to the garden. Cat, dog and other pet feces may harbor disease.

Manure that is several months old and partially broken down works best. Fresh manure can be full of weed seeds, which pass intact through an animal's digestive system. Fresh manure's relatively high concentration of nitrogen can also "burn" seedlings and create deformities in some vegetables. Carrots, for example, respond to fresh manure by forking or growing into weird shapes.

Although many ranchers and cowboys willingly give away horse and cow manure, most gardeners prefer purchasing bagged manure at local garden centers. Bagged manure is inexpensive—usually less than $2 a bag—and has typically been heated to kill weed seeds. Unless you own a truck or need huge amounts of manure, it is generally more convenient to purchase manure than haul it.

Aged manure can be applied anytime, even at planting. I routinely spread a half-inch layer on my annual flowerbeds and vegetable gardens each September so it is ready to be dug in when spring arrives. For perennial flowers, asparagus and trees and shrubs, manure can be topdressed or broadcast around the base of the plants.

Manure Tea

Manure tea is liquid fertilizer made by steeping manure in water. It attained a certain status when it was featured in Martha Stewart's popular *Living* magazine.

It is hard for me to imagine Martha herself really making this stuff—scooping up barnyard droppings and so forth—but she is an excellent gardener. Maybe she really does make her own smelly vat, who knows? The article *did* offer a recipe for her concoction.

I'm a bit less exacting; call me silly, but I'm not inclined to measure poop. I put a shovel full of manure in a coarse bag and let it stand for a few days in a big bucket or garbage can filled with water. The water browns as millions of tiny particles break away from the masses and become suspended in the liquid. Ideal tea is colored a weak brown.

Wood Ash

Don't add wood ash to your garden as a soil amendment.

Western soil tends to be alkaline, with a pH on the high side. Wood ash increases soil alkalinity, intensifying the pH imbalance.

If you've already thrown wood ash on your garden, don't panic: It takes pounds of wood ash to markedly effect the soil. Throw your wood ash in the trash, and save your eggshells and coffee grounds instead. Eggshells supply calcium and small amounts of nitrogen and phosphorus, and some gardeners swear that crushed eggshells strewn around the base of prized plants help keep slugs away. Coffee grounds contain nitrogen and a trace of phosphorus and potash. I sprinkle mine around the garden like mulch, eventually working them into the soil as I weed and dig.

Tip

Cardboard boxes are good for mulch. Cut them flat and water until soaked. Cover with a 3-4 inch layer of organic matter such as shredded leaves, straw or grass clippings. The top layer prevents the cardboard from blowing away.

Darker brews should be diluted with more water.

Manure tea is not a robust fertilizer, as there is only a small amount of nitrogen in it. I consider it more of a tonic. The tea carries soluble phosphorus that stimulates roots. Since liquids penetrate the soil and come in contact with roots rapidly, they are one of the easiest foods for plants to absorb. Generously ladle it out to give a boost to your plants and flowers.

Although I have a gardening friend who keeps a barrel of manure tea brewing all season (occasionally recharging it with a new batch of manure), Martha suggests one should not store the tea for lengthy periods because it will "ferment and smell objectionable."

Right on, Martha.

Fertilizer

If the soil test shows that the soil is deficient in nutrients, add synthetic fertilizers for a quick fix.

When I looked into purchasing good fertilizer to give my plants a boost, I found many brands on the market—so many that the average gardeners might be confused about what is best for their plants.

There are two general types of fertilizer available, organic fertilizers such as bone and blood meal, and inorganic, or chemical, fertilizers. Organic fertilizer is material derived from plants, animals and minerals that contains elements essential for plant growth. It can be dried, ground, chopped or processed in some other manner, but no chemicals or synthetic materials have been added.

Far more prevalent are inorganic, chemical fertilizers. While there are no requirements for nutrient analysis of natural fertilizers, by law every bag of synthetic fertilizer must carry a list of its ingredients. The numbers on the labels of chemical fertilizer bags, such as 10-10-10, or 19-7-9, represent the percentage by weight of the most important plant nutrients contained in the fertilizer: nitrogen (N), phosphorus (P) and potassium (K). If you are like me and forget whether the "K" stands for potassium or phosphorus, remember that fertilizer ingredients are always listed in alphabetical order.

A soil test will indicate what nutrients you need to add to your soil. While all three elements are necessary for good plant growth, nitrogen is the most important. Because it is rapidly leached away, it is also the element most likely to be in short supply in mountain soil. Plants with a steady supply of nitrogen are sturdy and sport rich, dark green foliage. Yellow-green, stunted plants indicate nitrogen is lacking.

Potassium is essential for developing strong stems and roots, making it a needed component for growing robust vegetables. Curled leaves and poorly developed root systems are signs of a potassium deficiency. Beets, for example, will be skinny and ripen unevenly. Potassium also intensifies the color of flowers. If new blooms appear faded, it could be a clue your soil lacks adequate amounts of this element.

Phosphorus contributes to early plant growth, strong roots and disease resistance. In vegetable plants a deficiency shows up as reddish purple discoloration of the stems, leaf veins and leaves. Lacking sufficient phosphorus, the plants won't mature and develop seeds and fruit.

A general-purpose fertilizer, with fairly even numbers, is usually a good bet. I occasionally buy name brands specifically formulated for trees, vegetable or flower gardens, with the appropriate number a bit higher.

If you choose a controlled release fertilizer (Osmocote® is currently popular), note that pellets must contact moist soil to diffuse the nutrients through the pellet's resin coatings. Controlled release fertilizers continuously feed plants for the number of months indicated on the bag when the soil temperature reaches 70 degrees. This means that in colder climates, time-release fertilizer lasts twice as long as it would in, say, the southern Utah desert.

Finally, be aware that too much fertilizer does more harm than good. Excess nitrogen causes carrots to fork, beets to develop huge leaves but

The best fertilizer is the gardener's footsteps

The key to composing in cold winter areas is pile size. Really cold, wet weather slows the compost process. Bigger piles are better insulated against cold, snow and even rain. The outermost layer of organic material provides protection for the rest of the pile.

no tubers, and tomato blossoms to drop. Follow the directions on the label of any fertilizer carefully.

I admit to using chemical fertilizers each spring; they are still the easiest and most inexpensive way to supplement soil nutrients. But I realize that other amendments should be added as well. Over time, soil that gets only chemical fertilizers becomes rock hard and devoid of earthworms and other good microorganisms. Plants don't care where they get their nutrients—be it a five-dollar bag of pellets or a scoop of horse manure—but these small life forms that restore nutrients to the soil need organic matter to survive. When I fertilize my garden, I also add rotting horse manure, compost, decaying straw and crumbling leaves. Half an inch or so spread on top will improve the soil as well as nourish the plants. Anyone who tills the soil has a responsibility to take care of it.

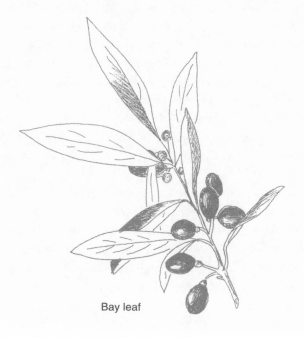

Bay leaf

The Plants

Only good plants grow good gardens. While working in greenhouses and nurseries, I've noticed that customers sometimes choose plants inferior to those left behind.

To choose premium quality seedlings and bedding plants, wise shoppers keep the following tips in mind:

→ Select stocky, well-branched seedlings with few flowers.
Though I regret to say and seldom do it, the blossoms should be pinched off before transplanting to encourage more branching. Maintaining flowers consumes a lot of the plant's energy that would otherwise be used in getting itself established in your garden.

→ Avoid stretched out plants more than six inches tall.
Smaller plants are less likely to be root bound and they will suffer less transplant shock than big ones. If you can sneak a peak when no one is looking, gently lift the plant out of its growing container and inspect the roots. The roots should be white, not brown, gray or mushy.

→ Choose seedlings with healthy, dark green leaves.
Pale, yellow plants are obviously unhealthy. On the other hand, if the color is so green as to be almost blue, the plants may have been over fertilized. I consider these "soft." A plant that has been grown slowly is a hardy plant.

I just come by and talk to the plants, really— very important to talk to them. They respond, I find.

Prince Charles

→ Check for insects.
No pesky bugs should be present, including aphids, whiteflies or other unnamed creepy crawlies.

→ Look for seedlings growing in multi-cell packs.
Cell packs cause less damage to the roots at planting time. If only old-fashioned communal flats are available, cut between the plants with a knife a few days prior to planting.

Gardeners with strict organic needs should seek a small grower—someone with a home greenhouse, for instance—who guarantees chemical free plants. Most large greenhouses use fungicides and possibly other chemicals, or they may ship in plants that have been sprayed at their growing site.

Your decision to buy shouldn't be based on just one factor. Instead, consider the overall vigor of the plant and how well it has been cared for. Don't buy plants that look neglected. Dried out, ratty plants can take a long time to make a comeback.

Ordering Plants by Mail

It is so satisfying to pour over glossy seed and plant catalogues in the winter months. The latter usually offer perennials that come back faithfully every year without replanting. I must admit that mail order nursery offerings are tempting, especially considering my winter-weakened will power. I want every plant they sell.

If you choose to mail order plants instead of seeds, keep in mind that shipping makes most mail order plants relatively expensive. Avoid ordering plants that can be easily found in your area. Why send away for a Shasta daisy when you can find them at your garden center? The advantage of mail order stock is obtaining unusual or collector plants—rare lilies, peonies, roses and medicinal herbs hard to find elsewhere.

Although you can and should request a shipping date, my experience is that companies often overlook it and send the plants when they process your order. Taking a lengthy vacation after you've called in your order may not be wise.

Plan on potting up your ship-ins when they arrive in containers you can pamper until weather permits planting. Don't be shocked if the small plants look nothing like the glossy catalog shot that seduced you to order: It would be prohibitively costly to ship a fully mature plant in a cardboard box.

Finally, be aware that it is hard on a plant to be sent in the mail. They must survive being dug up, wrapped up, tossed around in mailrooms and airports, and possibly getting overheated or very cold in mailboxes and shipping decks. If your plants arrive damaged or even dead let the company know. Most reputable mail order nurseries work hard to keep customers happy, and will often give a refund or a replacement.

Selecting Seed

I diligently study my seed catalogues each winter: cross checking, taking notes, marking pages. You know the routine. Over the years I've learned that much of the horticultural information presented is based not on the rigors of mountain gardening, but on experience elsewhere. A seedman's seducing prose, promises and pictures seldom take into account how utterly awful mountain weather can be. When a catalogue refers to "most climates," it's not talking about mine.

The Teton County Fair paints a truer picture. The best gardeners in this northern Wyoming county produce relatively small vegetables. No cabbage as big as bushel baskets, no softball size onions. Fairgoers praise the single green bean entry. What an accomplishment, to grow a bean. Spring flowers don't grace our gardens until mid-summer. Even peonies won't bloom by Memorial Day, as blithely predicted in Burpee's mail-order opus.

I tried, but it died.

Tip

To determine when to start your flower and vegetable transplants, count back 8-10 weeks from the date plants can typically be set out safely in your area.

This is not to suggest that gardening catalogues are useless to mountain dwellers. These helpful guides are often packed with solid gardening advice. To get the most from a seed catalogue, however, you need to sort through the information and read between the lines. Paying attention to the key elements listed below will help you make good choices for your mountain or northern garden.

Days to maturity

Look for "early," short season vegetables. Local garden centers often have a good handle on days to maturity for many vegetables and flowers in your hometown if you are unsure an item is a good bet. A quick call or stop at your county extension office will also tell you how many frost free days you can expect in an average summer.

Cold hardiness

Look for plants labeled "cold hardy." Over time, plants slowly change genetically in response to their climate and environment. Cold hardy plants are those that have adapted to cooler climates. How cool is determined by a hardiness zone rating.

Zone ratings and microclimates

USDA maps divide the United States into 11 zones by average minimum winter temperatures. The rating given a plant indicates it can survive average conditions in that zone; in very cold years, it may die. The zones are:

Zone 1	Below −50 F
Zone 2	-50/-40 F
Zone 3	-40/-30 F
Zone 4	-30/-20 F

Zone 5	-20/-10 F
Zone 6	-10/0 F
Zone 7	0/+10 F
Zone 8	+10/+20 F
Zone 9	+20/+30 F
Zone 10	+30/+40 F
Zone 11	Above +40 F

Most catalogues include a zone map. If you are not clear which zone you live in after checking the map, call a local garden center or your county extension office. My home in northwest Wyoming is in Zone 3. Through trial and error, however, I've found I have several microclimates on my property. Topography and manmade features make these areas wetter, drier, or warmer than the rest of my landscape. If I exploit the warmer areas—located next to a stone wall or building, a sunny south-facing fence or a pocket protected by a boulder—I can grow plants from Zones 4, 5 or even 6. Your catalogue selection expands if you pay attention to your private environment.

Light requirements

Take note of sun versus shade requirements, and adjust for cooler temperatures. Growing shade-loving plants in high altitude or northern shade may cause their demise. Here, shady spots stay cold: The soil and plants just don't warm during the day. I once planted a bed of impatiens, listed in the catalogue as a flower that likes shade, in a dark corner that craved color. My impatiens grew horizontally, hugging the ground, I suppose, in an effort to gain a degree or two of warmth. When I do my catalogue planning, I take into consideration that some intense, high altitude sunshine can be an asset to "shade" plants.

I consider every plant hardy until I have killed it myself.

Sir Peter Smithers

Tip

Most seeds will remain viable for quite some time, but toss out onion and parnip seeds that have not been used within a year.

After two decades of perusing the garden wish books that perennially brighten my mailbox, I've learned to live with diminished expectations. Catalogues exclaim and exaggerate, using close-up photos to make flowers appear more spectacular than they really are. (They sometimes even cheat by adding additional flower stems to a cluster. Shocking.) When a catalogue description reads "massive spires," "immense bloom," or "huge clusters," I take into account that I'm growing these plants in the merciless, mountain weather of northern Wyoming. In my painfully short season, respectable blooms, a short spire, and *any* clusters spell victory. I delight in harvesting half a dozen cucumbers or a bowl of ripe tomatoes; there are no surplus zucchini jokes in Jackson Hole.

Garden catalogues can be repositories of gardening wisdom, technique and advice. Just remember to keep your eyes open when reading them and hunt for clues to make good choices for your garden.

Seed Starting

I have to confess that I don't grow many of my garden transplants from seed. I often wish I had the time for such luxury: growing plants from "scratch" opens a world of possibilities. I could grow flowers in a wider range of colors, and raise heirloom vegetables and unusual plants not found in any garden center. And I wouldn't miss the magic of watching a plant grow from seed to harvest, reminding me that seeds are wondrous things. Starting seeds isn't really that tricky, although some require more coddling than others do. Many cool climate gardeners start seeds indoors. If you want indoor seed sowing to be more than a little winter recreation—a way to satisfy the need to get dirt under your fingernails when spring isn't quite here— following the tips listed here will increase the success of this immensely enjoyable project.

Develop a timetable

Unbridled enthusiasm can lead to one of the more common sins in seed starting: planting too early. A glorious March day arrives and your fingers start itching to plant. In go the cabbage, tomatoes, lettuce, and marigold seeds, even though outdoor planting weather is on the distant horizon. When the time and weather are finally right to set them outside, you've got leggy, root bound plants.

Utilizing information on the back of the seed packet helps rein in false spring fever. Their printed charts cover planting depth, temperatures that should be maintained and light conditions necessary for germination. Calculating when to sow seeds indoors is a matter of noting on the seed packet the number of weeks needed to produce a transplant of suitable size to set outside. Then count backwards from the average date of the last average frost in you locality and you'll know approximately when to plant the seed. There is no guarantee of when the last frost will occur in a mountain valley, but you might come close.

Don't over sow

I try not to sow seeds as thickly as I once did. Give each of the very tiny seeds at least one eighth inch of space from its neighbors. Medium seed needs one half inch of room and large seeds one inch.

Getting the seeds to fall where you want them can be tricky. Very fine seed, such as pansy or viola, can be mixed with sand to help distribute it more evenly. Some small seeds may be pressed into the soil, with a thin layer of soil sprinkled over them. Mid-sized seed, such as tomatoes which come about 20 to a packet, may be placed with tweezers.

Optimize growing conditions

Plants seeds in a moist soil medium (I prefer commercial lightweight

To plant a seed is a hopeful deed.

Cabbage, cauliflower, squash, marigolds, cosmos, zinnias, calendula and an assortment of other flowers can be successfully transplanted, and are good candidates for indoor starts. Although I prefer to sow lettuce seeds indoors and transplant them to my garden rows outside, most leafy greens can be directly sown outside right into the vegetable garden.

mixes formulated especially for seed starting), keep them warm and watered and give them plenty of light on a windowsill, under fluorescent bulbs or in a greenhouse. If the seedlings remain indoors for long, they'll probably need a weak solution of liquid fertilizer a time or two to keep them thriving until they are set outside.

Sowing indoors keeps little seedlings out of harm's way and gives the gardener a jump on the growing season by several weeks. For those of us who garden in a cold climate, getting this head start is key. But keep in mind that not all seeds should be started ahead inside. Some plants just don't tolerate being moved, and often die when transplanted. I suggest direct sowing—putting the seeds where you want them to grow—for sweet and garden peas, most wildflowers, poppies of all kinds, radishes, spinach, beets and turnips, carrots, sunflowers and beans.

Seed Starting Containers

Many containers can be used for seed starting. Some gardeners make their own; other folks use scavenged objects. Still others can't resist trying the latest gadgets. Convenience, cost and reusability will determine which container is best suited for you. A handful of the many options follows:

Polystyrene plug trays

> A gardening friend who grows about 1,000 seedlings each spring claims these are the best things she's ever used. She buys hers from the Park Seed catalog. These moderately priced trays direct roots downward instead of circling around the root ball, allowing plants to pop out easily without disturbing the roots.

Peat Pots

> Peat pots are not my favorite. They dry out quickly, last only one season, and roots may have trouble penetrating the fiber.

Newspaper pots

It is possible to make biodegradable pots out of old newspapers. Fashion the pots by shaping and taping newsprint around jars, or cut, fold and staple the sheets to form a small container (a good project to farm out to the kids). Plant your young transplants, pot and all; the newspaper will fall apart in the ground.

Recycled containers

Because I'm a frugal (i.e. cheap) gardener, I usually use recycled containers. Quart milk cartons cut down to size are both sturdy and stackable. Their depth makes them ideal for starting tomato transplants, which have large root systems. Yogurt and cottage cheese containers aren't as space efficient as square cartons, but are easy to label with a waterproof pen. And grocery store cake pans that have clear snap-on lids make good mini-greenhouses. Drainage holes, of course, must be poked in the bottom of any of these containers. I also reuse plastic pots I accumulate from garden center purchases. If you do this, too, disinfect them in a weak bleach solution before planting.

Avoid tiny seed starting containers, such as egg trays. The small spaces tend to let the soil dry out too quickly as the plants grow. Always use a fresh starting medium for new seed batches. Used soil can be mixed with batches of fresh soil to pot up larger plants.

Damping-Off: A Sneaky Thief

If you start your own plants from seed, at one time or another your seedlings have probably been attacked by a disease called damping off. This sneaky thief tends to strike quickly after planting, causing the untimely death of tender seeds and seedlings—often before they have seen the light of day.

I have great faith in a seed. Convince me that you have a seed there, and I am prepared to expect wonders.

Henry Thoreau

Damping-off, also known as black root and wire stem, is a rot caused by several genera of fungus parasites. The fungi live in the soil and attack seeds from the moment of germination until the seedlings emerge above ground. Cold, wet soil encourages the rot—a good reason not to rush your outdoor gardening endeavors. High humidity, inadequate light, overcrowding, and lack of air circulation invite the rapid multiplication of the fungus in indoor plantings. If damping off is present in the soil, it is bound to take its toll.

The first noticeable sign that damping-off has occurred is toppled seedlings. A close look reveals a discolored, shrunken stem unable to support the plant. The fungi continue to invade other parts of the seedling until it dies. Damping-off rarely kills older, established plants, whose developed stem tissue creates a barrier that foils fungal penetration. It can, however, infect their new roots and cause root rot. Poor growth and wilting are classic symptoms the plants have been infected.

Once damping-off gets started outdoors, there is little you can do to save seedlings. Drying the surface soil will temporarily check the disease, but it will resume growth with the next watering. I find the best plan is to throw out the whole batch of seedlings and dirt and start over.

You can prevent future damping-off by following preventative measures: It is possible to outwit the sneaky thief who has snatched your plants. First, consider creating a raised bed with pasteurized soil mix, widely available at garden centers, and make sure your bed is well drained. Delay planting until temperatures have warmed sufficiently to allow rapid growth. Sow your seeds thinly, giving them plenty of air, light and space.

Avoid recontaminating the soil by soaking your tools and containers in a mild bleach solution (one part bleach to nine parts water) for 30 minutes. It you are soaking a lot of tools and containers, be sure to soak in batches of fresh solution.

Damping-off is easier to control indoors than outside. Soil-less mixes containing peat, perlite and vermiculite are usually free of the damping-off fungi. I buy big bales of a soil-less medium called Sunshine Mix™ for indoor seed starting, as do many local growers, and have successfully avoided the problem. Make sure you don't over water or crowd your seedlings, and give them plenty of light.

Transplanting

The production of good seedlings ready to set out at precisely the right time requires a synthesis of observation, timing, experimentation, elbow grease and a measure of good luck. Don't waste the effort required to attain this fragile balance by introducing your little proteges to the great outdoors at the wrong time.

About a week or so before you think you will be transplanting, begin taking your seedlings to a sheltered spot outdoors. Near a wall, on a lightly shaded porch or under a tree are good choices. Leave the containers outside for about half a day, increasing the length of time each day and progressively moving them to a more exposed location. Gradually exposing young plants to harsher outdoor conditions is a process called "hardening off."

Hardened seedlings should be transplanted on a mild, overcast day. If you have to do the transplanting on a sunny day, wait until late afternoon when the strength of the spring sun and any accompanying winds are diminished. Late day planting also gives the plants all night to adapt to their new site.

Dig an appropriate-sized planting hole and gently remove your seedling or plant from its container. Check to ensure it is not root bound. If seedlings were started too early, their roots begin circling the limited container space. Left to themselves, roots may continue to circle instead of spreading out to collect the soil nutrients your plant needs to thrive and produce.

If the roots are sturdy, such as those on marigolds or tomatoes, use your fingers to loosen the roots from the growing circle and spread them out in the planting hole. Fibrous root bound plants form a tight

To dig and delve in nice clean dirt Can do a mortal little hurt.

John Bangs

39

root ball that is difficult to separate. I've found that kneading a fibrous root system back and forth helps stimulate the plant to start growing again.

When the transplanting is completed, water your newly planted seedlings well and check them frequently for several days. New transplants are particularly susceptible to stress. If the day following transplanting is bright, sunny and hot rig a shade of some sort out of newspapers, old sheets or other materials at hand. If the young plants look droopy and pale they may need more moisture.

Careful transplanting is the link between your seedlings and glorious summer color or healthy vegetables. Haphazardly plopped in the ground and forgotten is a sure death sentence.

Maintenance & Care

Watering

At this very moment, I guarantee that it's raining somewhere on our planet. But chances are it's not here in Jackson Hole—or at your high altitude home.

According to Jackson meteorologist Jim Woodmency, the annual precipitation in our mountain valley measures 16.5 inches, which breaks down to only one to 1.5 inches a month during an average summer. That means that our flower and vegetable gardens, lawns, newly planted trees and shrubs, and especially container plantings, need to be watered during the growing season.

Gardeners with automatic sprinkler systems should douse their gardens once a day for 20-30 minutes. I water my gardens by hand at least three times a week, thoroughly soaking them with the hose to keep the soil moist and crumbly but not waterlogged.

Water, of course, is essential to all living things. It is the lifeblood of plants, carrying dissolved nutrients and minerals from roots to the foliage and back again. Their survival depends on having enough of this magic solution.

In the arid West, it is important to use water wisely. The challenge is to get the greatest mileage out of the water we use, conserving it while also nurturing our crops. Applying the techniques and strategies that follow helps meet both goals:

Gardeners are not made by sitting in the shade.

Rudyard Kipling

→ Water slowly. Adjust water flow so that it does not puddle or run down the sidewalks. Water needs time to soak into the soil before more water is applied.

→ Apply water directly to the base of the plant. Water that lands any distance from the root zone is wasted. Soaker hoses, also known as weeper or oozer hoses, water deeply and well. If you can afford it, the most water-efficient system is automated drip irrigation. Drip systems reduce the stress of extreme moisture fluctuation.

→ Reduce irrigation during late summer and fall when growth has decreased. This allow leaves and shoots to harden off (toughen up). Plants then naturally lose less water, reducing their supplemental water requirements.

→ Build great soil. This is one of the most important ways to conserve moisture. A humus-rich loam created by adding lots of compost and organic matter holds the water it receives while simultaneously aerating the soil.

Watering a garden is certainly much easier today than it was for our ancestors. We seldom perform rain dances to the heavens (although that sounds like an excuse for a great party), haul buckets of water great distances, or dig miles of ditch by hand. Watering is as easy as turning on the spigot and unwinding a garden hose.

Often, though, I see long suffering plants that just aren't getting enough supplemental moisture. Keep in mind that while sudden mountain showers seem powerful, they often barely wet the garden's surface.

Weed Control

Any unwanted plant not native to an area—especially if it is growing there in abundance—is called a weed. A flower elsewhere might be a weed here and vice-versa.

Certain weeds need no introduction. Dandelions were probably the first plants we learned to identify as kids. Although their profuse bright yellow flowers are pretty in the spring, dandelions are non-native invaders. Weeds squeeze the life out of plants you want to prosper by competing for space, sunlight and soil nutrients. They must be controlled if you want your plants to survive. Mulching, landscape fabrics, and applying pre-emergent herbicides are all tools gardeners use to combat these pesky intruders.

Mulching

Mulching can save a gardener a lot of weeding. Most soil is packed with tiny weed seeds that burst into growth when warm weather arrives. Worse, digging stirs up a new batch of hundreds, if not thousands of dormant weed seeds from below.

However, weed seeds need light to germinate, and mulch prevents light from reaching the soil. A three to four inch layer of mulch effectively controls weeds. Weed seeds that do germinate are usually easy to pull because they become spindly as they struggle to push through the mulch. It will not smother established weeds, as many have grown strong enough to push through it. Before applying any mulch, the soil should be cultivated and weedy growth removed.

Mulch can consist of organic material such as leaves, pine needles, grass clippings, straw or shredded bark and wood chips, or inorganic gravel and sheets of black plastic.

In addition to weed control, mulch stabilizes soil temperatures for healthier plant growth. In cold winter climates, bare frozen soil thaws as it absorbs intense daytime sun, heaving up herbaceous perennial plants. When the soil refreezes at night, these displaced plants will likely die. By insulating the soil, mulch helps maintain a constant winter tempera-

Sweet flowers are slow and weeds make haste.

—

William Shakespeare

*Sunflower hulls con-
tain chemicals that
inhibit growth and
germination of many
vegetables and flow-
ers. Spread them
thickly as mulch in
areas where you want
nothing to grow, and
think twice about
planting under your
bird feeders.*

ture. Similarly, in summer mulches keep the upper inches of soil cooler in the daytime and warmer at night.

A layer of mulch also conserves soil moisture by shielding the soil surface, reducing watering requirements. Conversely, when it is necessary to water thickly mulched plants, make certain you water sufficiently. Check water penetration by pushing aside some mulch and probing the soil; really heavy layers of mulch can actually prevent water from reaching the ground.

Mulch can add beauty to your garden. It looks more attractive than bare ground, especially in newly landscaped areas. Your plants, flowers and vegetables don't become mud-splattered during or after a rain, and your grounds look quite tidy.

Mulch Drawbacks

Though there are many reasons to use mulch, it also presents some drawbacks. Mulch provides a favorable home for pesky critters. The cool, moist environment is a bonanza to slugs, which hide during daylight hours. Mice and voles, especially during periods of heavy snow accumulation, tunnel underneath mulch and feed on trunks, stems and even roots of perennial plants.

Straw and hay can be loaded with weed seeds and can add to your weed problems rather than reducing them. Use only clean straw and hay for mulching. Grass clippings must be free of herbicides. If you use weed killers on your lawn, pile clippings out of the way for at least six weeks or the chemical residue could damage your plants.

Sawdust is sometimes used as mulch, but caution must be used here as well. Fresh sawdust consumes nitrogen as it decomposes, creating a temporary shortage for the plants. If you use sawdust, scratch a sprinkling of nitrogen fertilizer into the soil before mulching.

I often see wood chips—which can be purchased in bags or bulk by the truckload—used as mulch. Wood chips give a pretty appearance to plantings and are long lasting. However, I only use them around permanent plantings such as trees and bushes. Used in an annual flowerbed—or anywhere that will be dug up and reworked—wood chips can be a nuisance. They get stuck in the soil and take forever to decompose. If you want to plant in an area covered with wood chips, scrape the layer away first before you dig.

Applying Mulch

Mulch applied to cold ground can cause germination problems. Apply mulches in late spring after the soil has already warmed. Cultivate your soil and remove weedy growth. The depth to which you mulch depends on what material you are using. Experiment to see what works. Usually a loose textured mulch can be applied more thickly than a finely ground one. No matter what you are using, I recommend a layer at least two-inches deep to have much effect. It isn't necessary to do a perfect job, but if you strive for a uniform depth when you mulch, the result will be more attractive as well as more effective.

Organic mulches break down and need to be replenished occasionally, although the more durable materials may last two more years without needing a fresh layer.

Landscape Fabrics

A number of years ago, someone came up with the idea of placing synthetic "landscape fabric" around plants to suppress weed growth. It didn't

News you can use

Newspapers can be used as mulch. (After all, they come from wood.) Although just a few sheets can be enough, I suggest putting down a 20-40 sheet thickness to ensure that any grass rhizomes, dandelion roots or weed seeds are starved for light. Overlap the edges of the newspapers by an inch or more to eliminate gaps.

Over time, the pulpy wet newspapers and the top cover of organic matter will become nutrient filled humus for your garden.

Of course, the problem with using newspaper for mulch is that, if you are like me, you'll find yourself sitting on the ground reading weeks-old news stories that you overlooked and getting little gardening done.

Hasten spring planting by warming your garden with sheets of clear plastic. Radiant energy passes through the plastic, trapping heat underneath it. As the soil warms, weed seeds are killed. Since black plastic shades the soil, clear plastic is the best choice. Place it directly on the soil.

take long for these synthetic fabrics to catch on: few of us relish constant weeding.

The fabrics are woven polypropylene or a combination of other synthetic materials. They are tough and dense but also porous to allow air and water to reach the soil. The best use for landscape fabrics is in permanent plantings around trees or shrubs. I don't recommend using them in places where you change plants often or where you may want to dig.

Landscape fabrics are easy to install. Simply unroll the fabric and cut slits (x's work the best) to fit the fabric over the plant. You may also fit the fabric around the plant. Overlap seams by at least three inches to close the gaps. Heavy nails or pins sold with the fabric anchor the outer edges.

After installation, completely cover the landscape fabric with two to three inches of organic mulch, such as wood chips or shredded bark. These products look nice, will help the fabric stay in place, and help conserve moisture.

Landscape fabrics have a long life span and will save the gardener many tedious hours of pulling weeds.

Pre-emergents

Some annual weeds (chickweed comes to mind) really go crazy in a garden, twining over, around and under anything growing beside them. Left unattended, they quickly crowd out all of your flowers.

Pre-emergent herbicide prevents rampant annual weed growth by killing weed seeds as they germinate. The weeds are eliminated before they ever see the light of day.

Water activated pre-emergents are generally applied as a granule. They are effective up to three months, so plan application to coincide with the time weed seeds are most likely to sprout, typically spring and early summer. Directions for application should be followed carefully and, of course, never use a pre-emergent in areas where you will be planting your own seeds that season.

Noxious Weeds

While we battle weeds in a small way in our yards and gardens, the West at large has a big weed problem. Because weeds have been introduced, the birds, insects, fungi and animals that kept them in check in their homeland may not exist in their new location. Further, most weed seeds can live in the soil as long as seven years. When they sprout, they produce millions of seeds that spread far and wide. According to Teton Weed and Pest Director Fred Lamming, the rate of weed spread in Jackson Hole is doubling every year.

Non-native plants' rapid growth threatens both range land and wildlife habitat, crowding out native species that provide valuable food chain and ecological links. The US Fish and Wildlife Service estimates that over 40% of our country's endangered and threatened species have declined as a result of encroaching exotic plants and animals.

Although government agencies are valiantly fighting to stop the invasion, we all need to take responsibility for controlling noxious weeds. Noxious weed is a legal designation given to plants that are particularly undesirable or difficult to contain. These are subject, by law, to control measures.

The first control step is learning to identify noxious weeds on your property or along your subdivision road. County extension and weed and pest control offices often stock informative brochures. Next, learn to properly destroy weeds when you see them. Controlling weeds can be done by pulling them out of the ground, chopping off their heads before they go to seed, spraying them with herbicides, or using weed-eating grazers like goats. Different control methods work best for different species.

Finally, be aware of weed seed carriers such as pets, mountain bikes,

Weed it and reap.

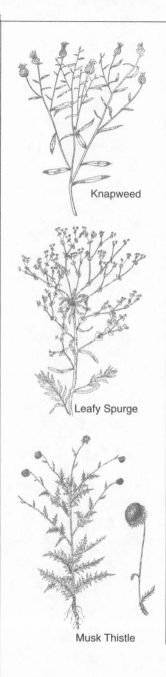

Knapweed

Leafy Spurge

Musk Thistle

the soles of hiking boots, vehicles and clothing. Clean your shoes, clothing and gear before leaving an area to avoid carrying seeds with you, and wash your vehicle after you travel backcountry roads, paying attention to your tires and undercarriage.

The principal noxious weeds in Jackson Hole and most of the Rockies are:

Spotted Knapweed

This weed flowers from June to October. It attains heights of 1-3 feet, and sports pinkish-purple, 3/4-inch tubular-shaped flowers. Bracts around the flower head have dark, divided tips; the plant's finely divided leaves have linear divisions. Spotted knapweed is sometimes confused with asters, which lack the divided flower head bracts. It was introduced from Europe and is well established on the East Coast. Its spread to the western United States has been swift. It typically grows along roadsides and in fields and pastures.

Leafy Spurge

Leafy spurge grows in thick, 1-3 foot high patches. Its branched stems are covered with narrow leaves. Yellowish-green bracts surrounding the tiny flower clusters are often mistaken for the plant's flower. If you break the stem, the plant emits a milky juice that may irritate skin and cause blisters or inflammation. Craighead and Davis report in *A Field Guide to Rocky Mountain Wildflowers* that leafy spurge can cause death if eaten in quantity, and hair loss among animals that frequently come in contact with it. Herbicides are an ineffective control measure for this poisonous plant. It frequents cultivated areas and moist roadsides.

Yellow and Dalmation Toadflax

Commonly called "butter and eggs," yellow toadflax's bright yellow flowers sport spurs and deep orange centers. The plant's leaf is long and narrow. Dalmation toadflax blossoms also have spurs, but are only tinged with orange. This plant's leaf is broad, waxy and heart-shaped. Toadflax is a native of Europe, and was likely introduced as an ornamental that subsequently "escaped" its flowerbed and border plantings. It thrives in grasslands and cultivated areas. Yellow toadflax contains a toxic glucoside that may be harmful to cattle.

Houndstongue

Found along sandy areas, dry roadsides, waste areas and on hillsides, this 1-3 foot tall branching plant bears 1/4-inch long reddish-purple flowers and numerous oblong-shaped leaves covered with soft white hair that feel velvety to the touch. It typically blooms June to August. Houndstongue is poisonous to animals, but rarely eaten because of its pungent smell and unpleasant taste.

Musk Thistle

Also called a bristle or nodding thistle, this noxious weed is difficult to control. Its broad 1 1/2-inch, solitary reddish-purple flower heads sway at the end of long stems, which are winged by a leaf base that curves downward. It reaches full bloom in July and August and is generally found in areas that have been heavily grazed, along roadsides, or in waste areas. The two species of musk thistle found in the Rockies were introduced from Europe.

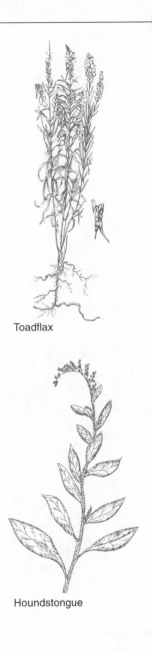

Toadflax

Houndstongue

49

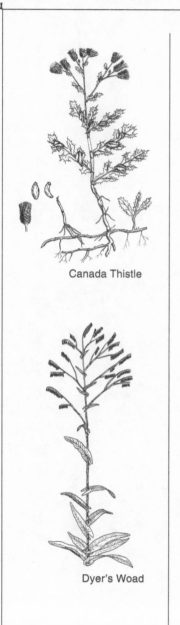

Canada Thistle

Dyer's Woad

Canada Thistle

The tenacity of this thistle has earned it the moniker "cursed thistle." Spread by deep, underground rootstock, one plant may cover as much as 20 feet above ground. Thousands of acres of farmland have been overrun. When the fields are plowed, the chopped up rootstock is dispersed, creating new points of infestation. The spiny stemmed and leafed plant grows in thick masses up to six feet tall. Each plant produces numerous pinkish-purple flower heads, which bloom June through August. It thrives along roadside and in cultivated fields and meadows at elevations up to 7,500 feet.

Dyer's Woad

This plant's small yellow, four-petaled flowers are not as identifiable as its numerous black seed pods. The slightly pear-shaped, 1/2-inch winged pods hang down. Each pod contains one seed. The plant grows 1-3 feet tall. Its lower leaves are oblong to lance-shaped; the upper protrude from the stem like ears. Dyer's woad prefers small cultivated fields and waste areas. It was introduced from Eurasia.

Common Tansy

This Eurasian species grows 2-5 feet tall on stems covered with finely dissected leaves. Its yellow button-like blossoms appear in August and September. It frequents sites that have been disturbed, such as roadsides.

Ox-eye Daisy

Ox-eye daisies grow 10-24 inches high. Their familiar, solitary white flower heads with yellow center appear June through August. Ox-eye's toothed, irregular leaves taper at the stem end. This perky white-flowered plant was introduced by European colonists. Most of the immigrants came mixed with crop seeds from the old country or stowed away in ballast and hay used for packing. A love-hate relationship soon developed as the ox-eye spread rapidly. While poets wrote of the "snows of June," farmers lacking weed killer were forced to fight the prolific invaders by hand.

Ox-eye daisies are a designated "noxious weed" in Wyoming. This wildflower, however, may not be considered a problem to everyone, everywhere. Ox-eye seed is unfortunately and occasionally found as an ingredient in commercial wildflower seed mixes. If you purchase packaged wildflower seed, check the contents carefully. The white daisy seed included should be Shastas and not ox-eyes.

Riding my bike down a road lined with ox-eye daisies this summer, I had trouble trying to dislike this so-called "weed". After all, the flowers are so pretty, so white and summery. Ox-eye daisy: We love you, we love you not!

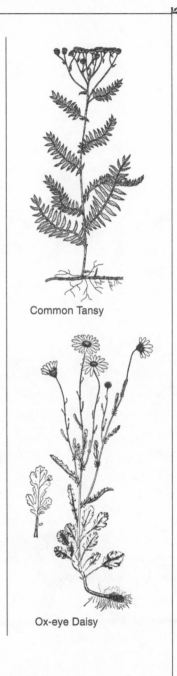

Common Tansy

Ox-eye Daisy

Slugs, Bugs & Other Critters

Wild Animal Buffet

The problems Henry David Thoreau encountered with woodchucks in his Walden Pond bean patch seem small compared to what Rocky Mountain gardeners put up with each and every season. We face an abundance of fauna among our flora. Our cool climate and brief growing season limits insect and disease problems created by six-legged pests—but the four-legged ones keep us on our toes.

I inhabit a small wood house situated on two wooded acres. Our property borders U.S. Forest Service land not far from Grand Teton National Park. Sometimes I wonder if an invisible sign reading, "Free Wildlife Buffet," is posted in my driveway. Greens are routinely mowed down and entire rows of broccoli heads have been neatly decapitated in a single night.

Because I've been the local newspaper's gardening columnist for so long, many folks seek my advice. Often I'm asked what they might plant to attract wildlife to their property. I think that they have a more romantic picture in mind than the nighttime visits I dread. "Plant lettuce, broccoli and cabbage," I tell them, "and petunias and berries and pansies. Then sit back and view the wildlife."

In a former life before marriage and kids, I was employed as a naturalist for U.S. Fish and Wildlife Service. Consequently, I harbor a schizophrenic, love/hate relationship with garden marauders. On one hand, I thrill at seeing a black bear in my backyard. On the other, I get fighting mad when he starts tearing apart my compost heap.

Little Chompers

The Uinta ground squirrel, commonly called a chiseler, is the most notorious of the varmints that vanquish vegetation in this area. These cute gray rodents are indiscriminate: They eat any kind of plant that I grow. Last summer as I was planting petunias in a long strip bed, I looked up to see a ground squirrel cartoonishly following me, methodically munching every plant I tucked in the ground. Had I been planting more slowly, I believe this little critter would have caught up and urged me to plant faster.

Everyone here has a chiseler story. My neighbor Suzanne remarked last spring that she had spent all weekend creating "chiseler habitat." She had, of course, simply planted her garden. One summer enterprising chiselers snuck under her tightly placed row covers and gorged themselves stress-free for a week. When Suzanne lifted the fabric to check her tender veggies, she found nothing left but stumps and a couple of plump, contented bandits.

Large Stompers

Endearing chipmunks live in the rock pile near my cabin. If they clear-cut my lettuce seedlings I'm usually not too upset; lettuce is easy to grow and I can always replant. But moose are another story. Just when my garden starts looking great, this largest member of the deer family

Sow seed generously. One for the rook, one for the crow. One to die and one to grow.

Tip

To easily disperse Irish Spring around your plants, shave the aromatic soap with the moon-shaped side of a cheese grater. The soap's strong scent masks plant odors, "hiding" them from munching critters.

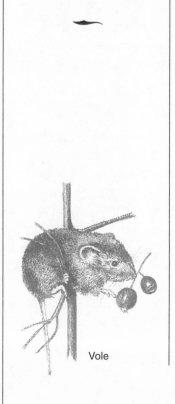

Vole

elects to hike through my garden, indelicately planting 1000-pound footprints on the Swiss chard. The last one to stroll the premises created six-inch wells in the spinach row.

A friend who lives and gardens a few miles north has a really large wildlife problem. Her property adjoins the spring migration pathway for the 400 or so bison that herd is this area. Bison love to wallow in bare dirt. It feels good and loosens the ticks and insects that plague them. What better place to wallow than a newly dug vegetable bed? Puts ol' Henry David's woodchuck problem into perspective.

Control Measures

One cool, crisp morning, loud bulging awoke me: Elk mating season was underway. This time my garden was spared, perhaps because the large, amorous bull became entangled in the badminton net as he trotted across the lawn. I was reminded that wild animals were here first and that I'm in their way. When autumn arrives and the aspens turn gold, I'm grateful for anything I've managed to grow. A bear trashed my honeybee hive the third year in a row, a moose devoured the brussels sprouts and pocket gophers ate the cabbage roots again. (If you see the top of the plant shaking a gopher is likely underneath wreaking havoc). But overall, my garden succeeded without me going to war against Mother Nature.

If you're not quite so philosophic (believe me, it's taken years), below are helpful ways to control wildlife nibbling in your garden.

Fencing

    Our property is too pretty to fence, although that is probably the only solution for keeping the large animals away. Small animals, of course, can still burrow underneath.

Movement

    Although nothing is 100 percent effective, you can deter wild-

54

life by hanging aluminum pie pans in the branches. Critters are wary of the moving, shiny items flapping in the breeze.

Scent

Try hanging mesh bags filled with a strong scented deodorant soap such as Irish Spring™. The soap's odor masks the scent of the tree, "hiding" it from animals. Human hair does the same thing. Collect bags of it from your barber or hairdresser and liberally spread it around the plants you wish to protect.

Sound

Several companies manufacture expensive ultrasonic units; I've found them to be minimally effective at best. Radios placed on a timer and tuned to a talk show are cheaper sound deterrents—but won't deepen friendships if you have nearby neighbors.

These measures may help. So can remembering that the most important tool a mountain gardener possesses is a sense of humor.

Slugs and Bugs

If mankind manages to destroy itself, bugs will likely survive. Gardeners know exactly where they'll live: in their vegetable garden. On their roses. Behind the tool shed. Bugs are a part of every gardener's life. Over the years, we've learned to recognize our many-legged and/or winged foes, and have devised clever ways to thwart their prodigious appetites. The usual suspects are:

Bug Blues

*There are bugs from
which you cower.
There are bugs you
squeeze with ease.
There are bugs that
bugs devour.
There are bugs that
bite your knees.
There are bugs you
hate with passion.
There are bugs at
which you scoff.
But the bugs what eat
your flowers.
Are the bugs that
tick you off.*

Tip

To easily pour small amounts of pesticide, don't remove the foil seal under the lid. Poke the seal with a toothpick or pin. The small opening controls the flow of liquid.

By summer's end I've heard many tales from local gardeners about their successes and failures with vegetables and flowers. Most often I hear stories about pests that had the audacity to get into a crop they had nurtured and cherished. "A porcupine pruned the raspberry bushes," "voles ate all the potatoes tubers," or "hungry grasshoppers ate everything." I've heard of slugs devouring petunias and "earwigs getting into strawberries."

Earwigs. Yuck.

Of all the garden pests, earwigs disgust me the most. This is probably because of their appearance. Sharp pincers protrude from the tail end of these 3/4-inch long, beetle-like insects. They make me cringe.

Besides being ugly, earwigs can do a lot of damage in a vegetable garden or greenhouse, especially in the spring. Earwigs are night marauders, demolishing plants by chewing their leaves. Though they also eat lots of decaying vegetation, they have a gourmet's taste for young vegetables. Lettuce seedlings and Chinese cabbage rate as favorite foods, and entire basil crops have been known to disappear.

If something is munching away on your plants and you don't see the silvery mucous trails typical of snails and slugs, earwigs may be the culprits. Quietly search your garden at night with a flashlight. Don't stamp or crash through the foliage as earwigs scatter in response to any disturbance. You may find earwigs clinging to the leaves.

Although earwigs aren't all bad (they act as scavengers and eat aphids) I would just as soon keep them out of my garden. If you feel the same way, keep your garden area tidy. A clean garden, free of old pots and trash, doesn't have much appeal to an earwig looking for a home.

If that fails to do the trick, try setting out traps. Loosely rolled newspapers, corrugated cardboard or sections of old hose and bamboo poles make good ones. Lay these materials out at night and each morning knock the insects into a pail of hot water. Saucers of beer placed around the garden also entice these pesky critters, which typically fall in and drown.

Slugs

Of all garden pests, none is more revolting than a slug (except, maybe, earwigs). Slugs have no fans.

These rather ugly soft-bodied creatures are about a half-inch long and look like their cousins, snails, without a shell. Eyes positioned at the end of tentacles move around like marbles on tiny Slinkys®. The only function these slithering creatures have that I'm aware of is filling a slot on the food chain. Snakes, birds and earthworms devour slugs.

I can't expect gardeners to see beauty in this notorious garden pest. Still, I am amused at the intensity of slug wars that take place in gardens across the country. Otherwise gentle, mild-mannered gardeners become bloodthirsty when they discover these slimy creatures in their lettuce row.

If you, too, are finding telltale silvery slime trails in the midst of munched plants, read on. I've written up a wicked list of mostly organic control strategies. One or several may work in your garden.

→ Hand-to-slug combat. Slug hunting (hand picking) early morning and evening every day for three weeks will greatly reduce the breeding stock.

→ Fork them. Definitely for the slime thirsty and those who don't like to touch the creatures with their bare hands. Pierce the pests with a fork taped to the end of a stick. Or, consider cutting them in half with trowels and clippers. Don't entertain the question, " Do slugs scream?" if you are serious about this.

Something in the insect seems to be alien to the habits, morals and psychology of this world.

Maurice Maeterlinck 1911

Tip

Clear Fuji film canisters allow you to measure herbicides and pesticides without contaminating your spoons. Use a spoon to measure 5 ml of water. Pour it into a canister and mark the water level with a permanent pen. Repeat three more times, marking each gradation. A full canister holds 25 ml. Save the marked canister to measure poisonous pest control products.

→ Create an irritating border. Slugs are reluctant to drag their tender bodies across rough-textured substances. A two-inch wide barrier of wood ash, eggshells, sharp sand or diatomaceous earth is a good slug deterrent.

→ Keep slug food at a distance. Remove all debris from the garden. A compost heap or garden trash pile should be a good distance from the garden. Though it is hard to believe, a slug can travel the distance of three city blocks a day.

→ Offer luxury lodging. Old boards, grapefruit rinds, banana peels, cabbage leaves, a stack of newspapers or overturned clay pots work as slug motels. Set them out at night and check them in the heat of the day. Destroy any and all slugs you find.

→ Sprinkle them with salt. Because too much salt is bad for the soil, it is probably better to scrape slugs into a bag of salt rather than sprinkling them 'in situ'.

→ Till the soil over and over. Tough tilling will slice up dormant slugs and unhatched eggs, as well as break up clods and destroy slug habitat.

→ Keep a flock of ducks. They have an appetite for slugs. Encourage garter snakes.

→ Mulch with pine needles. Old leaves and straw mulches are cozy nests for slugs.

→ Surround plants with slug fencing. Copper stripping can be attached to boards around raised beds. The metal holds up during rainy weather when other barriers break down. Slugs receive an electrical shock (they literally sizzle and foam) when they touch the copper. Ooooh!!!

→ Give your plants elbowroom. Thin or transplant seedlings so there is space between your plants. Hiding places will be eliminated and air circulation increased.

→ Sprinkle a very small amount of fertilizer (ammonium sulfate or ammonium nitrate) on the slimy creatures, causing them to dehydrate.

→ Use the famous beer trap method. Sink a shallow pan or bowl into the soil and fill with beer. Slugs are attracted to the yeasty smell of the brew and, once they are in it, they drown.

→ Have a party! If you feel the above is a waste of good beer, invite your friends to an evening "slug fest." Buy several cases of beer (Slugmeister anyone?) to consume while gathering slugs by flashlight. Who could ask for more fun than that?

Drawing by Diane Benefiel   BEER

You don't have too many slugs. You have a deficiency of ducks.

If you spy white cabbage butterflies in your cabbage, broccoli and cauliflower—touching down their black spotted wings to lay eggs on the undersides of leaves—watch for the worms that will soon follow. The velvety green larvae of this butterfly feeds on the leaves and heads of susceptible plants, and can quickly devour an entire crop.

Spider Mites

I was out of town last summer during a week of hot, dry weather. I returned to find a downright explosion of spider mites in my greenhouse. It appears that when adult mites aren't voraciously feeding, they're reproducing like crazy.

The cucumbers and little jewel dahlias were infested the worst. Clues of spider mite infestation appeared on their leaves, which had a few yellow or brown spots and an overall speckling of little dots known as leave stippling. This is a typical symptom that mites have attacked; tiny webs are another. Shaking a plant over a piece of white paper is likewise an effective diagnostic device. If the "dust" that falls onto the paper begins to crawl, your plant has spider mites.

Plants plagued by spider mites die a slow death. Though mites are tiny—about the size of the period at the end of this sentence—they suck huge amounts of nutrients from a plant's leaves. The weakened plant subsequently produces less fruits, vegetables or flowers.

I needed to counterattack. Actually, I'm into "peaceful" alternatives rather than all-out chemical warfare, though I'm sure spider mites don't find them peaceful at all. I use Safer's® insecticidal soap, available at garden centers and from mail order garden catalogues, to rid my plants of spider mites. Safer's does not harm people, pets, wildlife or beneficial insects. It is made of potassium-based fatty acids that work by bursting the cell membranes of sucking insects, which die when their body fluids drain away.

Safer's and other soap sprays are contact insecticides: They must be sprayed directly on the insect to be effective. Be sure to douse the leaves undersides, where mites often cling and hide. Spray every few days to keep the population in check.

The edges of large vegetable leaves, such as squash, sometimes brown after being sprayed with a soap solution. Soap concentrates on the tips of the leaves before it drips off, causing some burning. The edges then stop growing but the inner leaf continues to enlarge; eventually, the leaf curls.

In spite of this occasional disfigurement, I recommend a sprayer full of Safer's soap and water as one of the most effective spider mite weapons for organic gardeners.

The Good Guys

Every summer they seem to arrive—crawling, creeping, chewing, burrowing, biting and sucking their way into our gardens. Seems like the only good critter is a dead one. Not true. Some are villains; others are heroes. If you knock out anything that moves with a deadly chemical, you destroy the good guys along with the troublemakers.

Beneficials

Certain insects, worms, birds and bats all benefit our gardens. Insects that prey on ones harmful to gardens are called beneficials. They include:

Ladybugs
> The best known ally is, of course, the ladybug. Officially known as the ladybeetle, this plump, red and black insect and its larvae devour aphids by the thousands, earning them the nickname "aphid wolves." They also consume mites, and are commonly sold to commercial orchards to control harmful scale insects.

Green Lacewings
> Green lacewings are great all-purpose predators in the garden and greenhouse. This delicate pale green, broad-winged insect is common in the West. It is often seen in weeds, grass, and on

Let us permit nature to have her way. She understands her business better than we do.

Michel de Montaigne 1588

61

the leaves of trees and shrubs. Green lacewings' nasty-looking larvae have a ferocious appetite satisfied by aphids, mealy bugs, whiteflies, spider mites, thrips and moth eggs.

Ground Beetles

The ground beetle is another common beneficial. Ground beetles resemble tiny oil slicks in motion—black, glossy blobs with a trace of iridescence on their wing covers. This nocturnal insect hides during the day under objects on the ground; at night they often fly towards light. Ground beetles are superb hunters of numerous garden pests, including slugs, cutworms, cabbage maggots, fungus gnats, aphids and flea beetles.

Bees

Bees and flowers need each other. When a bee sips nectar buried deep within a flower, powdery yellow pollen sticks to its fuzzy body. The bee carries this fertiizing pollen from flower to flower as it gathers food, brushing some of it onto other flowers' stigma. The stigma, of course, needs pollen to produce fruit and seeds. In the course of feeding themselves, bees ensure plant survival generation to generation.

While it is possible to buy commercially reared beneficials through mail order catalogues, releasing them on your property is tricky. Often they will disperse and fly away, or stop feeding and exist on stored body fat. If you do succeed in introducing beneficials don't expect overnight miracles. Not as powerful as pesticides, these little creatures require time to work. Beneficials should be released early season when pest numbers are low. Gardeners must provide them with diverse habitat and food sources to keep them where they are needed.

It pays for gardeners to develop the curiosity of a scientist, to be interested and not squeamish about living critters in the garden. When you work in your garden, keep an eye out for the good insects and watch your step.

Worms

If your garden is full of worms, consider yourself lucky. Earthworms add more usable nutrients to the soil than any other organism. They take undigested organic matter and produce waste that is a blend of super nutritious substances plants can readily use.

Earthworms prefer cool, wet soil, so in very hot or cold weather they burrow deeply to reach more moderate temperatures. As they burrow into the ground—as far as six feet down—they aerate the soil, making holes for rain to penetrate and allowing much needed air to reach roots. In the hot dry summer months, worms may come to the surface only on cool, rainy nights to eat bits of organic matter on top of the ground.

Don't have any worms? Don't try to 'import' them: that rarely works. Very sandy or clayey soils simply don't offer worms enough to eat. Instead, attract earthworms by building good garden soil. Work lots of organic matter into your garden—materials such as compost, manure, old leaves and grass clippings—and earthworms will appear.

Using large quantities of high-nitrogen chemical fertilizers may cause the earthworm population to decline. The same is true of strong insecticides. Use only the amount of these chemicals you need, and distribute them directly around the plant rather than broadcasting them throughout the garden.

As an avid gardener I've come to love my worms. I've spent years amending my soil into a worm-welcoming condition and consider myself lucky to have many. They are my friends, my partners in the soil. Toiling unseen even while I sleep, worms are cheap perpetual motion garden assistants who never ask for a raise or vacation time.

Nature is
full of
genuises.

Henry
Thoreau

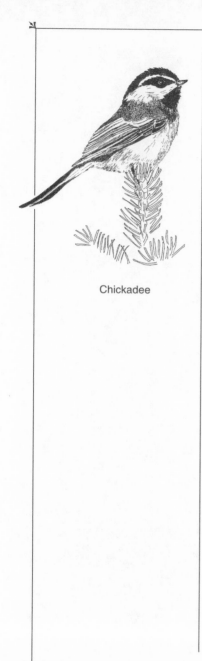

Chickadee

So embrace your worms. (Not literally, of course. It is impossible to hug a worm.) Treat them well. Sing to them. Avoid gashing them with the spade. Provide them with yummy rotting compost and protective leafy mulch each fall. Worms help feed your plants by improving your soil, and high altitude, Western soil often needs all the help it can get.

Birds

Our world would be a poorer place without birds. They fill our days with song and delightful activities. They also eat a lot of garden pests. I can't imagine a gardener who wouldn't want such useful and beautiful creatures around.

A welcoming landscape—one that provides food, water, shelter and nesting places—is the best way to encourage a variety of birds to visit and reside in your yard.

"Birdscaping" should include many kinds of plants. The more varied the plantings, the greater variety of birds you will attract. Remember to keep the colors and overall shapes of the plants to your liking, so you enjoy the garden, too.

The most attractive yards to birds include trees and shrubs. If you only have room for a few, choose ones that produce berries and fruit. Dogwoods, hawthorns, elderberries, chokecherries, serviceberries, roses, cotoneasters and honeysuckle are good candidates. These bushes provide fresh berries in the summer, and dried berries still on bare branches throughout the winter. The bright orange fruit of mountain ash and crabapple trees is also apparently good dining for birds. I've seen entire flocks of Bohemian waxwings foraging for days on their branches. Rounding out the list of potential trees and shrubs are alders and birches, whose small seeded catkins are a good source of nutrition for our feathered friends.

Over-tidy gardens offer birds poor pickings. Leave some fallen leaves, as they are home to insects birds eat. And don't cut all your garden flowers down in the fall. Birds will pick their seed heads clean during the winter. The seeds of cosmos, bachelor button's, zinnias, phlox, sunflowers and asters are particularly delectable to a host of songbirds. It should go without saying that if you want insect-eating birds to visit your yard, don't purge it with chemicals.

Supplement what your habitat lacks by hanging an assortment of birdhouses and feeders filled with seeds, grains and suet. Conscientiously keep your feeders full. This is especially critical during the winter. Your feathered residents elected to stay because food was available. Don't let them down.

A consistent supply of fresh water for birds to drink and bathe in is another essential component of birdscaping your garden. Birds are never far from water in the wild. Place a birdbath close to sheltering plants so birds can easily reach protective cover from house cats and pouncing predators.

For some, a garden is not a garden without birds in it. Keep birds in mind when you landscape, and you'll multiply your pleasure many times over while ridding yourself of garden pests.

Bats

A few years ago bats became rather trendy. Gardening catalogues advertised bat roosting boxes and one even sold seed collections to create a "bat garden."

It is refreshing to see these long-maligned creatures viewed with interest instead of revulsion. Bats are benign, night-flying mammals that benefit the gardener by eating hundreds of noxious insects an hour, including beetles, moths, flying ants, leaf hoppers and mosquitoes.

To welcome bats into your neighborhood, propagate plants that entice night-flying insects. Night-blooming flowers such as four o'clocks, moonflowers and nicotanias are great choices. Other candidates include

This is the place where birds fly through, so watch where you sit, whatever you do.

bachelor buttons, phlox, salvia, honeysuckle, spearmint and phlox.

It is recommended that bat houses be hung 12-15 feet above ground in an area warmed by the sun.

Truthfully, I haven't had much luck attracting bats—nor has anyone else I know. Perhaps our bat houses were in the wrong places. Bats prefer to be around a water source, and my property lacks a nearby creek or pond. Or, maybe there aren't any bats in the area. If you'd like to try, your best bet for bat watching may be to position an outdoor light near the garden. This would attract the bat's food and improve the chances of seeing these tiny, flying critters in action.

Closing Up Shop

As the growing season winds down, I slow down as well and start pondering and daydreaming about all sorts of things. This morning I began to wonder about the creatures I encounter as I putter around the garden. What happens to them when winter comes? How do these varied life forms survive in snow country?

Where do butterflies go in winter? What about my resident garter snake? Or the toad that hangs around my greenhouse all summer? Do earthworms survive the winter, and what about all those slimy, soft slugs?

Research yielded some answers and strategies. Butterflies, I found out, either migrate or winter in egg, pupae (cocoon) or adult forms. The adults that winter here are able to do this by producing glycerol in their blood, an insectivorous antifreeze.

As for my garter snake and his kin: Snakes seek out safe winter hiding places under decaying logs, in deep protected rock crevices or even in burrows of other animals—wherever they can escape sub-freezing temperatures. Toads may also seek out underground burrows for hibernation, digging themselves into soft soil with their hind feet. Oxygen is absorbed through their skin during these periods. Earthworms survive the winter by burrowing deeper underground. Ants move from their nest to deep passageways where they won't freeze.

Finding out the whereabouts of slugs during the deepest, darkest part of the year took a bit of searching. Those very creatures that destroyed your lettuce last summer do not survive the winter. Most die when the weather turns really cold. No need to rejoice, however, for their offspring emerge next spring from over-wintered clusters of dormant egg masses laid in the fall. Ladybugs survive the winter in large groups. When the weather gets chilly, they cluster up by the thousands under leaf litter and rocks.

The more I ponder, and more questions pop up. Does a woolly bear caterpillar's reddish brown belly stripe tell how cold the winter will be? (Folklore holds that wider the band, the milder the winter: the thinner the band, the more cold and snow.) Is the size of a bald-faced hornet's paper nest another indicator of a severe winter? (We've got a whopper hanging from our roof.)

Large or small, beautiful or strange, each plant and animal has developed a means of species survival in even the grimmest conditions. Pretty exciting stuff to think about, wouldn't you say?

Fall Checklist

Ah...fall. The time of flannel shirts, raking leaves and road trips. The time to kick back and close up shop.

But only after the final gardening chores are done. The damp, chilly mornings and bright colorful afternoons of autumn are the perfect time to complete tasks that benefit your garden when springtime rolls around

N

Now is the time of the illuminated woods...when every leaf glows like a tiny lamp.

John Burroughs

Tip

Pull out stakes identifying your flowers when you put your garden to bed. If you don't, your beds will look like a fairy cemetery all winter.

again. As the years have gone by, I've found more and more to do each fall. It has become, in fact, one of my busiest seasons. Always the optimist, I compile a checklist of work I hope to get done before the snow flies. Here it is:

→ Clean up and turn over the vegetable garden. Clear away old vines, leaves and plant detritus that may harbor pests or diseases and toss it in the compost heap.

→ Cut back perennial flower plants to a few inches in height. Leaving a stub of the stems standing helps catch and hold protective snow.

→ Topdress garden beds with manure. I buy it in bags, or get a truckload of well-aged manure from a local rancher.

→ Clean out and re-dig annual flowerbeds to get a jump on spring work when the snow melts.

→ Mow grass one last time, to a maximum height of one-and-a-half to two inches.

→ Fertilize lawns. Grass roots send down reserves in the fall. Well-fed grass responds more capably to spring weather.

→ Harvest culinary herbs for winter use. I chop and freeze French tarragon, chives and cilantro, and dry parsley and thyme.

→ Gather seed from my favorite marigolds and store them in jars. Remember: if you save seeds from hybrid plants, they may not breed "true." The next generation may produce unexpected mixes and colors.

- Rogue out perennial plants that just didn't work. In fall, I can still remember which plants I'd hoped would grow tall but turned out short, and which ones that should have been short grew too tall. Some may have become straggly; others never bloomed, no matter what I did. Fall is a good time to dig into a flowerbed and correct mistakes.

- Empty and stack clay pots. Low-fired, porous Mexican clay pots are particularly vulnerable to cracking.

- Cut back fuchsias to approximately 6 inches and bring them indoors to rest over the winter. Ditto with geraniums.

- Plant garlic cloves and shallots. Mark the spot so you won't forget that they are there. Find a spot for critter resistant daffodil bulbs; little beasties seem to savor tulip bulbs in the winter when they get hungry.

- Watch for terrific nursery clearance sales. Perennial flowers, trees and shrubs can still be planted. Be sure to keep them watered till the ground freezes up.

- Prune tree branches that cast shade on a sun-loving garden.

- Dig potatoes after the first hard freeze blackens the vines.

- Store battery operated timers where they won't freeze.

- Drain and roll up hoses and bring in any ornaments and decor that could be damaged by winter weather.

Shed no tear—O, shed no tear! The flowers will bloom another year.

John Keats

Tip

Cold weather is tough on clay pots. Wet soil expands if it freezes and cracks the clay. When you clean up in the fall, knock out the soil and store pots upside down. The drier the pot is in freezing weather, the longer you'll have it.

Finally, when everything seems to be done, put away your tools. Ideally shovels, rakes, spades, pruning shears, trowels and so forth should be cleaned, oiled and sharpened. Truthfully, I don't always get to this maintenance.

I do these tasks regretfully—not because I dislike the work, but because I have trouble really letting go of my garden. Perhaps it is because we mountain gardeners know all too well how long it will be until we can dig in the rich, warm dirt again.

Geraniums

To add color to our long mountain winters, I always bring in a few outside geranium plants before the first frost. You can, too: It is nice to see fresh green leaves in January.

If your plants are in big tubs, transplant them into smaller pots. If they are already in workable inside containers, proceed with these simple steps:

→ Set your pots in a nice bright spot (not necessarily direct sun) that is preferably cool at night and chop them down to four to six inches of stem with leaves. (You have to do it; I sometimes cheat and leave more.) If your plant stems are very woody near the bottom, make your cuts about two inches above the hard brown section.

→ Water well after transplanting and cutting back.

→ Fertilize only with the initial watering. Geraniums need to rest in the deepest, darkest part of winter. When the days lengthen around the end of February, start fertilizing again.

→ Water only sparingly during the winter, allowing the soil to dry out between waterings. Yellowing leaves are a sign of both over and under watering. Check the soil: If it is wet all the time, cut back on the water. If it is very dry, step it up.

→ Cut your geraniums back again in March. This is hard to do, because the plants look great. Take heart in the fact that the cut doesn't have to be as severe, and you can save the cuttings to propagate new plants. Cut at a 45-degree angle just below a leaf node and remove the flower leaves. I root these cuttings by placing them in a jar of water for a few weeks, but they can also be rooted in a 50-50 mixture of damp sand and potting soil. If you have florescent grow lights, use them; otherwise, place the cuttings in a warm spot out of direct sunlight. They should root in about a month, then be transplanted into small pots. Pinch off growing tips for bushier plants, and look forward to lots of brightly colored blossoms all summer.

Overwintering Plants

Sometimes I've gardened so hard and frantically all season that frost-blackened plants don't bother me; I finally have some time off! Occasionally, though, I have favorite plants that would be heartbreaking to lose (like the $8 scented geranium I carted from Washington to Wyoming one summer.) These I pot up to preserve indoors over the winter, with hopes of replanting them in next year's garden.

Life on the inside can be tough on plants. Winter days are short and humidity is low. I figure that I have about a 75 percent success rate for overwintered plants. I don't bother with cheap, easy to grow annuals such as petunias, marigolds and violas. I only try to save unusual, expensive plants or ones that I've become emotionally attached to. This year I'll overwinter some rosemary and lavender plants, a couple of asparagus ferns, English ivies, vinca vines and licorice plants from my container plantings.

To bring a plant indoors, dig it up and shake the soil from the roots.

Autumn is a season immediately followed by looking forward to spring.

71

Tip

Cabin fever can afflict cats as well as people. Help yours through the long, cold month by growing greenery for them to nibble on. Oat grass is a favorite. Buy oat seed at a feed store and grow in a sunny spot, or purchase a pre-packaged kit of "cat grass" at your pet store.

Check it closely for pests and diseases. If the plant is large, the top as well as the roots may need to be pruned before being potted. Expect some yellow leaves initially; this is a traumatic operation for a plant. Keep your potted up plants well watered and fed—and your fingers crossed that they survive.

Winter growth may be spindly and it may be necessary to cut the plants back again in the spring at the time of replanting outdoors. I've found that an extra year or two is all I can get from these plants. After that, they become woody and a grower should probably start over with fresh plants from cuttings or a nursery.

Fall is the time to plant spring bulbs.

The Gardens

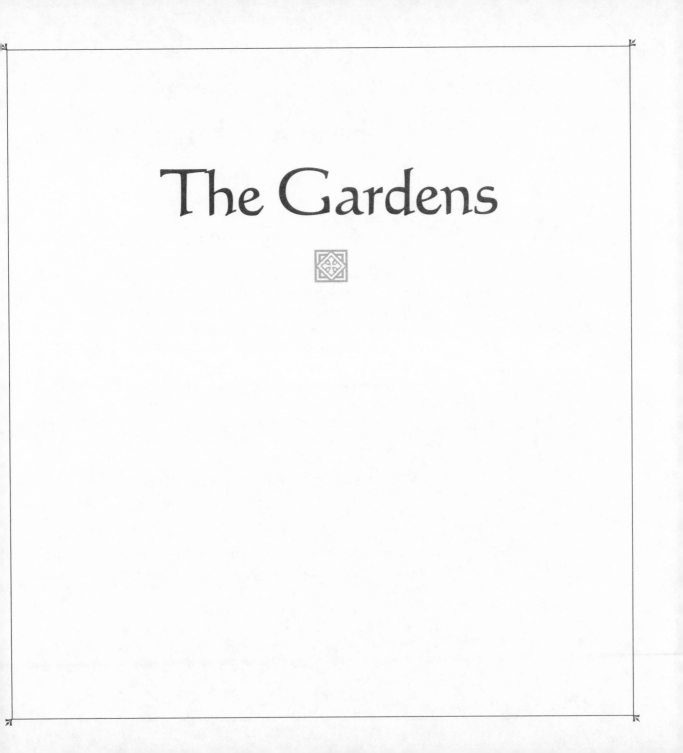

Flower Gardens

Annuals

Because the growing season above 5,000 feet is so short, annual flowers are often a mountain gardener's best bet. They provide color quickly: From seed to seed, they are over and out in one glorious summer, completing their entire life cycle in a single season. Their quick growth and the nearly unlimited variety of colors, heights, forms, versatility and continuous summer bloom make annuals invaluable for all gardeners.

Annuals are used in mass plantings, as fillers in perennial flowerbeds and borders, for edging, in window boxes and container plantings, and temporarily between newly planted shrubs. It is not surprising that they are among the most familiar of garden plants, gracing public places and planters everywhere we go.

Whether you grow your own or buy annual flower starts in garden centers, prepare them for harsher outdoor conditions by "hardening off." Move them outside for a few hours a day for several days before planting. Starting in a sheltered spot, gradually work up to the intensity of direct sun. I sometimes leave my trays of annuals in the car overnight to acclimate them, utilizing my back seat as an instant and convenient cold frame.

If it is not snowing, or cold and rainy, the toughest annuals can be set out around mid-May in Jackson Hole, about the time the aspens begin to leaf out. To be safe, wait until Memorial Day or even the first week of June to set out your more fragile annual flowers. In this mountain

Lupine

valley, there is no sure way of knowing whether the last frost was really the last until the next frost comes along.

Annual flowers grow best in rich, well-drained prepared soil. Working organic amendments into the soil before planting time makes a big difference in how well the plants grow.

When you provide regular water and fertilizer, annuals respond with a steady supply of blooms all season. I place granulated time-release fertilizer in my annual flowerbeds and containers each spring to feed them for the season. Some folks swear a diluted solution of Miracle Gro® or fish emulsion keeps their plantings robust and healthy.

Deadheading

Deadheading refers to the task of removing faded and spent flowers. If this simple chore is done with regularity, it will not only greatly improve a plant's appearance but may prolong the blooming period or even initiate a second flush of blooms.

Why is this so? If blooming plants are allowed to set seed, flower production stops: The plant has done its thing for the year. But if withered flowers are plucked off before they mature and form seedpods, the plant keeps trying to produce seed to ensure its survival.

Deadheading is especially important maintenance for annual plants. As I water and weed I carry along a bucket and fill it with snipped spent flowers of petunias, pansies, violas, calendulas and marigolds.

"Top Ten" List of Favorite Annuals

Sweet Alyssum
> 3-4 inches. Low growing and spreading. This sun-lover softens the edges of flowerbeds and paths with hundreds of fragrant tiny white or purple blooms in billowy mounds. I put alyssum in planters and let it spill over the sides.

More than anything I must have flowers.

Claude Monet

75

Edible flowers are back in vogue. Orange calendula and marigold petals add color and flavor to rice and pasta dishes and pansies, violas, nasturtiums and blue borage flowers are a striking crowning touch to a tossed salad. Just remember to present your garden masterpiece before you add the dressing. Delicate petals wilt under the weight of gooey Thousand Island or ranch dressing.

Calendula

12-30 inches, depending on the variety. Large orange and yellow blossoms decorate these sturdy plants. Grows exceptionally well in cooler weather and usually survives light frost.

Pansy

8 inches. Extra hardy, these low growing plants shrug off frost. Pansies come in many colors including blue, yellow, white, purple and apricot as well as bi-colors. Some pansies have faces that make me smile. Grow in partial shade and keep them watered for continuous summer bloom.

Petunia

Up to 12 inches. Petunias are likely America's favorite bedding plant. Dozens of varieties have been developed that are useful in boxes, barrels and beds. "Grandifloras" have tuba-sized blooms, "multifloras" have more blossoms but are smaller.

Dianthus (aka pinks)

6-12 inches. I set these frost tolerant plants out early. Most are low growing in shades of pink. Blossoms have a sweet fragrance.

Snapdragon

6-inches to 2 1/2-feet tall. Vertical, frost hardy flower spikes in wide assortment of colors. Snapdragons make good cut flowers; dwarf varieties work well in borders. I plant medium snaps in tubs and other plantings, and tall varieties such as "Rocket" as background plants in an annual flower bed. I buy snaps as seedlings from a garden center; they need to be started indoors very early for mid-summer bloom. Kids love this flower if you show them how to pinch (or snap) the individual blossoms and make a "dragon's mouth" open and close.

Marigold

>6 inches with small blooms, to 2 feet tall with huge flower blossoms. Almost everyone recognizes the unmistakable scent of this multi-petaled, orange and yellow flower. Because marigolds are extremely frost sensitive, I set them out late. Easy to grow from seed. Plant marigolds in the sunniest spots you have.

Lobelia

>4 inches. Low growing, trailing plant. A truly blue delicate flower, 'Crystal Palace" is my pick for tubs or as an edging plant along borders. Does best in partial shade and moist ground.

African daisy

>Low growing. This sun-loving annual flower comes in soft shades of yellow and orange and is nice in massed plantings. I use them often in beds in city parks, and find them able to withstand cold weather. They make a poor cut flower because the blossoms close at dusk.

Aster

>8 inches to 2 1/2 feet. One of my personal favorites, these cold tolerant flowers are not used enough in beds and borders. They bloom late in the summer with chrysanthemum type flowers that are pink, purple and white. Asters prefer full sun.

Featured Annuals

Sweet Alyssum

Anyone who grew up with a garden recalls a snowy border of sweet alyssum gracing or framing a plot of flowers. Mounds of sweet alyssum

My garden was at its peak last week. Sorry you missed it.

Tip

Scraping your finger-nails across a bar of soap and applying lanolin hand lotion before gardening— even if you wear gloves—makes hand cleanup much easier.

soften the edges of mixed flowerbeds and are good filler in a rock garden. And I love alyssum in container plantings. It obligingly cascades over the sides of whisky barrels, redwood tubs and window boxes in a mass of blooms.

White is the most familiar color of sweet alyssum, but rose, purple and even apricot—a recent introduction—are also available. "Sweet" refers to the honey-like fragrance that surrounds each clump of this appealing annual. Plant it in a sunny spot and take note of how many small low flying butterflies are attracted to the sweet perfume of its profuse blossoms.

Alyssum is one of the easiest annuals to propagate. The seeds germinate quickly and produce blooms in only five to six weeks. Once the bloom starts, it continues until hard frost arrives. Alyssum will even occasionally reseed itself.

I start this annual in my greenhouse or on a sunny windowsill around the first of May. I sprinkle a few seeds in plastic pots filled with potting soil, pat them lightly and water. In a few days—voila!—fresh green sprouts begin popping up. A four-inch pot of alyssum grows into a clump at least twice that width when planted outside. I let it get about an inch high with several layers of leaves. When weather permits, I transplant it into my garden bed or plants. Each alyssum plant has hundreds of tiny blooms. As one seed catalogue suggests: "Sweet alyssum is reminiscent of Victorian lace—very fine little spots which all work together for an overall illusion." I like that: Delicate, fragrant lace in my flower garden.

Calendula

I love the bright scarlets, clear yellows and vivid oranges that color annual flowerbeds—but I and other mountain gardeners know that many of these bright, fiery flowers require hot weather to do their best. An exception is festive calendula, a reliable and hardy annual that I plant each spring.

Calendula takes light frost in stride. While I fret about when to set out marigolds, ageratums, begonias, and impatiens, I don't lose sleep over this delightful annual. I know that any calendula planted before the arrival of late frost will pull through—which is probably why I plant so much of it: "Late" frost is inevitable where I live.

If you are like me and wish to start some of your flowers indoors from seed, calendulas are a good choice. I have never had a problem getting this plant's seeds to germinate. Even when spring is excruciatingly slow to arrive and my calendula seedlings grow leggy, I've found they usually bush out in a few weeks and eventually fill my flowerbeds with their colorful blooms.

There are named calendula hybrids in many shades, from palest yellow to darkest orange. If height is a consideration, then read the plant tags carefully. Dwarf types, such as Bon Bon or Dwarf Gem do well in containers. The taller varieties, such as Pacific Beauty, grow upwards of 2-3 feet and are best planted in a border.

Pinching out the growing tips of calendula plants encourages the development of side shoots and more blossoms. Regular deadheading also

Annual, biennial or perennial?

The distinction between annual, biennial and perennial plants can be confusing because climate and cultural practices affect a flower's growth cycle. For example, rose campion may be listed in some gardening books as a short-lived perennial, and black-eyed Susans are often grouped among self-sowing annuals. Sweet William, foxgloves and forget-me-nots bloom their first year if started very early.

For some biennials, flowering is triggered by temperatures slightly above freezing, a response called vernalization. Others may respond to lengthening spring days. Some may need both signals before they blossom. Some biennials will even remain in a non-flowering leafy state indefinitely if not exposed to low temperatures. These plants must 'think' they have been through a winter before they flower and produce seed.

Tip

Soak sweet pea seeds in a saucer of water for 24 hours before planting to soften the seed coat and hasten germination.

induces the plants to keep blooming.

In milder climates, calendulas may self-sow, becoming—believe it or not—a "problem." I surely don't mind any of those vigorous little volunteers, however, even if they are not always in the proper place.

Calendula blossoms are surprisingly long lasting when cut. My final kitchen bouquets of the season are always those of bright orange calendulas, one of the best annuals of a mountain climate.

Nicotiana

To look at their pretty flowers, you would never guess that nicotiana is a member of the notorious tobacco family. Other names for this showy annual are "tobacco plant" or "flowering tobacco."

As the name implies, this plant contains nicotine, which is why it is practically pest-free: nicotine is a potent poison to many insects and animals. (The plants, however, aren't harmful unless you eat them.) These easy growers are sun-lovers, but will tolerate a little light shade or afternoon shadow. I recommend limited use of fertilizer. One season I over-fertilized a planter full of "Nicki Bright Pink" plants. They grew huge leaves but had sparse flowers and looked, well, like a barrel full of tobacco plants.

The short, stocky new hybrids are good for container plantings and come in a rainbow palette of burgundy, mauve, lavender and white, as well as chartreuse. (Now, there's a flower color you don't see every day.) Mixing all the colors in a whisky barrel would create a riotous display of hues.

Although nicotianas are famous for their fragrance, the hybrids, which are usually what is sold at greenhouses, have little scent at all—at least to my nose. To enjoy the old-fashioned, perfumed nicotianas you will have to buy seed and germinate it yourself. A couple of varieties reach gigantic proportions and could be grown at the back of a flowerbed. Others are real oddities with lime green, night opening blossoms.

Nicotianas are good hummingbird plants. These feathered little jewels love to dip their beaks in the trumpet-like blossoms for a drink of nectar.

So there you have it: the lowdown on nicotianas. Birds like them. People do, too. If you don't eat them or smoke them, nicotianas will be a good addition to your plantings this season.

Sweet Peas

Ah, sweet peas…Their bright velvety blossoms make the best of all garden bouquets and few flowers match their heady fragrance. If these aren't reasons enough for growing this vining annual, here's another: Sweet peas (*Lathyrus odorata*) are frost hardy, allowing them to thrive in mountain valleys.

Plant annual sweet peas in well-dug trenches immediately after the soil thaws in spring. The early timing satisfies our desperate post-winter need to plant something—anything—and sweet peas don't mind cold feet. Soaking the seeds in water overnight before planting hastens germination, which seems excruciatingly slow if the weather is, and stays, cold.

For years a good friend of mine has grown sumptuous sweet peas by her creekside cabin. The secret of her success lies in picking a sunny spot to ensure abundant bloom and never allowing the plants to dry out. She routinely picks bunches of blossoms every three or four days during peak bloom so seed pods don't form, which stop the vines from flowering. And, she moves her sweet pea bed every two to three years to maintain maximum vigor. Her favorite variety is "Royal Mix" because it blooms early—a real plus in a short season locale.

A pink and white perennial sweet pea (*Lathyrus latifolus*) also grows well at higher altitudes. Although it comes up faithfully year after year, making replanting unnecessary, perennial sweet pea sadly lacks the annual's' memorable perfume. It is this wonderful fragrance that keeps

The Earth laughs in flowers.

Ralph Waldo Emerson

81

my love affair with sweet peas strong. I have no doubt that the romance will last a lifetime.

Unusual Annuals

When I moved to Jackson Hole many years ago it was a small, isolated Western town. I felt lucky to find common bedding plants to fill my planters and boxes each spring, and drove long distances to find plants other than petunias, marigold and pansies. Today, numerous valley outlets sell uncommon annual flowers.

For a gardener who likes to experiment (and don't we all, eventually?) the list of annual flowers candidates is long. Recent upstarts are really just old-fashioned flowers that have made a comeback as the interest in gardening has grown. Sky blue cornflowers, nemesia, bright blue larkspur and colorful cosmos are some of the unusual annuals I've come across the last few years. All have been around for decades. Why not try something new to you? The list below will get you started.

Scabiosa
> A short round headed flower in soft shades of white, pink and lavender.

Sapiglossis
> Two-foot tall cousin of the petunia that has striking dark-veined blossoms.

Godetia
> Also known as satin cups. This pretty pink poppy-like plant attracts attention wherever I plant it.

Nirembergia
> This wispy plant makes a great filler plant in containers

Diasica
> A pale pink flower that also makes a wonderful filler for containers.

Purple Heliotrope
      This fragrant flower won't grow as big or bloom as prolifically as it does in warmer climes, but it's a showstopper anyway.

There are more: extravagant schizanthus (aka butterfly flower), ferny love-in-a-mist (grown as much for its seed pods as its blue and white flowers), and yellow, small flowered sanvitalia, a good trailer for the edge of a container. Bright orange California poppies can be tucked into planters for a "wildflowery" look or a gardener may find a new color of a zinnia.

The possibilities go on and on, and for gardeners like me it is an addiction. I'm always searching for new plants and when I find one, I have to try it.

Saving seeds

Flowers are said to be food for the soul. Unfortunately, feeding one's soul has become rather expensive these days as the cost of seed goes higher and higher. Price escalation has prompted me to save some of my flower seeds each fall. Seed saving requires only the smallest amount of attention and labor, and is well worth the effort.

The first step is obviously letting your flowers go to seed. I'm a relentless deadheader (as in removing spent blossoms, not Jerry Garcia) and must make a conscious effort to leave a few plants be. I've discovered in the process that seedpod heads can be beautiful, too.

The next step is determining when to harvest seeds. Immature seed will not have full viability and keeping quality. Careful observation is necessary in order to catch the harvest.

Flowers fall into two categories for seed collecting purposes: those that scatter or disperse their seed quickly and must be bagged or watched carefully, and those that hold most of their seed and can be left in the garden for harvesting later.

All the flowers of all the tomorrows are in the seeds of today.

Chinese Proverb

After harvesting, spread seeds out to dry for a few days in a warm, dry place out of the sun. Store the seeds in a cool place in a sealed container. I use jars with screw lids.

I've successfully saved seed from old-fashioned perennial standbys: mullein pinks, Shirley and Oriental poppies, sweet Williams, hollyhocks, gaillardia daisies, rocket, columbine and flax. I've also saved annual marigold, cosmos and zinnia seed.

If you save the seeds from hybrid plants, those grown from crossing varieties, remember that they won't breed "true." The next generation may produce unexpected mixes and colors.

Biennials

Biennial flowers were the cornerstones of old-fashioned gardens. Gardeners of yesteryear commonly included tall-spired foxglove and hollyhocks, sweetly scented rocket, yellow evening primroses, orange wallflowers and beautiful Canterbury bells. They grew sweet William for cutting and honesty plant for its silvery pods. Perhaps no garden was without endearing forget-me-nots, feverfew and English daisies.

Nowadays, gardeners cultivate these independent plants less frequently. Although biennials grow as easily as annuals and perennial flowers, they require more planning and patience.

Biennials are plants whose life cycle is stretched to two years. The plants produce only foliage the first year, flowers and seeds the second. After reproduction, they succumb to old age or cold temperature and die. Because biennials are champions at self-sowing, a patch of them may seem as long-lived as any of the perennials. At an old Montana hot springs, I found stands of multi-colored hollyhocks that had naturalized along the roadside, enduring for generations.

A gardener in a hurry can usually find biennial plants for sale at local garden centers. Often they are benched with, and undistinguished from, true perennials. A more economical way to acquire biennials is to

84

buy inexpensive seed packets and start them from scratch yourself. I've had success directly seeding many biennials in my flowerbed. The seedbed should be loose and well amended with organic matter. The best time to sow seeds outside in prepared beds is when plants naturally set seed, which varies area to area from mid-May to late summer. Because I live in the Northern Rockies, I plan my seeding to give plants at least three months growth before the onset of hard, nightly freezes.

Because biennial plants are exceptionally easy to transplant, they can also be started from seed in flats indoors or in a cold frame. I follow directions on each flower's seed packet regarding soil depth, watering and light requirements for germination. The seeds sprout promptly but grow slowly, waiting for spring. Fortunately, once you get biennials introduced in your garden, they will freely re-seed themselves and you'll enjoy new blooms for many seasons. Remember two important points about growing biennial flowers: you must allow them to go to seed (absolutely no deadheading) and you must leave some open ground where fresh seed can land. Heavy mulches, such as chipped bark, discourage biennials from sprouting.

The Language of Flowers

Once upon a time, a fellow gave his true love a red rose and she melted into his arms. A fairy tale, perhaps, but modern romantics still use this time-honored stratagem to capture hearts: Florists sell millions of red roses as Valentine's Day approaches.

We have the Victorians to thank for this day of romance. With time on their hands they formalized both the message of love and the language of flowers, thus creating an international phenomenon. Each flower and herb was assigned an emotion; nosegays were composed of several flowers to convey a thought.

"I am worthy of you," stated a bouquet of white roses. "I am innocent and telling the truth," declared daisies and chrysanthemums. Red carnations cried, "Alas! My poor heart!" Geraniums signified true friendship. Pansies whispered, 'You occupy my thoughts,' and violets indicated faithfulness.

But not every posy was rosy. Lavender connoted distrust and marigolds broadcast jealousy. Basil meant hatred. The Victorians thought of something for everyone.

Over the decades the language of flowers has mostly been forgotten, except for the simple message of the red rose: "I love you."

Who could forget that?

Tip

What will the weather do? Nature gives us clues. Flowers smell sweetest right before a rain. Birds fly lower before a storm. When they fly high, fair weather is on the way.

For a steady supply of seedlings, I routinely shake each plant's seed heads around my garden when I do fall clean up. New plants pop up wherever seeds happen to drop, creating different and delightful flower combinations each year. Be certain you know what seedlings look like. If you are missing feverfew in your garden this season, perhaps it is because you pulled it up last summer!

Cottage-style flower gardens have become quite popular as gardeners renew their interest in simple, old-fashioned plants. Combined with annuals and perennials, the results are glorious. Each spring my garden briefly turns into a sea of blue as carpets of self-sown forget-me-nots bloom. I'm glad that I, too, have discovered how rewarding biennials can be. They are well worth the wait.

Favorite Biennials

Forget-me-not (*Myosotis sylvatica*)
> 6-12 inches. Ranges in color from blue to pink. Prefers moist soil and partial shade. Great companion for early spring bulbs.

Canterbury bells (*Campanula medium*)
> 2-3 feet. Blue, pink and white. Showy, late blooming, bell-shaped flower.

English daisy (*Bellis perennis*)
> 4-6 inches. White, pink. Can be grown in dappled shade or sun; good in rock gardens and edging.

Foxglove (*Digitalis purpurea*)
> 3-4 feet. Pink, cream, purple, yellow. Can grow in partial shade

Evening Primrose (*Oenothera hookeri*)
> 3 feet. Peach, yellow. Strong evening fragrance. Mulch for winter protection in very cold areas. Prefers full sun.

Honesty plant (*Lunaria annua*)
> 30 inches. Purple. Silvery, coin-like pods used for dried arrangements; also called money plant.

Sweet William (*Dianthus barbatus*)

>8 inches to 2 feet. Red, pink, white, salmon. Clove-like fragrance. Good cutting flower. Plant in full sun.

Hollyhock (*Alcea rosea*)

>Up to 8 feet. Red, white, pink, rose, yellow. Spectacular tall stems of large flowers. Plant in full sun.

Dame's or sweet rocket (*Hesperis matronalis*)

>3 feet. Purple, white. Sweet scented, long blooming.

Feverfew (*Chrysanthemum Parthenium*)

>2 feet. White clusters. Excellent garden filler. Petite, daisy-like flowers good for cutting

Rose Campion (*Lychnis Coronaria*)

>2-3 feet. Magenta. Soft, silver gray foliage is a striking contrast.

Featured species

Forget-me-nots

I think flower gardens are at their finest in spring. It is then that gardens look so fresh and green, bursting with the promise of a beautiful summer.

My spring garden contains daffodils, tulips and fat clumps of perennials. Nestling in and amongst the bulbs and showier blooms are my forget-me-nots, carpeting the ground with their sprays of tiny blue flowers. Years ago I planted less than a half-dozen of these

Blossom Ballerinas

When I see hollyhocks in bloom, I'm reminded of the blossom ballerinas I made with my twin sister when we were kids. Making hollyhock dolls is a delightful way to while away a summer afternoon. This is the way to do it:

1. Pick fully opened blossoms plus a handful of unopened buds.
2. Pinch out the middle of the flower (the pistil) and extend a toothpick or sharp twig through it to attach the head of the blossom.
3. Use a bud for the head. Peel off the green part to expose the "eyes" and push the head onto the toothpick with the point up.
4. You can fancy the dolls up if you please. "Skirts" can be layered underneath by adding a number of hollyhock blossoms to the twig. A pretty blue bellflower could be added for a hat.

Real pros can make the dolls without a toothpick, but it takes more skill, and the dolls can't stand much handling.

Tip

Never plant a peony too deep. The eyes— the white or pink canine tooth-like nubs at the crown of the plant—should be no deeper than two inches below soil level.

charmers: Forget-me-nots have a habit of coming up anywhere they want to. Left to themselves they readily self-sow, persisting all over the garden for years.

Forget-me-nots are usually biennial. They set seed and begin to die soon after they flower. During this especially unattractive period they grow leggy, dry up and often suffer powdery mildew—a truly sorry sight. I have to resist pulling them up and discarding them so they will mature and drop seed. Even though they are good at self-sowing, I admit to sometimes shaking old plants around the garden to ensure lots of new plants and blue flowers the following spring.

Forget-me-nots are widely available at greenhouses. Although you may occasionally find them for sale with pink or white blossoms, it is the blue ones that I find most endearing. In my opinion, a forget-me-not in any other color than sky-reflecting blue just isn't genuine.

Members of the borage family, forget-me-nots prefer cool weather and moist soil. They do their best in lightly shaded areas but can be grown in sunny spots if they are kept well watered.

Forget-me-nots make beautiful companions for spring blooming bulbs and perennials and are wonderful in masses. When planning and planting your gardens, remember the forget-me-nots.

Perennials

I use perennial flowers as the backbone of my gardens. Perennials give vertical dimension and mass, against which spring bulbs and summer annuals can display colorful blossoms. In a climate where spring may be painfully late, perennial flower plants awaken as the snow retreats, dressing up otherwise bare areas with a bit of refreshing green weeks before annual flowers can be planted.

Perhaps because I'm so starved for green after long months of winter, I have come to love these early spring gardens best. This brief time is a tonic to me: tender columbine leaves unfurl, red nubs of bleeding hearts poke up, mounds of Shastsa daisies and Oriental poppies come to life and the withered clumps of hen and chicks plump up in the lengthening days. There may still be snow squalls in April and May, but the vibrancy of my perennial flowers gives me faith that it won't be long until I can get some dirt under my fingernails again.

Perennial flowers need good quality, well-drained soil, since their roots continue to develop year after year. I amend my beds liberally with rotted manure, compost and peat before I plant. Annually, I side dress the plants with manure and a balanced fertilizer.

Although perennial flowers are deeply rooted, they still need watering throughout the season. Western gardeners can seldom depend on rain to do our work. Violent mountain thunderstorms pass over quickly and seldom do more than wet the surface. I recommend giving perennial beds a good soaking at least three times a week.

If you have dependable snow cover, as I do, then mulching for winter protection is probably unnecessary. In fact, the year I decided to cover my plants with straw proved disastrous. The numerous voles burrowing under the mulch had a feast on the crowns of many of my flowers.

Division

Many perennial flowers magically gratify us with blooms year after year, with little or no attention. Ironically, problems arise because these plants do so well with so little. They can spread into massive clumps, sometimes developing crowded woody centers. As the size of the clump increases, flowering may decline. Blooms reduced in size and number are a sure sign of densely crowded roots.

It is time to divide. I divide my perennials when new growth is just emerging from the ground in early spring. Since different perennial flowers awaken at different times and break their winter dormancy, the work usually spaces itself out nicely. Although it is possible to do this chore in the fall, the erratic weather can turn suddenly cold, giving the

When gardening I have a gift you won't find in any manuals. I know it's strange, but I can change perennials to annuals.

Dick Emmons

Tip

Chicken wire makes a great invisible and cheap growth support. Bend a section of wire in an arch and place it over plants when they reach one-third of their mature height. Secure the ends of the arch with bent pieces of hairpin-shaped wire or coat hanger. Plants will grow through the wire, which will soon "disappear" but lend needed support.

newly moved roots scant time to put out fibrous feeder roots.

Start by digging up a well established, good-sized plant, roots and all. Loosen the soil deeply so you can lift the entire plant without yanking. Now look for natural divisions—clusters of young stems that have their own roots—and firmly pull them away from the clump. On some perennials, such as lilies of the valley or daisies, these divisions are easy to find. Others, such as yarrow, have a mat of slender, shallow roots that you just have to tear apart with your hands. Plants with crowns, such as coral bells, need to be decisively cut apart.

A few varieties have such dense, tough crowns that they have to be literally sawed or whacked apart. I speak from experience. Trying to divide a large and very woody clump of Autumn Joy sedum one spring, I first tried to split it up with a sharp spade (couldn't do it) and then to coax it out of the ground with a digging fork (my back turned into a pretzel). Then I spied the ax sitting beside the woodpile...

Wielding this trusty tool with a strong arm, I split the sedum into four wedges in a matter of minutes. Although I tried to aim my cuts between major shoots and buds, in the end I chopped the plant up however the ax fell. No matter. All the pieces grew into nice clumps with little nurturing on my part.

Since my first success with the ax, I've used it to divide other plants with dense crowns or root clumps. I hacked apart a lady's mantle that had grown big as a bushel basket. I axed old clusters of Shasta daisies and an enormous Maltese Cross. I easily cleaved a large oregano. Yes, I probably lost some shoots—but all the divisions survived.

Transplant a new division as you would a small container grown plant. If you can do it on an overcast day, plants will suffer less shock than on an intensely sunny one.

Most perennials should be divided every 3-4 years for the health and beauty of the plant. There are, of course, exceptions: baby's breath, heliopsis, lychnis and columbine resent being disturbed. My rule of thumb? If a plant looks good, leave it alone.

90

Unless you are expanding from a yard to a park, you'll probably have more little plants than you can use. This gives you the opportunity to share. There is no greater act of friendship between gardeners than the promise, "I'll give you some when I divide it."

Staking

While on vacation one summer, I visited Canada's world-famous Butchart Gardens. A team of 50 full-time gardeners had so skillfully staked massive flowering plants—five foot dahlias, spires of delphiniums, Asiatic lilies and clumps of sunflowers—that I had to get down on my hands and knees to find the supports.

Regrettably, I didn't take the time this season to stake my own perennials. By mid-August, the flower garden registered my neglect. Floppy plants had collapsed on their neighbors; tall ones had toppled over. The whole mess looked like a wilted tossed salad. It drilled home what I already knew: It is important to stake plants that need support if you want them to look good, and to use the right technique and materials.

Most perennials should be gently confined within open supports, rather than corralled in rigid columns. Stake them with their natural leaning tendencies in mind so their characteristic silhouette is not lost. Many mail order catalogues and nurseries sell plastic coated metal stakes and support circles. Though pricey, these last for years and are generally worth the money.

Staking single stems is the best method for tall plants. I have a supply of green bamboo rods on hand for these varieties. Tie stems loosely to the stakes with a soft, flexible material such as jute. Strips of old panty hose are great for this task. Very tall stems should be tied to the stakes in more than one place, keeping the top tie well below the flowers so the plant doesn't look like its being strangled.

Grids with detachable legs work well for heavy plants such as peonies. Placed over the entire plant in the spring, the grid completely disappears

9

If you are not killing plants you're not really stretching yourself as a gardener.

—

J.C. Raulston

as the plant fills in. L-shaped linking stakes can be used to brace heavy, overgrown plants that were not supported as they grew.

If you take the time to plant, take the time to stake. It makes a big difference.

Tried and true perennials

When it comes to choosing northern perennials, the bottom line is winter hardiness. I use hardiness ratings in seed catalogues as a starting point for selecting plants but have found that some rated for warmer zones succeed as well. A flower bed on the south side of a house with good drainage, full sun during the growing season, protection from cold north winds, and consistent snow cover may actually allow me to plant flowers that are rated for a zone or two warmer than my area

The best way to find out what will grow in your yard is to try the plants that you want and see how they do. After years of experimenting, I've come up with a list of some of the most reliable summer flowering perennials for Northern and mountain gardens with elevations of 6,000-8,000 feet. Though it is possible to grow all from seed, most are readily available as plants sold at nurseries.

Shasta daisies

Perhaps the classic perennial flower, I use them often in sunny locations. I prefer the single petaled forms, choosing Silver Princess or Little Miss Muffet for short 12-inch plants, or Alaska when height is needed. These white daisies bloom in my area for much of August. To keep Shastas flowering well, divide the clumps every 3 or 4 years.

Heliopsis

Rugged mountain winters don't keep this tough perennial from a shining performance year after year. Its perky yellow sunflower-like blossoms keep going from mid-summer till frost. "Summer Sun" is a good choice. This trustworthy variety produces semi-double flowers on 3-foot stems, making it valuable for the back of a flower border. Heliopsis is sun-loving and does better than most in dry soil.

Columbine

No mountain garden seems complete without this delicate flower. Considered a spring flower elsewhere, columbine blooms at my high elevation in June. "McKanna" is a popular hybrid with long spurred flowers in a wide range of colors. Because it thrives in partial shade, columbine is a useful plant. However, I add it to my list with reluctance because in our locale, leaf-eating larvae seem to find columbine as attractive as I do.

Oriental poppies

These bloom in my yard in early June before many other perennials. If the huge, brilliant orange flowers aren't shattered by wind or rain, this poppy is a show-stopper for a good 2 weeks. I think of this plant as a BIG perennial. The flamboyant flowers may be 6-10 inches across and are borne on 3-foot stems. The large clumps of hairy foliage go embarrassingly dormant in late summer so I'm careful where I plant them. Oriental poppies can be very long-lived, lasting for decades.

Gypsophilia (Baby's breath)

If you have room for the big 3-4 foot mounds of this airy flowering plant, by all means include it in your garden. A mid-season bloomer in northern and higher elevation gardens, its lacy stems and myriad tiny flowers add grace to any summertime bouquet. Since this perennial doesn't spread, clumps can remain undisturbed indefinitely. Baby's breath is so tough that I've found

A morning glory at my window satisfies me more than the meta-physics of books.

Walt Whitman

escaped plants blooming beautifully in total neglect along roadsides.

Lychnis

The most trustworthy of this group is one variety called Maltese Cross. A dependable, handsome plant, it bears clusters of bright scarlet blossoms atop 3 to 4 foot stems. Maltlese Cross does best in full sun; good drainage is essential in cold areas. I've left my plants undivided for more than a decade and they still bloom predictably each July.

Campanula

Though there are many bellflowers, I find *Campanula carpatica* to be one of the most cold hardy and garden worthy. Blue Clips, a compact plant for rock gardens or the front of a border, blooms in late July. Large upward facing, widely-opened bells add a nice garden blue for almost a month. Blue Clips can be grown in sun but will also flower in light shade. Plant in good garden soil and water regularly.

Lupine

This big member of the pea family must have plenty of sun and well-drained soil to produce dense spikes of blue, white, yellow and pink flowers. The "Russell Hybrids" are striking. I find the plants decline somewhat after about five years and probably should be replaced.

Delphinium

These back of the border plants can grow tall up to four feet depending on the variety and may need staking as they come into full bloom and splendor. Although they need lots of sun, they prefer moist ground. Take care not to let them get too dry.

Hardy geraniums

These geraniums are entirely different plants than the familiar red and profusely flowering potted plants sold at every garden center in the spring (which are more correctly called pelargoniums.) Hardy geraniums may be less confusing if referred to by the name cranesbill. There are dozens of varieties, from tiny rock garden plants to taller types and mounding forms that are good in perennial flower borders and beds. "Johnson's Blue" is a personal favorite because—like many of the true geraniums—it has the simple charm of wildflowers.

Veronica (speedwell)

Growing these long lived perennials is a good way to get that much sought after "true blue" in the garden, although varieties do come in shades of pink, purple and white these days as well. Taller forms are reliable and trouble free and short forms are good for edgings and rock gardens. I grow "Crater Lake Blue," "Red Fox" (a deep rose pink) and "Sunny Border Blue." All have many small blossoms on 2-6 inch spikes. I plant the veronicas in sunny spots but they are said to do equally as well in filtered shade.

Gaillardia daisies

Also called blanket flowers, these cheerful daisies bloom all summer long with red and yellow pinwheels. "Monarch" is a hardy form that grows to 30 inches, while dwarf "Goblin" top out at a mere foot. Easy to grow from seed and somewhat drought tolerant, gaillardias need full sun and will self seed if you can get a stand of them going.

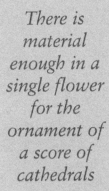

There is material enough in a single flower for the ornament of a score of cathedrals

John Ruskin

Daisies

An abundance of flowers lay claim to the name daisy. The round yellow center in many types greet us like the sun or "day's eye," shortened to " daisy." Even small children readily recognize this common bloom, whose petals have been used for decades to poetically test romance: He loves me, he loves me not.

Daisies should be included in all perennial gardens: I can't imagine one without some. Most varieties are easy to grow. If you provide a sunny location, keep them watered and their roots well drained, you will be rewarded with plentiful flowering. Among the many flowers called daisies, I choose Shasta, heliopsis, gaillardia and the varieties described below to include in my own gardens. All make good cutting flowers.

Painted daisy

This bold mix of rose red and pink colors add beauty to a garden. Be liberal with the garden hose; painted daisies don't like to dry out.

Gloriosa daisy

I think of these black-eyed Susans as a "soft" perennial: sometimes they lack enough vigor to make it through the winter. They are nice if you can keep them going.

Golden marguerite

This is a small daisy that reseeds readily. Pinch without mercy to keep marguerites compact.

Though definitely not fancy or rare, these daisies have always been favorites among gardeners. Refreshingly simple, they complement any combination of annual and perennial flowers, shrubs or foliage plants. All can be grown from seed or purchased as potted plants from local garden centers.

If blossoms diminish in size and number, the clumps probably need to be divided. Division will invigorate a planting, so I try to get this task done in very early spring every three or four years.

Bleeding Hearts

It is no mystery how bleeding hearts got their name: long wands of winsome heart-shaped flowers arch gracefully over the foliage on these delightful plants. These May and early June bloomers have long been a favorite of mine.

There are several varieties of bleeding hearts. Old-fashioned *Dicentra spectabailis* is very hardy and does well in a mountain climate; white *Dicentra alba* is less vigorous than its pink cousin, but charming nonetheless.

While it is not difficult to grow bleeding hearts, you must follow cultivation instructions carefully. Plant bleeding hearts in the spring. They can grow in areas that receive only part day sun, a boon to gardeners who have lots of shady spots in their yards.

Choose a well-drained site and enrich the soil with lots of organic matter. Be sure to keep the soil moist; bleeding hearts may not survive if you let them dry out. Finally, top dress your plants annually with manure.

If you follow the above procedures, you should be rewarded with

The blooms of bleeding hearts are perfect plants for pressing. Tuck them between the pages of a thick dictionary or other big book and the flowers are flattened into perfect little hearts. When thoroughly dry, they can be glued on notecards and valentines or whatever suits your fancy.

big, shrub-sized plants that have enough sprays of valentine-shaped flowers for bouquet cutting.

Although it is possible to propagate bleeding hearts from root divisions in the spring, I am reluctant to dig up established clumps unless they really need to be moved. The fleshy roots are extremely brittle and break easily, literally falling apart as they come out of the ground.

Bleeding hearts may go dormant in August and turn a sickly yellow. Some of the newer hybrids flower until fall.

Columbine

Columbine

A mountain garden without lovely columbines seems incomplete. Light and airy and lacy, columbines soften the look of any garden—and today, more kinds and colors of this beautiful perennial plant are available than ever before.

"McKanna Giant" is an excellent choice if you are looking for tall plants. This long spurred columbine comes in many hues. Shorter and more compact, but just as pretty, are the "Music," "Dragonfly" and "Songbird" varieties.

Relatively new to the market are double columbines. A rather odd one I frequently see for sale is named "Nora Barlow." The flowers of this double hybrid are unlike any other columbine. Spurless and pompom shaped, it doesn't even resemble its elegant relatives. Nora Barlow makes me wonder why plant breeders tinker with flowers of outstandingly beautiful form!

Columbines need rich well-drained soil that is kept moist all season. High elevation gardeners can plant them in either sun or filtered shade, subject to the usual trade-offs. In sunny locations, the plants will be sturdier and produce more flowers. Planted in shady spots, the flowers will last longer and the colors of both the leaves and flowers will be more intense.

Columbine roots prefer to remain undisturbed, so plant them where you want them to grow. This plant's long taproot also makes it a poor candidate for container planting.

Hen and Chicks

Hen and chicks are a longtime favorite of mine. This perennial's funny name reflects the tendency of its new shoots to grow around the mother plant like chicks around a hen.

Like most plants in the succulent world, hen and chicks (whose Latin name, *Sempervivums*, means, "live forever") are drought tolerant and tough. Uprooted clumps start to put out roots unaided, and potted plants quickly multiply. An occasional "chick" perishes and many "hens" pucker and sag during the cold winter months, only to plump up and look delightful when spring arrives.

Hen and chicks can root in crevices containing sparse soil, making them an ideal rock garden plant. Their juicy rosettes also admirably decorate places less hospitable to other plants: pockets in stone walls, cracks in flagstone steps, bases of birdbaths or sundials, corners of garden steps, troughs, outdoor dish gardens and strawberry jars (clay vessels with flared side openings.)

There are many species of this odd little plant. Some are as small as a dime, others as big as a grapefruit. Others may be colored in a palette of greens and maroons and covered with fine hair. Their decorative value makes their drab, pinkish flowers of secondary importance. Mine bloom so sporadically that a flower surprises me. Sending up a thick flower stalk apparently so exhausts the hen that it dies, yielding its space to a new generation of chicks.

Rarer varieties are found at specialty greenhouses or can be ordered by mail. Better yet, ask a gardening friend to give you a chick plucked from its mother. I don't remember where I acquired my common hen and chicks years ago, but I do know it has thrived in my garden for a long time.

I used to love my garden, but now that love is dead. I found my bachelor buttons in my black-eyed Susan's bed.

To transplant hen and chicks, simply dig an area a few inches deep and cover the attached succulent stem with dirt. Since hen and chicks are masters of growing in uncompromising conditions, the soil they are grown in doesn't usually need to be amended.

Keep the transplants moist until the hen gets busy and starts producing chicks. You can then ease up on the watering and let them more or less take care of themselves. If I think of it, I water them when it is hot and dry—but even if I forget, these funny little plants seem to keep on growing, and reproducing, without me.

A few starts will quickly fill up a pot and perhaps even send out a few chicks to dangle over the edge.

Lamb's ears

I'm always looking for plants that bloom into the fall. After all the annual flowers have frozen, it's nice to have some of the garden still looking pretty during precious Indian summer days. A few tough plants keep us gardeners from getting depressed. They allow us to reassure ourselves that the season isn't really over, that winter isn't too close.

Lamb's ears is a hardy perennial that hits its stride in August and early September, sending up thick stalks of small whorled, purple flowers. Also known as stachys or wooly betony, its tongue-shaped leaves are coated with silvery white "wool" that give them the appearance and feel of lamb's ears. I love to pick them while I'm out in the garden and rub them against my cheek. They are very soft and furry, and feel delightful.

Like other members of the mint family, lamb's ears is a simple plant to grow. It spreads easily and will fill in large spaces if you let it go. In fact, within a few years of planting gardeners are able to divide and move lamb's ears to other areas, or give away chunks of it to other gardeners in the spring.

Melanie Hess, a local artist who creates dried flower wreaths, pictures, and potpourris, grows a large quantity of lamb's ears. She uses

Lilies of the Valley and Fairies

A wealth of colorful and delightful legends surrounds the origins of plants and flowers. One of the best known concerns Narcissus, who became so fascinated by his reflection in a pool that he pined away, leaving only a flower bearing his name to preserve the memory of his vanity. Lilies reportedly sprang up from Eve's tears, shed as she fled the Garden of Eden with Adam.

The dainty lily of the valley is a fragrant herald of spring, thanks to faeries and gnomes—or so the legend goes. It is one of my favorite tales. I think of it each spring as I gather delicate nosegays of this sweetly perfumed flower.

On the eve of May Day, the faeries were preparing for a grand party. They recruited the gnomes to gather nectar for refreshments. But the gnomes, being notoriously unreliable, collected only a few drops before they tired of the task and decided to dance in the moonlight instead. They hung their baskets on blades of grass and soon forgot about them completely.

Hours passed in merrymaking, and before the gnomes knew it, dawn was breaking and the faeries were assembling for the party. Only then did they remember their undone chores. They hastened to retrieve their buckets, but alas, the bails on the pails had grown fast to the blades of grass!

Luckily for the naughty gnomes, the Queen of the Faeries merely laughed and waved her magic wand, changing the porcelain pails into pearly white bells tolling merriment in the breeze. If you doubt this is how the lily of the valley began, look into one of its bells. You will find a drop of nectar gathered by a gnome before he hung up his pail to dance in the moonlight on May Day eve.

If you don't already have a patch of lilies of the valley in your yard, buy or beg a division this spring. Plant the "pips" (the little shoots that appear along the roots) in a shady niche. Lilies of the valley make a good ground cover on the north side of a house or in any moist shady spot. Plants should multiply and last for years with very little care, thanks to the Queen of the Faeries.

the air-dried flower stalks and foliage in her products. The silvery leaves make good additions to wreaths and add contrasting color to potpourri.

A "flock" of lamb's ears highlights any garden. The sky-reflecting lightness of these silver and pale gray plants soothes the strong colors of other flowers during the peak blooming season. Best of all, lamb's ears is a plant that looks great right through the fall.

Oriental Poppy

The Oriental poppy is one of Nature's small miracles: Few flowers can match its sheer eye-catching color and form. Its beauty is regrettably fleeting. The fiery, six-inch flowers generally last only two weeks, less if the weather is rainy and windy.

Despite a short bloom, in good soil Oriental poppies can spread up to three-feet across in just a few years, taking up more space than you had planned. To contain your poppies or get better bloom of the ones you have, poppies should be divided and transplanted—tricky acts that require good timing if the plants are to survive.

Division is best accomplished when flowering is long finished and the plant is fading into a yellowish, unattractive dormancy. Cut into the crown to create separate clumps. Because poppies have a long taproot you'll have to dig deeply to get as much of the fleshy underground plant growth as you can. Don't be surprised if roots left in the original hole send up new shoots in the fall. You can dig up and replant these young plants, too, if you wish.

Oriental poppies should be replanted at the same depth that they were growing before division; if you replant too deeply, the plants will be smothered. Of course, they'll need to be kept moist their first season and watered in subsequent years much as you would other perennials.

Oriental poppies (*Papaver Orientalis*) aren't the variety grown commercially for bread seed, though their edible seeds have a similar taste and crunch. Poppy seeds used in baking are from a pink annual

(*Papaver somniferum*), the source of opium in other parts of the world. Sensitive drug tests can detect the presence of opiates in someone who has recently snacked on baked goods peppered with poppy seeds. To my knowledge, no one has been arrested for indulging in a poppy seed muffin binge.

Bulbs

Over the course of time, many perennial plants have developed fleshy underground bulbs to store food during adverse weather until growing conditions became favorable. Today's mountain gardeners benefit from this adaptation, with thousands of varieties of "bulbs" available. But in truth, only half of what we call bulbs are bulbs. The rest are corms, tubers or rhizomes.

A true bulb is a complete miniature of a plant encased in fleshy scales that contain starch and sugar. That's why it is hard to fail with bulbs their first season: the flower and food are already there for sure-fire blooming. A daffodil is a bulb; so is a tulip. Because of differences in structure, lilies are called scaly bulbs and onions, truncated bulbs.

A corm is the base of a stem that becomes swollen and solid with nutrients. Corms may be rounded, like crocus, or flat on top like gladioli. A tuber also stocks food in an underground stem. It has a tough skin that grows roots all over its surface rather than just at the bottom, like bulbs and corms. Begonias and anemones grow from short, fat knobby tubers.

How many of you have seen the thickened rootstock of iris, growing horizontally and weaving along the surface of the soil? These roots are called rhizomes, another form that is technically not a bulb.

All of these plants have one trait in common: They gather food from their leaves during the growth cycle and pack excess nutrients into their unique storage bins to provide food for future plants. Being technically correct really doesn't matter. A gladiola is just as pretty whether you call it a corm or a bulb. But I find the more you learn about

Bloom, damn it.

103

plants—what they are and how they grow—the more interesting gardening becomes.

Bulb farms

Most of us associate bulb flowers with Holland. The Dutch are well-known masters of breeding and producing high quality bulbs. But did you know that many bulbs are grown in the northwestern United States? The Washington Bulb Company is, in fact, one of the world's largest tulip and daffodil producers.

Washington's commercial bulb industry is headquartered in Skagit County. Most of the 45 million bulbs grown there are sold in the US, but a percentage is exported to Holland. Skagit Valley has hundreds of acres devoted to tulip growing and twice that many planted in daffodils.

It takes 2-3 years to produce a mature bulb that is ready to sell. Beware of "bargain" bulbs: They may be mere babies that will not produce the results you want. In each of the bulb's immature seasons, the flower heads are topped between full bloom and the petals falling to the ground. One day a field may be a carpet of vivid colors, the next just snipped stems. With the flowers removed, the bulbs begin to absorb the stem as food, turning it into energy for future flowering power.

Mature bulbs are harvested in the summer when the bloom is done and the leaves are dry and brown. Machines slowly dig up the dormant bulbs and load them into wagons. The bulbs are cleaned, sorted and graded right in the field to be shipped to customers around the country.

Planting bulbs

Spring without blooming bulb plants is a disappointing affair filled with longing and regret. From the first brave crocuses and daffodils to fragrant hyacinths and flamboyant tulips, bulb flowers are a tonic after a long and colorless winter. But they don't plant themselves. Because planting bulbs is one of the last chores of the season, tired gardeners too

Tulip

often neglect it. Think spring, grab your gloves and dig in: your industry will be rewarded.

Try to plant early to mid-autumn. Although bulbs can be planted up to the time the ground freezes, bulbs planted late fall bloom late the following spring. They have little time to grow roots before the freeze sets in. Rooting will be postponed until spring thaw, delaying the appearance of flower stalks. I once planted 100 daffodil bulbs in November, the day before a blizzard turned the valley white. The daffodils bloomed the following year—but not until the end of June.

Well-prepared bulb plantings tend to be more productive than spot plantings. The following guidelines will help first-time gardeners (and even us old hands) create memorable bulb gardens.

→ Check the merchandise. Buy only bulbs that are firm and solid. Bypass those with mold, bruises, holes, scars or soft spots, or ones that have dried out in packages or storage bins. Large-sized bulbs (in comparison to cheap undersized bulbs) produce bigger flowers.

→ Choose bulbs appropriate to your area. Voles and pocket gophers, critters that are common in the West, find tulip bulbs very tasty. If these little animals are abundant on your property, consider planting daffodils, which rodents won't eat. Similarly, fancy hybrids are less hardy than standard varieties in a cold climate.

→ Don't skimp. A single daffodil may be beautiful in the pages of a catalogue but it needs company in a garden. When it comes to bulbs, it is hard to overdo. As a rule of thumb, six of a kind is the minimum for making a worthwhile cluster.

→ Pick a site with excellent drainage that receives full sun. Bulbs may fail in waterlogged soil, and although bulbs can be planted in areas that receive filtered light, most perform best in full sun. Bulbs that

Flowers seem intended for the solace of ordinary humanity

—

John Ruskin

I dig up and store the tubers from my tuberous begonias for a repeat performance the following year. At the beginning of September I cut back on watering and lift the tubers when the plant's foliage begins to yellow. I then clean, dry and remove the stem from each tuber, and store them in dry peat moss in a cold (40 degree) spot over the winter. I've discovered favored plant started from older tubers produce big, voluptuous blossoms.

receive too little sun are unable to store enough energy to bloom a second season.

→ Spade to a depth of 8-12 inches, working in organic matter such as compost, peat moss and well-rotted manure (fresh manure will burn bulbs) to improve the soil. Digging a hole that deep in higher elevations can be a problem if the ground is hard and rocky. I dig down as far as I can and add surface mulch after cold weather sets in to make up the difference in depth.

→ Toss a handful of Bulb Booster®, a fertilizer especially formulated for bulbs, in each planting hole. It and comparable bulb fertilizers are widely available at garden centers.

→ Plant in clumps rather than straight rows for a more natural look. Place bulbs in the planting holes with the pointed end up. (Don't laugh: I get asked this question every fall.) Bulb roots grow downward and outward so be sure they are properly spaced and planted deep enough. Large bulbs such as daffodils and tulips need to be planted approximately 8-inches deep and 6-inches apart. Smaller bulbs—crocuses, grape hyacinths, etc.—should be planted 3-4 inches deep and 3-inches apart.

→ Firm bulbs in place. If the bulbs are all planted at the same depth, they'll bloom together.

→ Your planted areas should be watered lightly to encourage rooting.

→ Mark the spot. Labels (or sticks) remind you where your bulbs are when they are dormant, so you won't dig them up while planting summer flowers. If you should accidentally dig up established bulbs simply set them back in the ground or move them to another place.

Unless they are sliced open, they should be fine.

I've given up using clever bulb diggers advertised each fall. For a small area and in loose soil they are indeed convenient, but I've had little success digging holes with them in the dense or rocky soil of our valley. Likewise for bulb augers that attach to electric drills.

Bulbs are among the easiest garden flowers for beginners to grow—but there is one hard and fast rule: You can't enjoy their spring flowers unless you plan ahead and plant them in the fall.

Forcing Bulbs

Okay, okay: You're only human. The first six-inch snowstorm has arrived and a bag of bulbs you never got around to planting is still in your garage. Now what? Store them in the refrigerator until spring, placing them in a place where they won't freeze. Keep them away from apples, which give off ethylene gas as they ripen. This gas is harmful to bulbs.

Unplanted bulbs can also be forced for mid-winter bloom. Chill them in your refrigerator for at least 12 weeks, then plant in potting soil. Water thoroughly and set the pots on a sunny windowsill. Keep the

Tulips

Tulips aren't reliable after the first year's spectacular display. Blooms become less numerous, noticeably smaller and in some cases nonexistent. For this reason, some gardeners treat them as annuals and replant them each fall to guarantee beautiful, full-size blooms in the spring.

This is fine if you don't garden on a budget. I personally want to get more from my spring bulbs that one good showing. While browsing through bulb catalogues look for varieties described as good repeaters to increase your chances of success. Tiny species tulips have worked well for me.

soil moist. This deceptive use of light and temperature "tricks" bulbs into believing they've experienced a winter-spring span of five months. Depending on the type of bulb you plant, you'll have blooms in 3-6 weeks.

I've had good luck forcing daffodil and hyacinth bulbs. Crocus and tulips seem to be more difficult, but are worth a try. Paperwhite narcissus and amaryllis bulbs, intended to be grown indoors, are the easiest bulbs to force. Pre-potted bulb kits usually show up in stores around the holidays. Complete with growing directions, they make great gifts. A dramatic, trumpet shaped amaryllis is a present no one is likely to overlook. The colors and enormous flowers make amaryllis plants an exuberant antidote for a gray, wintry day. And paperwhite's sweet fragrant can fill an entire room.

After the blossoms fade, I discard the paperwhites but save the amaryllis. Its foliage makes an unusual houseplant, and it can be forced to rebloom after a period of dormancy.

Forced hyacinths and daffodils may be saved for replanting outdoors. Gradually dry the bulbs as the leaves start to yellow and set them in a cool room till spring. Plant the bulbs outside as soon as the ground can be worked and allow them to replenish themselves; they must get back on the proper timetable before you can expect more blooms.

When the days are short and the light low, forced bulbs help mountain and northern gardeners wait a little more patiently for spring.

Ugly Foliage

Although spring bulbs are lovely in bloom, I hate the sight of their drying leaves when the flowering period is over. And I'm definitely not alone. We gardeners do crazy things to hide the ugly remnants of bulb foliage, robbing the bulbs of food for next year's display.

Admit it. I'll bet like me, you've cut back the leaves and stems of spring flowering bulbs when they were still green. I've tied withering

Amaryllis

daffodil leaves together and bent them over. One year I even braided the leaves into silly coiffures in an attempt to tidy their appearance. The leafy hairdos not only looked stupid—they didn't allow the foliage to manufacture enough food.

One really has only two choices: Put up with the dying leaves (its ok to curse them) until they yellow or loosen from the bulb, or hide the unsightly foliage by interspersing plants that grow around and above it. Vinca and other evergreen ground covers make ideal companions for small bulbs such as snowdrops and crocus, but tulips and daffodils need heartier choices. In sunny spots, disguise ratty bulb beds with catmint, cranesbill or lady's mantle. Good choices for lightly shaded areas include hostas, columbine and mid-sized forget-me-nots.

Naturalizing

Among plants to naturalize, none are easier than bulbs. Naturalizing is the term used to describe informal plantings that get minimal maintenance. I think it is more than that. Naturalizing, to me, means planting as though it was Nature's idea instead of mine: generously planting bulbs in the wooded outskirts of your yard, by the dozens in a fresh green meadow, in irregular drifts by ponds and streams, or along winding paths and rough banks. Places where plants take care of themselves.

When selecting bulbs for naturalizing, choose those that endure neglect. Single flowering varieties last longer than double flowering types. A bulb closer to its wild form is more durable than a showier complex hybrid. Little bulbs such as glory of the snow, botanical crocus, winter aconite and snowdrops are good choices.

Daffodils are perhaps the supreme flowers for naturalizing. Sweeping down a hillside or rambling in patches beside a creek, they symbolize springtime. Success with these hardy, long-lived bulbs is almost assured, making them a good choice for beginning gardeners. By mixing early,

F

Flowers are beautiful hieroglyphics of Nature, with which she indicates how much she loves us.

Wolfgang von Goethe

Tip

Perennial borders that peak mid- to late summer often look dull in the spring and fall. Give them color and spice by mixing in appropriate spring and fall bulbs.

—

mid-season and late daffodils, it is possible to get a month or more of bloom.

Tulips, unfortunately, are poor naturalizers. Fancy hybrid tulips lose their vigor after a year or two. Others must be divided every two or three years and some, like the big Darwin tulips, are just too stiff for informal plantings.

If you choose to naturalize, clear your mind of boundaries. Plant quantities of bulbs in large clumps but do not fill the whole space: It is important to leave some quiet reaches for the eye to rest upon. On every piece of property, whatever the size, there should be an area of complete naturalness—a little hidden path where wild things grow or an out-of the-way corner. There may be a time when such a spot will mean more to you than any garden, no matter how fine and finished the latter is.

Autumn Crocus

Autumn crocus (colchicum) is a strange bulbous plant that flowers several weeks, usually starting around late September and lasting into October. Each spring colchicum sprout strapping leaves. Come summer, the leaves die back and one tends to forget them entirely. They quietly sit beneath the ground until the flowers pop out in the fall. Single flowers grow directly out of the bulb with no stem or leaves for company, earning them their cheesy "naked boys" nickname.

Although autumn crocuses look like bigger versions of the pretty spring crocus, they are members of the lily family. They are only available for fall planting, and sometimes arrive from the supplier blooming in their bags. This won't hurt them a bit; just tuck the big bulbs in place in filtered shade or full sun and enjoy their beauty.

Minor Bulbs

There is a grab bag group of flowers classified officially as "minor bulbs." This title does a disservice to these early blooming diminutive plants, for if they are planted well in the fall they have a major impact in the spring. Many are the first to appear when the last of the snow has melted, providing sorely need color.

Minor bulbs are practical. They are true perennials that can persist in the garden for decades in self-maintaining colonies. Without help they will often multiply, spreading both by dropping seed and by offsets around the base of the mother bulb. As the number of bulbs grows, the rate of increase is accelerated so, in time, one can end up with a carpet of these Lilliputian charmers.

In spite of their many advantages, many of the minor bulbs are little known. While tulips and daffodils have become almost a springtime cliché, a gardener may have to resort to mail order catalogues to even find some of the species. Some of my favorites include grape hyacinths, glory of the snow and chinadoxia.

When deciding where to plant the small bulbs, their pint-sized stature should be considered. Plant them where they will be seen. As with any bulb, good drainage is essential. Minor bulbs can be planted in areas that receive either full sun or filtered shade, and are sometimes even planted under deciduous trees. Other planting possibilities include unmowed hillsides and among low-growing ground covers. The shortest ones—crocus, grape hyacinths, glory of the snow or winter aconite—can rim the front of a perennial flower border or peek out from deciduous shrubs. Their compact size makes them ideal candidates for rock garden plantings, where a full sized tulip would look out of place.

Because minor bulbs are delicate, gardeners must plant them in profusion for a fine show. A dozen is a drop in the bucket; a hundred is more like it. Alone, a miniature bulb has little impact other that to offer a delightful surprise on a dreary gray day, but planted closely and generously in drifts they give us something to swoon about, and look like a natural colony of wildflowers.

Planting dozens of these little bulbs is relatively easy: the smaller the

If of thy worldly goods bereft and of thy meager store two loaves are left Sell one and with the dole, buy hya-cinths to feed thy soul.

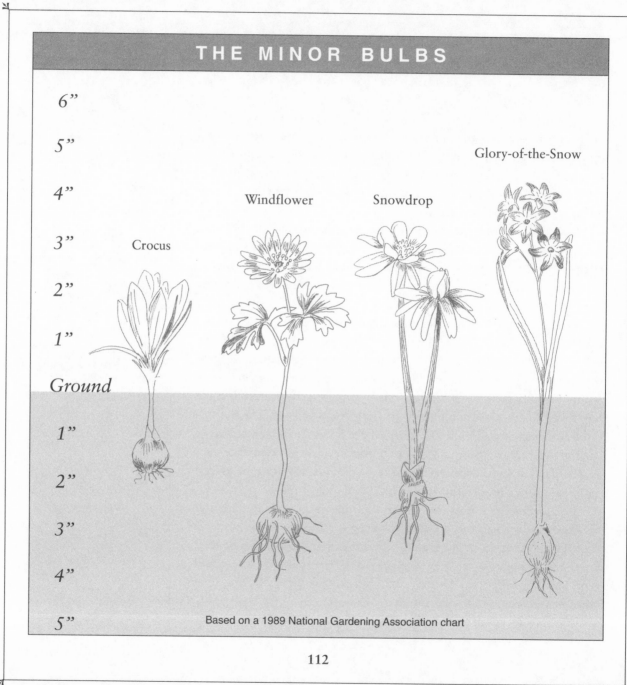

THE MINOR BULBS

6"

5"

4"

3"

2"

1"

Ground

1"

2"

3"

4"

5"

Crocus

Windflower

Snowdrop

Glory-of-the-Snow

Based on a 1989 National Gardening Association chart

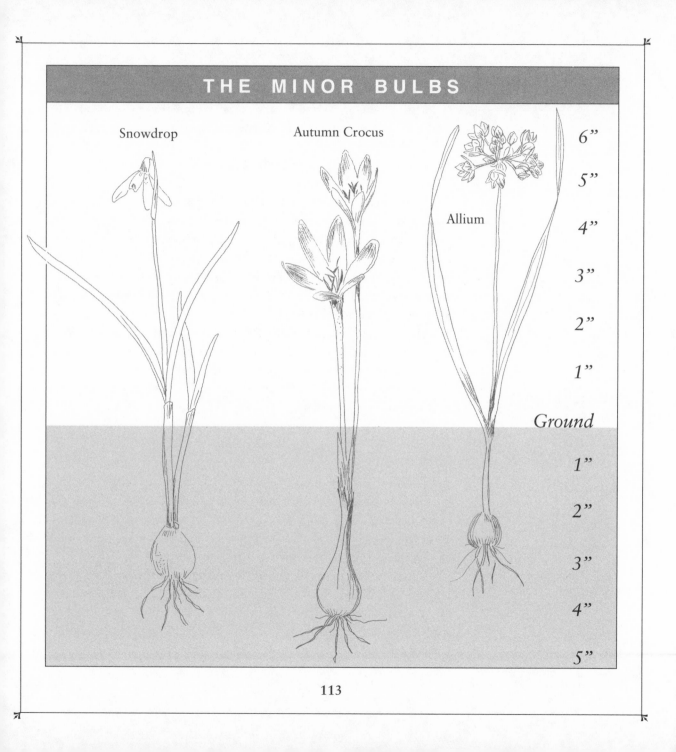

THE MINOR BULBS

Snowdrop

Autumn Crocus

Allium

6"
5"
4"
3"
2"
1"
Ground
1"
2"
3"
4"
5"

Tip

Enter your best flowers in the county fair. It's fun, and the cash prizes will help pay for the seeds and plants you splurged on in the spring.

bulb, the more shallowly it is planted. The old rule of green thumbers applies: plant bulbs to a depth of three times the diameter of the bulb.

Minor bulbs are spring's wake up call. When they poke through the cold ground we know that the gardening season has finally arrived.

Cutting Gardens

How often I've wavered between cutting a bouquet in my garden or leaving the flowers on the plants so my beds won't look bare. This psychological torture of whether to pick or not to pick—of actually going at a garden in its prime with beheading in mind—can be alleviated by creating a special bouquet garden. It is a lot easier to take scissors to your plants when you know the only purpose of a particular plot is to provide a steady supply of cut flowers.

Cutting gardens are more about utility then design or perfect grooming. In fact, the classic cutting garden is a row by row planting, much like many vegetable gardens. There is no reason that the garden shouldn't be pretty, but really, the test of a successful cutting garden is how nice it looks in a vase.

Cultivation

A cutting garden should be placed in a sunny, out of the way spot. You don't want to showcase it center stage, since this is the plot you raid in its prime. As with any plantings meant for harvesting, good soil is a good friend. Poor soil should be improved in the usual way and should be dug up, at least a foot down, before planting.

Like any other flower garden, a cutting plot thrives only if it is maintained. Water when needed and religiously cut spent flowers. If flowers are allowed to go to seed, plants will simply stop putting out fresh crops of bloom, which of course defeats the whole purpose of a cutting garden.

Choosing flowers for your cutting garden is easy. Just about everything you grow could be a likely candidate, but the obvious ones are the longer lasting varieties. (For example, I wouldn't include daylilies because, true to their name, they only last a day). Consider blowsy, large flowers that have a brief season of bloom, as well as plants you like but can't seem to fit into your landscape.

Cutting gardens can be comprised solely of annual flowers, and often are, but it is possible to extend your blooming season by also planting bulbs and perennials. Rows of tulips and daffodils make wonderful cut flowers early season and should be included. Perennials can be placed at one end of the garden as well. Although most folks think "long stemmed" when thinking of cut flowers, many excellent choices have short stems. To me, nothing is sweeter than a tiny vase filled with small blue violas, dwarf zinnias or tiny marigolds. Good cutting candidates include:

Perennials	Snapdragons
Shasta daisy	Asters
Yarrow	Larkspur
Black-eyed Susans	Blue cornflowers
Peonies	Marigolds
Feverfew	Sweet peas
Perennial scabiosa	(should be trellised)
Sweet William (biennial)	Carnations
Delphinium	Godetia
Baby's breath	Calendula
Bleeding hearts	Pansies
Love in a mist	**Bulbs**
Annuals	Tulips
Cosmos	Daffodils
Zinnias	Asiatic lilies

If I had a single flower for every time I think of you, I could walk forever in my garden.

115

Tip

Gardeners who suffer from allergies should choose plants with bigger, brighter leaves. Smaller plants have tinier, wind-pollinated grains that are easy to inhale. Wearing sunglasses helps keep pollen out of the eyes, and using black plastic mulch minimizes dust and mold growth.

Being able to snip to my heart's content—with no sense of esthetic loss—is truly a luxury.

Cut Flowers

We've all seen those pretty advertisements: A lovely woman gathers flowers from her garden or sunny meadow and charmingly lays them in a wicker basket on the crook of her arm.

Nice—except I know that if I treated a garden bouquet like that, it would be wilted by the time I reached home.

What I carry to picking spots is an unromantic bucket of water. It's not a catalogue shot, but the daisies on my kitchen table are.

The longevity of cut flowers can be dramatically increased be taking a few precautions when cutting and handling them. First, most blossoms should be cut in the morning or early evening when they are full of water. Use sharp clean tools; sharp scissors or a kitchen knife usually work better than blade and anvil clippers, which will crush the stems.

Choose flowers that have not quite reached their prime. An indicator of age is the presence of pollen in the flower's center.

Cut the stems on a slant and quickly plunge the stems into water. If you want really long-lasting bouquets, harden the flowers by placing them in a cool darkened place for several hours or overnight. A basement or the refrigerator is a good conditioning place. In the dark the stomata, the minute pores in the stems and leaves close to reduce water loss.

Remove any foliage that will be below the water line in your container. Though I rarely use them, some people swear by commercial flower preservative powders, available in small packets at floral shops. I've also been told that adding a tablespoon of 7-Up® or an aspirin to the water will extend the life of cut flowers.

Finally, place your bouquet out of direct sun and away from heat sources. Check the water daily, adding more or changing it altogether if necessary.

Vegetable Gardens

Growing vegetables in a mountain climate isn't going to save the gardener money. A wonderfully efficient system brings a year round supply of produce to supermarkets, often at reasonable prices.

I slave away in my vegetable garden because growing my own veggies offers other advantages. When just picked, their flavor is at its peak. I can choose varieties that are frequently tastier, have a more delicate texture (only sturdy, hard skinned varieties ship well) or ripen over a longer period of time. Vegetable gardening is great exercise and outdoor recreation to boot. It couldn't be healthier.

If you don't already have a vegetable garden on your property, begin the planning process by considering a site. Vegetable gardens require at least eight hours of direct sun a day, with midday sun being the best. A well drained, gently sloping south or southeastern exposed plot away from competing trees is ideal. If it is near a water source, even better, because most northern and mountain gardens need supplemental watering.

Garden size, of course, depends on what you want out of your plot. An area that is too big is as bad as one that is too small. Remember that the larger the garden, the more maintenance it requires.

Let my words, like vegetables, be tender and sweet, for tomorrow I may have to eat them.

Try planting in wide rows. Lettuce, spinach, carrots and beets are a handful of the many vegetables that thrive planted in bands 5-12 inches wide rather than in single-file rows. As the plants grow, their leaves cast shade that helps keep the ground moist and curtails weed growth. Weed carefully until the plants become established.

Raised Beds

Once you've selected a site, consider creating a raised bed. Gardening in many parts of the West is a challenge that can break a spade. (Really—it's happened to me.) Our exceedingly obdurate soil is an underground obstacle course of rocks, rocks and more rocks. Quarrying is probably not what you had in mind when you decided to start a vegetable garden. A raised bed will save your spade, back, and temper.

Raised beds offer good drainage and loose soil that is easy to amend with organic matter—an ingredient we sorely miss in most of Wyoming. In these optimal conditions roots grow down instead of sideways in search of nutrients and moisture, allowing crops to be planted closer together. Moreover, the soil in raised beds thaws quicker in spring than it does at ground level. Since we mountain gardeners endure long winters, that time advantage can spell the difference between success and failure.

A raised bed is essentially a framed, bottomless box that holds soil. It should not span wider than you can comfortably reach across and into. Framing wood must be rot resistant to withstand constant contact with moist soil; redwood is a good choice. If you use pressure treated wood, expose it to the weather for several months to leach out undesirable chemicals before framing. I recommend making your frame a minimum of 12-inches deep to accommodate the root depth of most vegetables.

I love the tidy appearance raised beds give a piece of property. Grass is conveniently kept from creeping in and strong architectural form is added to the garden. And, the vegetables I've grown in raised beds have thrived.

What to Plant

The fun part is deciding what to plant. Climate-challenged gardeners must select "early" varieties. Most seed packets include "days to harvest" numbers. Gardeners in my mountain valley are taking a big chance planting anything that requires more than a 70-day growing period. If seed packet directions say "sow indoors," this implies that the plants need a long frost-free season to develop—also risky in the mountains.

Obviously, not all vegetables thrive in cool climates. Tomatoes, cucumbers and corn need a longer, hotter season than mine to produce well outdoors. On the other hand, any of the leafy greens produce a good crop. Spinach, chard, arugula, lettuce, kale and endive thrive in my valley. Ditto for root vegetables. Mountain gardeners will find success with carrots, onions, leeks, potatoes, turnips, parsnips, radishes and beets. The cole crops—cabbage, broccoli, kohlrabi and brussels sprouts—grow well in cool weather places, too, as do peas.

Planning Your Garden

The final planning step is to commit your tentative selection to paper. Draw your garden to scale (reduce the number of feet to the same number of inches). A garden sketch helps you determine if your selection is realistic size-wise, and provides a year-to-year planning guide and reference for crop rotation. Plot out what is to be planted in each part of the garden. Tried and true tips include:

→ Tall crops, such as trellised peas, should be planted at the north end of the garden so they will not shade other plants.

→ Allocate space that will be left undisturbed for perennial vegetables and plants such as rhubarb, asparagus, chives and horseradish.

→ Don't plant crops requiring lots of water at the garden's edge; they'll dry out faster.

Zucchinis terrific. Like bunnies, profilic.

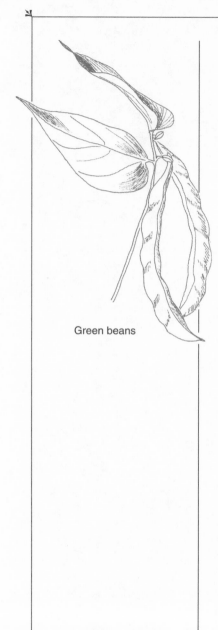

Green beans

→ Plant small quantities of a variety of vegetables rather than very long rows of a few.

→ Plant only crops that you and your family enjoy. When I started growing our own food, I quickly discovered that no one at my house would touch beets with a stick. I quit planting them long ago.

Companion Planting

When planning your garden, consider companion planting. Over the years, observant gardeners have discovered that certain plants grown with other plants are healthier than when they are grown by themselves. The favorable pairing results in increased vigor for both plants and the ability to repel insects. Much of this knowledge has been passed down as gardening lore.

Although lacking hard scientific evidence, companion planting seems to make the garden a more harmonious community. This no doubt has to do with the chemical effects of root secretions, plant odors and insect attracting or repelling substances that influence the growth of neighboring plants.

Most herbs possess companionable characteristics: mint repels ants and cabbageworms, sage repels carrot flies and when grown near cabbage is said to make it more digestible. Garlic repels potato blight, and parsley attracts lacewing insects and honeybees. Horseradish may protect the garden from wild animals that don't like its smell. Aromatic herbs supposedly increase the vigor of plants they grow near, and because basil is one of the sweetest herbs, it is considered to be an especially valuable companion.

Choosing the wrong companions may have a detrimental effect. Strawberries should not be planted near the cabbage patch and onions are said to inhibit peas. Dill will reduce the carrot crop if grown too close.

Interplanting certain kinds of flowers can help keep pests away and attract helpful bees as well, and will certainly make your garden a prettier and more interesting space. Why not give companion planting a try? It is fascinating and may result in the best garden you have ever grown.

CROP	PLANT BY:	KEEP FROM:	REMARKS
Basil	Most crops	Rue	Basil repels flies & mosquitoes and enhances the growth and flavor of tomatoes and lettuce.
Carrots	Lettuce, onions leeks, peas, chives Cabbage, potatoes		Leeks and onions repel carrot flies.
Garlic	Tomatoes, roses Cabbage	Peas, beans	Garlic deters Japanese beetles and aphids.
Kohlrabi	Cabbage family	Tomatoes	Kohlrabi stunts tomatoes.
Lettuce	Carrots, radishes strawberries	Cabbage family	Lettuce tenderizes radishes.
Oregano	All crops		Oregano deters many insects.
Peas	Carrots, beans Early potatoes	Garlic, onions leeks, shallots	
Swiss chard	Kohlrabi, onions	Pole beans	
Thyme	All crops		Thyme deters cabbage moths.
Tomatoes	Cabbage family Sage, rosemary, Basil, carrots	Potatoes, kohlrabi, fennel	

Timing

Don't let cabin fever trigger you to start your seeds too soon. Seedlings planted in a pre-spring fervor often look as spindly and weak as anorexic basketball players when the ideal transplant date arrives. I recommend waiting until the middle of April to start vegetable seeds indoors.

Likewise, a few balmy, sunny days can cause spring fever to run high, but suppress the urge to dig up the garden beds too early. If you work the soil when it is wet, you will end up with cement-like clods when it finally dries out. A cover of clear plastic over the garden can help warm the soil and keep spring rains from saturating it further.

Maintenance

Once your garden is planted, take care of all those little seedlings. Water on a regular basis. Generally, your garden will require about an inch of water a week throughout the growing season. It is best to water deeply, soaking the ground for a considerable distance down.

Regular weeding, and mulching if you are so inclined, are important to keep your vegetables growing at a steady pace and to prevent disease and pest problems from getting out of hand. You may also have to fertilize if your soil hasn't been improved to it's fullest potential.

I'm always urging gardeners to thin their vegetable seedlings to the suggested spacing that's listed on the back of the packets. Thinning, the task of pulling out enough seedlings in a row to give adequate space for the remaining ones, is a job I no longer neglect. I've learned (over and over) that crowded plants don't grow or produce well. Root vegetables are particularly susceptible to deformation if they are growing too close, and packed greens become weak and spindly. I thin by hand after the plants have become established but are still mere babies, selecting the Strongest of the lot as I pull plants from the row.

If it is a good year, nature might do most of the work, supplying the warmth and moisture and natural fertilizer that plants need. Other years, you may feel Mother Nature is working against you…and winning. However your garden grows, it will hopefully be a rewarding experience.

Words of warning are probably appropriate here. Vegetable gardening is habit forming. Once you've picked that first bowl of succulent salad greens, or pulled up a bucket of your very own brightly colored carrots, or felt the pride of digging a bucket of the nicest potatoes you've ever imagined …. you're hooked.

Featured Vegetables

Lettuce

During the dormant and dreary gardenless months of winter, I daydream of picking succulent, leafy greens from my vegetable garden. When spring has finally sprung, one of my first garden tasks is to plant a row of lettuce for an early fresh salad.

Nowadays, there is a fabulous array of lettuce forms, colors and textures for the home gardener. In just one of the seed catalogues I receive, entire pages are devoted to gourmet lettuce seeds. The dozens of kinds of seeds on the market can be grouped into several main types. These I'll explain to simplify your seed selection:

Crisphead
> This is the most familiar form of lettuce: everyone has purchased "Iceberg" in the supermarket. Head lettuces ship well, but can be challenging for home gardeners to grow.

Butterhead
> This lettuce is semi-heading. It is sometimes called Boston or Bibb lettuce. Of all lettuces, butterheads are my favorite be-

I don't remember planting this.

Tip

To increase your harvest of lettuce and leafy greens—especially if frost and insect damage have been a problem—try a floating row cover. They are sold at garden centers and by mail order companies. Lay the white, wispy cover lightly over your plants. The plants readily lift the cover as they grow. The cover helps keep pests out and provides extra warmth and humidity.

cause of their smooth taste. Their foliage is softer but more flavorful than the crispheads.

Cos or Romaine

These lettuces have a distinctly upright shape and long, narrow leaves clustered around crunchy hearts. This is the lettuce of the classic Caesar salad, a weekly staple at my house.

Loose-leaf

Some of the easiest types of lettuce to grow are the loose-leafs. The leaves grow up and out, creating a loose rosette. Often called "cutting lettuces," I can harvest individual leaves as I need them. Loose-leaf lettuces come in a delightful range of leaf shapes, colors and textures. The red varieties, such as Red Sails and Red Salad Bowl, have become very popular in the last few years.

Many varieties are too fragile for shipment. For a truly wonderful salad, people should grow their own lettuce, which for the most part is an easy task. In this area, slugs pose the greatest challenge. Wash your greens thoroughly at harvest time to avoid extra protein on your turkey sandwich.

Marauding deer and moose, and even an occasional chipmunk also relish the lettuce crops in my garden. I don't really mind too much. My lettuce grows well and there is usually enough to share.

Swiss Chard

Every season, I grow new flowers and vegetables, partly to keep my gardening challenging, but also to give me something new to write about. After 16 years as the local paper's gardening columnist, I need fresh ideas!

This season I experimented with scarlet runner beans, canary bird flower (a failure), bicolored gourds and my first crop of Swiss chard. Last week, my chard was ready for harvest: tall, crinkly leaves topped fleshy stems. As I picked a bowl, I belatedly realized I needed advice on how to cook this leafy vegetable.

I called a friend who is also a professional cook; she had much to say about chard. Its succulent stems add extra crunch to stir fry dishes; its leaves can be used the way many cooks use spinach. Chard can flavor soup, be tossed with pasta or sautéed with lots of garlic and layered in lasagna.

I concluded that chard is as easy to cook with as it is to grow.

Swiss chard is related to beets, a fact I keep secret from my family. This biennial vegetable tolerates cool temperatures, which makes it successful in our mountain valley. Chard seeds are commonly found on greenhouse racks, and seed catalogues are filled with choices. I grew "Fordhook," a standard green variety, but chards also are available in shades of red, orange and yellow. It can be grown wherever lettuce can be cultivated and tastes a lot better than most non-chard eaters' suspect.

The more I learn about chard, the more I wonder why I waited so long to grow it. It is a storehouse of vitamins A, E, K, some B vitamins, and magnesium and potassium. It also contains cancer-fighting antioxidants. It is the best "new" plant I've grown this season, and I'm sure I'll try it again next spring.

Arugula

Nothing tastes better than those first spring greens from our gardens. After a winter diet of pale imported iceberg lettuce, the crisp textures and lively flavors of freshly picked greens is a treat.

Arugula—also called rocket and roquette—is one of the easiest greens to grow in a mountain garden. A quick maturing cut and come again plant, it is a good choice for high altitude areas that have intense sunshine but cool weather. As with most members of the mustard family,

One good thing about rutabagas is that they provide something for turnips to taste better than...

125

arugula is very tolerant of harsh weather, and will poke its leafy head up even in the midst of spring snowstorms. It has a nutty, peppery flavor that wakes up mixed green salads with its unusual bite: A little goes a long way.

Seed arugula directly in your vegetable garden, thinning seedlings to stand five or six inches apart. Keep your plants well watered for a good crop. I recommend planting a new crop every two or three weeks for an ongoing supply of fresh, bite-sized leaves (older plants are over-poweringly pungent). You can raise a wheelbarrow full of this salad sparker for the cost of a few seed packets.

Arugula has been savored in Europe for centuries. It is admittedly an acquired taste. I've come to enjoy its spicy, unusual flavor and I think many folks will come to like it, too.

Red Orach

Red orach (*Atriplex hortensis*) was a favorite summer green with homesteaders. This heirloom vegetable has recently come back into vogue, with regional seed companies marketing both red and green varieties.

Orach is a mild, slightly salty tasting green. It can be cooked like spinach, but I prefer red orach served raw. It adds interest and color to tossed salads.

It is also striking in the garden. The entire plant is a beautiful red-dish-purple with triangular, spinach-shaped leaves. Easy to please, it's unusually tolerant of alkaline soil and dry conditions. With good soil and sufficient water, red orach really shines. Its large, tender leaves become thick, meaty and profuse on upright stems.

Plant orach as soon as the ground can be worked in the spring. Don't bother to start seed indoors; orach's fine roots hate transplanting. Sow seeds in a sunny spot in rows 12-inches apart. Thin to 4-6 inches between plants.

Red orach is basically trouble-free. Don't be surprised if it grows several feet tall. Keep plants low and bushy by pinching tops back occasionally. If you allow red orach to go to seed, it will self-sow abundantly all over the garden.

Kohlrabi

Last fall a friend of mine gave me a bag of kohlrabi. These strange, pale green vegetables are members of the cabbage family. Their bulbous aboveground growth with long-stemmed leaves shooting out in all directions has led some to call them mini-satellites or vegetable sputniks.

Kohlrabi derives its name from the German words for cabbage (kohl) and turnip (rabi). It is grown for its delicious dense globe, which is actually part of the stem. Its firm, crisp texture is reminiscent of a potato, its nutty sweet flavor a cross between a mild turnip and an apple.

Since kohlrabi is a cool weather crop—and cool most often describes our growing season—this vegetable does well in a mountain climate. I recommend starting kohlrabi seeds indoors in the spring and transplanting the seedlings to your outside vegetable garden when the weather has warmed the soil. Kohlrabi can even take light frosts; in fact, a few frosty nights in the fall make the globes sweeter.

The generous friend who gave me a share of her kohlrabi crop suggests covering the plants with a floating row cover. She uses spun-bonded polypropylene "reemay" cloth and finds that the extra warmth and protection from pests it provides gives her a superior yield.

The fastest growing of all the brassicas, kohlrabi prefers the rich soils that also grow good cabbages. The round globes should be harvested between the size of a golf ball and a tennis ball; larger, they tend to become tough and pithy.

German and Hungarian cookbooks are good places to look for kohlrabi recipes. Kohlrabi can be steamed, but I really love the fresh crunch of eating mine raw. Fresh kohlrabi is an excellent source of calcium,

Onion skin very thin, Mild winter coming in. Onion skin thick and tough Coming winter cold and rough.

Old English rhyme

phosphorus and potassium and has more vitamin C than orange juice—though I doubt you could talk your kids into switching kohlrabi for oranges in their lunch buckets.

It just might be too hard for them to love a vegetable that looks like it should be orbiting the earth.

Carrots

When I first started gardening I believed carrots would be one of the simplest vegetables to grow. But I've found that for this nutritious root vegetable to be a true gastronomic delight, it must be properly grown. And that means putting some elbow grease into the carrot patch.

The secret to growing really good carrots is to thoroughly prepare the soil in which you plant them. Carrots like loose, friable soil. They don't like rocks, and they don't like clay. Stony soil yields misshapen, forked or stunted roots. As for clay, carrots languish in it. Aim for stone-free dirt at least 12-inches deep—which doesn't sound hard unless, like me, you live on top of glacial cobble—and add lots of organic matter to break up the soil. After working in organic matter, I add a couple of buckets of fine mason sand to my carrot row to ensure good, loose soil. Mason sand is available at most construction companies for a small fee.

Novice gardeners will tell you that carrot seeds never sprout. It only seems that way. If the soil is cold, it takes weeks for them to poke up through the soil, and when they do the tiny plants look like goners. They do better, however, than seedlings started indoors. Never try to transplant carrots. The result will be twisted and otherwise deformed vegetables. Direct sow the seeds where you want them to grow. Soaking them between wet paper towels overnight may speed up germination.

Carrot plants must be thinned to thrive. When carrot tops are two inches long, go through the row and pluck out enough plants so your seedlings are roughly three inches apart. If you

What's up, Doc?

don't thin, you'll end up with skinny, poorly formed roots due to over-crowding. Never use high nitrogen fertilizer on carrots. Excessive nitrogen will cause the tops to grow large while the size of the root suffers. And keep your plants moist. If you allow the soil to dry out, the roots may crack when you irrigate.

At one time my carrot crop was so gnarly and ugly that even Likely, our pet rabbit, refused to eat them. But since I've worked to improve their ground, I'm growing better and better bunny food. Heck, I might enter my carrots in the county fair this year and see if they win a prize.

Specialty Potatoes

It used to be that a potato was just a potato. Not so anymore. Home gardeners today have a choice of potatoes with personality—ones with variety, color, form, texture, unusual size and great flavor—instead of the cheap, gnarly brown spuds that inhabit the grocery store. Europeans have always preferred yellow potatoes to white. After growing creamy, moist and tasty "Yukon Gold" and "German Butterball" varieties last year I can see why. I've also found fingerling potatoes to be a real taste treat. These small, slender tubers are surging in popularity as gardeners discover them.

Be bold and experiment with your spuds. Some you'll like, some you won't. While my Yukons and fingerlings were a hit, the new blue varieties fell flat. My "Peruvian Purple" spuds turned murky gray when cooked. (My son, Cooper, actually refused to eat them.) I've since learned that adding a tablespoon or two of vinegar into their cooking water will retain their full beauty and may even improve their taste. I doubt I can convince my family to eat a bowl of intensely blue mashed potatoes; perhaps I'll try "All Red" or "Huckleberry" next. Their bright red interior should hold more appeal.

Specialty spuds are planted no differently than other potatoes. Cut seed potatoes purchased from a retail or mail order nursery in pieces.

Potatoes and marriage, as an Irish aying goes, are two things too serious to joke about.

129

Each piece should have at least two strong eyes. Leave plenty of flesh around the eyes to nourish the plant during its first few weeks of growth. Let the pieces air dry for a day or two. Plant them 6-8 inches deep, cut side down and 10-14 inches apart. Lightly tamp the earth around the potato and water well.

When your stems are approximately 8-inches high, carefully use your hoe to scrape dirt around both sides of the vine, a processing called hilling. The potato experts at Rominger's Seed & Potato company explain why it is important: "Hilling puts the root system deeper where the soil is cooler while the just scraped-up soil creates a light fluffy medium for tubers to develop into."

Hilling is recommended again in 2-3 weeks, and yet again two weeks after that. In seven to eight weeks, your potato vines will be in full bloom, and small tubers will be big enough to eat as "new potatoes." Dig the main harvest when the vines freeze back in the fall.

Potato Scab

In cool mountain climates, rust isn't a big problem on strawberries. Fungus stays manageable and pesky slugs hole up and disappear when the weather turns chilly.

But even our challenging climate is hospitable to a widespread malady: Potato scab.

Scab is found virtually everywhere spuds are grown. A fungus that develops in the soil causes the disease. If you notice raised, pitted areas on your garden tubers, where the skin is rough and bumpy with a corky texture, you've got scab. Once introduced, the disease may linger for several years. Keep scab away from your potato patch by avoiding the use of fresh manure as a soil amendment. Fresh manure often harbors scab fungus. If your soil needs improvement, incorporate compost or well aged and rotted manure into your garden.

One potato, Two potato, Three potato, Four. In high altitude climates, you'll get a lot more!

Infestation tends to be most severe in dry, alkaline soils. Acidify your soil several weeks before planting by adding small amounts of elemental sulfur. Keep potato hills moist but not waterlogged during the growing season. Scab can also be controlled by crop rotation. Don't grow potatoes in the same location more than once every three years. And, of course, don't save scabby spuds for next year's seed stock.

Luckily scab usually doesn't rot or decay the inside of the potato, which remain safe to eat if cooked. I simply peel off the disfigured areas of my tubers when I'm scrubbing them up for dinner.

Tomatoes

A juicy homegrown tomato in the Northern Rockies is an object of wonder. After all, the tomato is by nature a Southerner, having originated in South America and Mexico.

Logic be damned: We mountain gardeners want them. Long for them. To us a heated greenhouse may be more prized than a warm garage. We send away for cold hardy "early" tomato seeds with hopeful names: "Siberia," "Sub Arctic" and "Groshovka" (a tough Russian variety). Surely *these* will grow in Wyoming.

And they do, sort of. None are the two-pound "Beefmasters" of our dreams—but they are far superior to most store-bought ones.

Determinates are one of two distinct types of tomatoes. Once they reach a certain height, these sturdy, bushy plants form a terminal flower cluster and cease growing. Tomato fruit grows at the top of the main stem. Determinates produce one early, good yield, then fruit production stops. Because these bush tomatoes stay compact, they are a good choice for container gardening. "Oregon Spring" and "Stupice" are my favorite determinate varieties.

Indeterminates are climbing vine plants that grow indefinitely, producing tomatoes all season long. Their marathon vines need to be supported; I use one inexpensive wire tomato cage for each plant.

Early to bed, early to rise. Work like hell and fertilize.

Emily Whitey

131

Tip

For sturdier plants, set transplanted tomatoes deeply in the soil. Dig a hole deep enough to accommodate the root ball as well as part of the stem. Set the plant in, fill the hole, and water thoroughly.

Although I mainly grow determinates, I always plant at least two pots of the terrific indeterminate "Sweet 100," a cherry tomato. Most cherry tomato plants are weedy and rampant, growing vines as long as 10 feet tall. The vines may even collapse on themselves and shade out the bottom of the plant. To prevent this, I start pruning my indeterminates in late July. As the season draws to a close, I also tip prune to direct the plant's energy into maturing existing tomatoes rather than forming new fruit that will be killed by frost before it matures.

No matter what the variety, growing a good tomato in Jackson Hole isn't easy. I'm one of the lucky gardeners in this valley, for I do in fact have a small home greenhouse on my property. I plant my tomatoes in black, plastic nursery cans and usually start harvesting ripe fruit by August.

Green Tomatoes

In spite of all my nurturing, I always seem to end up with more green tomatoes than red ones at the end of the season. One cold mountain summer I had so many hard, green tomatoes that I used them to play catch with my dog. I surely hate to toss them out, as I've spent the entire summer nurturing those rambling vines. But these green beauties are even harder to give away than surplus zucchinis—and they can't be eaten raw.

Cooking, however, will make these unripe fruits palatable. Green tomatoes have a unique, tangy flavor that partners well with spices such as cinnamon and ginger and, surprisingly, chocolate. Try the recipes on the opposite page!

Ornamental kale

A few months ago I received a letter from the editor of *The Hardy Gardener,* a small gardening newsletter. He invited me to share any ideas I might have about extended season gardening, particularly on growing vegetables in a "potentially threatening climate."

The letter arrived at the end of one of the worst growing summers I'd experienced; there's no doubt the request had been sent to the right location. My 6,800-foot elevation garden is threatened each season by ridiculously late and early frosts. It has fallen prey to earth tremors; marauding porcupines, moose and deer; hungry chipmunks who love to nibble on garden seedlings; and to my once small son, who pulled up all the tiny carrot plants to see if they were ready to eat.

Much of this adversity I have no control over. (Who could have guessed it would snow on the Fourth of July?). I face the challenges as they come, in ways that limit my exposure and time invested. Since I lack the time to set up cloches, cold frames and the like, I've learned to grow extra hardy vegetables and flowers that can withstand the cool, short growing season.

Some of my favorite and most successful plants are ornamental brassicas, the decorative cabbages and kales. I grow these sturdy plants around the edges of my raised beds for their beauty. Although edible, the flavor of

Green Devil Cake

Your friends will never guess what makes this cake so wonderfully moist!
  2 cups flour
  1 cup brown sugar
  1 tsp. each baking powder, cinnamon and soda
  4 oz. melted unsweetened chocolate
  1 cup sour milk
      (Mix 1 T vinegar with enough milk to make
      1 cup. Let stand 5 minutes).
  1 cup pureed green tomatoes
  1 cup softened butter
  2 eggs
  1 T grated orange peel
Combine the first 5 ingredients. Add chocolate, milk, tomatoes, butter, eggs and orange peel. Beat with electric mixer for 2 minutes. Pour into a greased and floured 13 x 9-inch pan and bake at 350 degrees for 33-40 min.

Indian Relish

Chop fine:
12 green tomatoes
12 tart apples
3 peeled onions

Boil:
5 cups vinegar
5 cups sugar
1 tsp each red pepper, turmeric, salt
3 tsp. ginger

Add chopped ingredients to boiling mixture and stir together. Lower heat and simmer for one hour.

Tip

Never let a zucchini squash grow longer than 8-inches. Zucchini is most tender and flavorful when it is small. Even in mountain climates, where there' never a real surplus, you can't give club-sized zukes away.

ornamentals frankly tends to be somewhat pungent and bitter for my taste.

At maturity, the plants form rosettes of gloriously colored leaves that look like huge flowers. Frost intensifies the color of ornamental kale and cabbage, highlighting the garden until snowfall.

Because the growing season here is so brief, I start my own seedlings indoors on a sunny windowsill or under lights well before it is time to do outdoor planting. Mail order catalogs offer several kale and cabbage varieties, including extra frizzy, peacock, white pigeon and red chidori. The smooth-leafed varieties are called flowering cabbage, the fringed-leafed varieties flowering kale. All have centers that turn white, pink or vivid purple as the weather turns colder.

Ornamental brassicas are bold plants. Well after the last calendula has bloomed and even the last viola has given in to winter, the kales and cabbages are still hanging in there, looking a little odd but still rather cheery. They are definitely a plant for the far north and its 'potentially threatening climate."

Power Veggies

For decades, Popeye has eaten spinach and Bugs Bunny has munched on carrots. I, for one, think they are on to something.

That "something" is nutrition. As research has made clear, good fresh foods are the best way to supply nutrients to our bodies—and there is no better place to find fresh food than in your vegetable garden. Scientific advances have produced a whole new crop of "power veggies," enhanced nutrition varieties as easy to grow as the old standbys but better for you. Breeding advances have increased the carotene content in squash and carrots and the vitamin C content in tomatoes and peppers. They've also developed nutritious, high vitamin vegetables that even kids might find interesting.

Hot off the breeder's bench is a pastel cauliflower the color of orange sherbet and a Chinese cabbage with a lemony orange center. Both have higher than normal carotene levels. Perhaps the most fascinating high carotene newcomer is an orange fleshed cucumber. Because we are so used to green, bright orange cukes seem odd—but I'm game to try them. This cucumber packs a vitamin A level equivalent to that of musk melon (ordinarily cucumbers have none.)

Of course, the health conscious gardener should grow broccoli or its close relative, broccoli rabe (pronounced 'rob'). Both are excellent sources of folic acid. And having a row or two of greens should go without saying. While many Americans may still make their salads from iceberg lettuce and believe that the dandelion is their enemy, our knowledge of greens today is worlds away for what we knew as children. A vast variety of edible greens from all over the world await our discovery. Many grow well in mountain climates.

Try growing some of the unusual greens: peppery rocket, cress, red orach, French sorrel and corn salad. All combine splendidly with loose leaf lettuce and spinach for fresh green salads. Other leafy vegetables that are nutritional powerhouses include kale and mustard greens. Shepherd's Seeds offers "Piquant Mix," a variety of tasty salad greens seed. Keep in mind that the darker green the leaf, the higher the vitamin content.

For the best flavor and nutrition, pay particular attention to harvesting. Greens are quite perishable, so if possible, pick them only as needed. If you can't use harvested greens immediately, store them in plastic bags in your refrigerator's vegetable crisper.

Popeye and Bugs had it right all along.

Who knew?

Gardeners know all the best dirt.

135

Sage

Herb Gardens

An herb garden is one of those rare things in life that is not only pretty but useful as well. Herbs are valued for their savory, medicinal and aromatic qualities—attributes that define a broad spectrum of plants. If you can cook with it, garnish a salad with it, soothe a burn or scratch with it, make a tea from it, perfume your sheets with it, kill a bug with it, treat a disease with it, weave, dye or spin something with it, or cast a spell with it, the plant is likely an herb.

Site Selection and Size

Herbs can be scattered among vegetable gardens or flowerbeds, but I find it convenient to group them together in their own garden site. When I made a garden especially for herbs, it focused my interest on these nifty plants, and I was soon reading about and searching for even more to include in my collection.

The first and foremost step in establishing an herb garden is selecting a good site. The garden must be in full sun for your plants to thrive. Good drainage is equally important. Raised beds provide the latter and are ideal for herb gardens.

Herb gardens planted primarily for culinary use should be situated close to your house. Gardeners are far more likely to use herbs in cooking if they can quickly step outside for fresh snippets.

Most herbs require very little space. You can grow a wonderful herb garden in only a small plot. Aim for variety, not quantity. For perennial herbs, one plant of a kind is usually enough; for annual herbs, try a small patch or short row of each kind.

Herbs are said to be tolerant of dry conditions, but my experience says the Rockies are often too dry even for drought-tolerant plants. I water my herb garden at least once a week, and find that annual herbs require even more moisture. Once my plants are in the ground and growing, I fertilize them with a mild, low nitrogen fertilizer once a summer and leave it at that: too much nitrogen diminishes herbs' flavor.

With a little planning, an herb garden can and should be a feast for the senses. The most artful collections are a pleasing arrangement of heights, color, textures, and shapes. This is not difficult to attain, since herb plants are so varied. Woolly thyme is fuzzy, rosemary is shrubby, and dill and fennel have fern-like characteristics. Others, like lamb's ears, have pretty silver-gray leaves. Sometimes I add bright flowers—orange marigolds and calendulas, a few johnny jump ups and pansies or some colorful patches of dianthus—for a splash of extra color.

Don't overlook a bit of ornamentation as well. A sundial, birdbath or Victorian gazing globe would make an already interesting herb garden even better. The most delightful herb garden that I've ever planted was graced by a small metal sculpture of a crowned girl with outstretched arms. She is my Queen of the Garden, welcoming plants all season long.

Obtaining herb plants

Starting herb plants from seed takes longer than most other seed crops. Patience is required and I seem to lack it. I usually purchase herbs and plant them outside when the weather warms. Local garden centers and the garden sections at retail and grocery stores often carry an assortment of popular culinary herbs in the spring, semi-hidden amongst larger vegetable seedlings and bedding plants. Parsley, basil, chives, sage, rosemary and mint are typically sold at these locales. Occasionally, more unusual ones are also shipped in bulk orders, such as chervil, lemon

As rosemary is to the spirit, lavendar is to the soul

balm, tarragon, garlic chives or burnet. Snatch these up: They are hard to find and difficult to grow from seed.

Planted in very small pots, most high altitude supermarket/garden center herbs have been shipped a considerable distance from warmer, out of state climes. If you grab them when they've just been delivered you'll likely take home plants that are healthy and well worth the money. Look for good color and firm leaves and stems.

Avoid buying the last outdoor stragglers. Chances are they've been baked in the sun and dried out several times, a trauma from which they may not recover. They've often lost their labels or, worse, been mislabeled from a jumble of loose tags being randomly stuck back in the pots. It's always a good idea to ask when the plants arrived, and when the next shipment is expected.

Division

Exchanging or obtaining starter plants from friends is a wonderful way to expand or begin an herb garden. Some mature herbs are easily divided. I've had good luck with all of the mints (there are dozens of varieties), oregano and thyme. I divide in early spring when the plant is just beginning to send up new growth.

To divide herbs that grow in clumps—such as chives, tarragon or oregano—dig up the entire plant and tear it into smaller pieces. Or, chop it in chunks with a spade. For herbs with shoots, such as mint, simply cut off the starts and treat them as young transplants. Replant all herb divisions at the same depth as they had been growing, and keep them well watered until they become established.

Mail Order Nurseries

If you become an addicted herbalist, you'll likely want to grow more than the common herbs available locally. Mail order nurseries are a good source for rarer varieties. It is, of course, cheaper to buy herb seeds than herb plants. Annual herbs, such as dill, basil, cilantro, sweet marjoram and borage, are a cinch to germinate. But many perennials, such as lavender, are difficult to grow from seed. If you only need one or two plants, buy seedlings.

A selection of reputable mail order nurseries that specialize in herbs are listed below. Use them to augment your local offerings.

Mountain Valley Growers
38325 Pepperweed Road
Squaw Valley, California 93675
Phone: 559-338-2775 • Fax: 559-338-0075
Email: mvg@spiralcomm.net • www.mountainvalley growers.com
> In business for 15 years, Mountain Valley Growers is the largest certified organic mail order plant nursery in the United States. The company's plant list numbers over 400 varieties, but it will contract grow anything. You can order a free catalogue or save a tree and view its entire catalogue on-line. Its Web site includes botanic name cross-references, informative articles, tips from past issues of its newsletters and a query section.

Lingle's Herbs
2055 N. Lomina Avenue
Long Beach, California 90815
Phone: 800-708-0633 • Fax: 562-598-3376
Email: Info@linglesherbs.com • www.linglesherbs.com
> Lingle's informative, on-line catalogue features over 150 plants. The family-owned nursery's plants are organically grown outside instead of greenhoused, factors that the company says "makes for the hardiest, healthiest and safest herbs. " The company, like all those featured here, guarantees safe delivery.

Accept a sprig of basil and true love will follow.

139

Good Scents
1308 N. Meridian Road
Meridian, Idaho 83642
Phone: 208-887-1784

> Good Scents grows over 400 varieties of potted herbs. All of its plants are propagated by seed, division or cuttings. None are wild harvested, as many wild medicinal herb varieties are endangered. The nursery has particularly nice selections of lavender, rosemary and scented geraniums. A full plant list with descriptions can be obtained by sending $1 to the address listed above.

The Thyme Garden Herb Company
20546 Alsea Highway
Alsea, Oregon 97324
Phone: 541-487-8671
Email: herbs@thymegarden.com • www.thymegarden.com

> This family owned and operated nursery organically grows over 700 varieties of herb plants. It ships well established herbs in 4" pots. Shipping is a bit more expensive, but the company notes that the larger size increases the survival rate of sending plants through the mail. Thyme Garden's 72-page catalog is short on pictures but long on useful information. It features herb seeds and plants, dried herbs, seasoning and tea blends. To obtain a copy, send a $2 check or money order to the address above.

Richters Herbs
357 Hwy. 47
Goodwood, Ontario LOC1AO, Canada
Phone: 905-640-6677 • Fax: 905-640-6641
Email: info@richters.com • www.richters.com

> Richters is one of the largest herb nurseries in North America,

offering over 800 varieties of culinary, medicinal and aromatic herbs. Plants, seeds, dried herbs, books and videos are included in the company's offerings. You can browse its on-line catalogue or request that a catalogue be mailed to you.

Culinary Herbs

To a gardener who loves to cook, fresh herbs from his or her own garden is one of life's luxuries. Fresh herbs add flavor to food, especially if you are cutting down on fats and salts, and can turn an ordinary dish into something extraordinary. The most commonly used culinary herbs you'll want to include are:

Chives

> Perennial that grows 12-inches tall. Clumps are easy to grow and will survive even the coldest winters. Chive's delicate light onion taste flavors cream soups and sauces, cheese, eggs and, of course, baked potatoes with sour cream. This pretty herb's round clover-like pink flowers are edible and can be used as garnishes.

Cilantro

> Hardy annual that grows 2-feet tall. Cilantro's fast growing and aromatic foliage and flowers are often used in Mexican cooking and salsas, though the flavor takes some getting used to. The dried seeds are called coriander and are also used in cooking,

Dill

> Gangly annual that grows 3-feet tall. Matures quickly from seed directly sown in the garden. Feathery leaves used to flavor salads, eggs, vegetables, seafood and chicken, and for making herb butters. Dill seeds, which are more pungent, are used to flavor potatoes and pickles.

Though an old man, I am but a young gardener

Thomas Jefferson

French tarragon

Perennial. Grows 3 feet tall. Undistinguished in appearance, true French tarragon doesn't form seeds. Gardeners will have to buy plants or start new ones from root divisions in the spring. Seed packets labeled tarragon are probably Russian tarragon, a tasteless imposter. French tarragon's anise-flavored leaves are good with chicken, eggs, and rice and for making your own salad dressings.

Mint

Perennial. Grows 1-3 feet tall. Numerous varieties are available; the most popular are peppermint and spearmint. Dividing the roots in the spring can create new plants. Mint is an aggressive herb. Be careful where you plant it, or it will take over. Mint's cool, refreshing taste is used to flavor teas, fruit salad, jelly, peas, salads and Middle Eastern yogurt and grain dishes.

Basil

Tender annual that grows 8-12 inches tall. Basil is extremely sensitive to cold; I grow mine only in moveable pots. It is easy to grow from seed, but pinch flower heads to encourage new growth. Wherever a cook's imagination leads, basil will follow. This very versatile kitchen herb is essential in most Italian dishes.

Parsley

Biennial. Grows 1-2 feet tall. Parsley is slow to germinate from seed. Flat-leafed varieties have a stronger flavor than curled types, which is most often used as a garnish. This celery-flavored herb can be used to flavor almost anything, and is often used in soup stocks, cream sauces, salad dressings, salads and on all types of vegetables.

Oregano

Perennial. Grows 18-inches to 2-feet high. This shrubby plant has a spicy fragrance and pretty purple flower heads. Harder to find but more pungent is Greek oregano. Try oregano in Italian and Greek recipes as well as meat dishes and soups and stew.

Rosemary

Perennial. Grows 1-2 feet tall. Shrubby and strong flavored, rosemary plants should be purchased, as it is extremely slow to germinate. In northern climates rosemary often won't make it through the winter. I plant mine in pots and bring them inside each fall. Use rosemary's needle-like leaves sparingly to flavor lamb, Italian dishes and sauces.

Sage

Perennial that grows 1-2 feet tall. A bushy plant with silver green leaves, sage should be cut back once or twice each season to produce a large number of tender stalks. Purple and golden sage are varieties that are ornamental as well as edible. Sage is the classic, distinctive ingredient in poultry stuffing.

Marilyn's Pesto

Basil is really a tropical plant that thrives in warm, humid conditions. Arid Wyoming's low humidity is great for outdoor recreation, but not ideal for lush, tropical plants. I plant my basil near the base of tomatoes I grow in large pots. Well-watered all summer, it grows the best it can.

The harvest isn't bountiful, but I always grow enough of the spicy leaves to make a batch or two of pesto.

2 cups fresh basil leaves
1/2 cup parsley leaves
1/2 cup olive oil
2 garlic cloves
1 teaspoon salt
1/2 cup grated Parmesan cheese

Puree the basil, parsley, oil, garlic and salt in a blender or food processor to a coarse texture. Stir in the cheese. Store leftover pesto, in the refrigerator with a thin layer of oil on top, or freeze.

Thyme

Perennial. Grows 10 inches tall. Summer pruning keeps plants full and bushy. There are many varieties of this herb, including English, orange, lemon and French thyme. Thyme's small pink flowers attract bees. Its tiny, pungent leaves are used to season chowders, stuffing, sausage, sauces, poultry and vegetables.

Featured Herbs

Garlic

When the last vegetables have been picked from the garden and frosts are occurring nightly, the time to plant garlic has arrived. Planting this hardy bulb in the fall results in a larger harvest the following season. Garlic has been beloved by herbalists, witches and gourmet cooks for centuries. Excluding vampires and werewolves, it is popular with almost everyone. I, personally, never seem to grow enough of it.

Two types of garlic are commonly found in gardening centers and mail order catalogues: hardneck, which has a woody neck and bigger cloves, and softneck, often seen decoratively braided at farmers' markets. If you buy garlic heads at the supermarket to break apart and plant, you'll be getting softneck. It is not as cold hardy as hardneck, but keeps longer.

Plant garlic in a site that gets lots of sun and that won't be disturbed (I mark my garlic patch with stakes and flagging or I inevitably spade it up in the spring.) Work the soil well, incorporating plenty of organic matter as you dig down. Next, break garlic bulbs into cloves and set individual cloves 4-6 inches apart, root side down, in the prepared site. Cover with 1-2 inches of soil. Fluctuating winter temperatures can heave the plants out of the ground if they are too shallow. After the ground freezes, apply several inches of organic mulch, such as straw,

144

on top of the site. Remove the mulch as soon as the snow melts in the spring.

Garlic is ready to harvest when the plants' leaves begin to yellow or brown off in late summer or early fall. Check bulb readiness by loosening the soil around it with a spading fork and gently pulling a plant up. (This is also the best harvest technique.) If papery skin has formed around each clove, its ready to be harvested. As you harvest your bulbs, gently brush the soil away from the roots, but don't wash the bulbs in water, as they cure when drying. Freshly dug garlic should be moved out of direct sunlight as soon as possible.

Garlic can be planted as a companion crop to cole and potatoes, acting as a natural plant insecticide by repelling cabbageworms and flea beetles. It also benefits the health of humans. Recent medical studies conclude that eating this flavorful bulb lowers cholesterol levels.

Maybe there is something to the old proverb, "Garlic is better than 10 mothers."

Horseradish

Although horseradish is a mouthwatering, eye-stinging, sinus clearing condiment, I love the vile stuff. This tall, white-flowered herb is a member of the mustard family. It is propagated not by seeds but by root cuttings from mature plants. Ask a friend for cuttings or buy them from a nursery.

Horseradish prefers deep, moist soil and full sun. To plant, place the end of the cutting 2-5 inches below the soil surface and pack the soil firmly around it. I suggest planting horseradish in an out-of-the-way corner of the garden. It can grow up to three feet tall and several feet in diameter, surpassing even vigorous rhubarb plants. A small piece of root left in the ground soon becomes a full-grown plant, whether you want it or not: One of the devilish features of horseradish is the difficulty of eradicating or containing it. When you plant horseradish you are forever in bed with it, so plan carefully.

Garlic makes a man wink, drink and stink

——

Apperson 1590

145

Horseradish's tough, stringy roots should be harvested just before winter sets in, as frost triggers the pungent qualities of the plant and improves its flavor. Dig up a bowl full of roots to make into a relish before the ground freezes solid. Wash and peel them until you are down to snowy white flesh.

Before food processors were invented, cooks suffered preparing horseradish. An invisible eye irritant is released during hand grating that gives even the most stoic tear ducts a workout. These days, chopped pieces of the root can be painlessly ground in a processor. Salt the ground horseradish to taste and mix it with white vinegar (cider vinegar gives the relish a yellowish cast) until it attains a paste-like consistency. Put it into jars and refrigerate. While vinegar allows the relish to last indefi-nitely, it begins to lose its zing after three months.

Chamomile

One of the easiest herbs to grow is chamomile, a well-known me-dicinal herb. In *The Tale of Peter Rabbit* by Beatrix Potter, Mrs. Rabbit gives her undisciplined son chamomile tea. Like a cup of warm milk, this soothing, quieting nighttime beverage reputedly calms digestion and helps young ones (bunnies or kids) drift off to sleep. Although clinical studies probably don't exist to support these claims, the collective expe-rience of millions of people over the centuries does.

Feathery foliage and small white, daisy-like blossoms characterize this pretty plant. I scatter its tiny seeds over freshly dug garden ground and let a stream of water from a hose settle them in.

Pleasant, apple-flavored chamomile tea is made from the plant's flow-ers. Steep a teaspoonful of dried chamomile flowers in boiling water for 3-5 minutes. Remove the flowers and sweeten with honey, if desired. People with allergies should be aware that chamomile flower tea con-tains pollen, and although rare, people sometimes have allergic reac-tions to this gentle brew.

Cilantro
(Coriander)

Ethnic fare has become standard fare in the West. Every town of any size seems to have Thai, Chinese and Mexican restaurants. Thus, the culinary herbs used in these foreign dishes—little known or grown 20 year ago—have become common as well.

Cilantro is one of these. It has become of our most popular seasonings in the past decade. This versatile plant has many uses, and several names depending on what part of the plant you seed. The dried seeds are called coriander. The fresh leaves are referred to as both cilantro and Chinese parsley.

I've grown cilantro in my vegetable garden for years with great success. It thrives is cool weather, something high altitude and Northern gardeners have in abundance. Because the plants have long taproots and don't transplant all that well, I plant the seed where I want it to grow for the season. Like most herbs, the plants do best in a sun-drenched spot with average, well-drained soil.

Cilantro has a reputation for going to flower within weeks of planting. Hot weather encourages rapid flowering, and I've seen puny little plants grown in cell packs crowned with blossoms.

I order "Slo-bolt"—which as the name suggests, is slow to go to seed or bolt—from mail order seed companies. Slo-bolt grows large and lush before sending up seed stalks, so I'm able to harvest leaves many times. By late summer even Slo-bolt is unfurling parasols of pinkish white to lavender florets at the top of two-foot stems. Because the plant's pollen is pink, your garden will soon be humming with rosy-knickered bees. This aromatic plant is a terrific attractor of pollinating insects. I'd even go so far as to say the swirl of activity around coriander's delicate mauve flowers is reason enough to grow it.

In the fall, the shiny, striped fruits will turn into fawn colored balls. Gather in your sweet smelling harvest quickly before the balls shatter.

Never enough thyme.

Curiously, I've found that some folks can't stand the spicy smell and flavor of the green, feathery foliage. It seems people either love cilantro (as I do) or detest it.

If you are one of the lucky ones who favor cilantro's bold taste, try growing some in your garden. You'll find it rewarding the easy to grow—something that can't be said about all plants in our climate.

Troublemakers

Lovage

My gardening encyclopedia says, "lovage makes a good background plant." Seed catalogues describe lovage as "a giant among herbs." I should have taken these descriptions as a warning.

At three years, lovage reaches its colossal mature size of seven feet. Seven, bushy feet. My lovage grew so huge my Yukon Gold potatoes were in danger of being shaded out. My onions disappeared in its foliage and the lettuce I'd planted two feet away never had a chance. Every summer I dramatically chop it down only to have it grow back as prolifically as a magic beanstalk.

Why did I choose this monster? Because I like to cook, and perennial lovage is listed as a good kitchen garden herb. It resembles celery in taste and use and its dark green leaves may be used as salad greens or to add flavor to soup. The amount of this strong flavored herb I use in relation to its size, however, seems absurd. If I don't soon find ways to include bushels of it in my diet, it will have to go.

If you dare, you can start lovage from seed or division. I've lately noticed that anyone who has lovage plants is generous about giving hunks of it away. Lovage prefers moist, well-drained soil and thrives in full sun or partial shade. I don't often let my plant flower but when it does, flat umbels of small yellow flowers reveal its relationship to carrots and parsley. Be forewarned that established plants reseed freely and sprout all over the garden. On second thought, perhaps I'll keep my enormous lovage. Its stems have a hollow center that gardening books suggest can be cut and used as straws. They optimistically note that, "children love to drink through lovage straws."

Lovage straws. Now that's what I call an essential herb.

Comfrey

Beware the medicinal herb, comfrey. Once planted, this hairy plant with its six-foot taproot and ability to withstand -40 degrees presents a real problem if you ever want to move or get rid of it. This hardy perennial produces new plants if even a trace of root is left behind, making it very difficult to eradicate.

This wouldn't be so annoying if comfrey was a pretty plant. But it's not. Its large leaves resemble donkey ears. Small, inconspicuous purple flowers nod on top of hirsute, four-foot stems. So, one wonders, why is this herb *ever* planted in the first place? Occasionally offered for sale in the herb section of plant nurseries, comfrey seedlings are cute, fuzzy little plants in two-inch pots.

Don't be fooled. These swans grow into ugly ducklings.

Herbal and Flower Crafts

The growing season in the Northern Rockies is brief. Like many mountain dwellers, I suffer gardening deprivation during the long months of winter. Herbal and flower crafts help extend the pleasure and beauty of gardening long after the first snows whiten the landscape.

Everlastings form the backbone of most projects. Everlastings are plants whose flowers, seedpods or foliage retain their beauty, color and form when dried. Air drying, desiccants such as sand and silica gel, and glycerin are all methods that can be used to preserve plants.

Gardening is an instrument of grace.

May Sarton

149

Tip

Regularly feed your everlastings with low nitrogen products to produce more flowers and less foliage. For easy harveting, take rubber bands to the garden and bundle blooms as you cut them.

—

I don't have a place in my garden dedicated to growing everlastings. I find that they are all pretty enough to mix in here and there in my flowerbeds and borders. I avoid planting groups of everlastings in my display gardens, however. Flowers I want to preserve must be cut when they reach peak bloom, or in some cases before they have even fully opened, leaving little to display outside.

Like most garden-grown plants, everlastings require well-drained soil and plenty of sun. Water them well and keep the weeds out, of course.

Air Drying

I consider true everlastings to be plants that can be air dried. The list of candidates is substantial. Some of the more popular plants harvested and air dried include:

Annuals	**Herbs**
Strawflowers	Chive Blossoms
Statice	Lavender
Globe Amaranth	Oregano
Celosia	Sweet Marjoram
Amobiam	Bee Balm
(Winged Everlasting)	Wormwood
Xeranthenum	Sweet Annie
Helipterum	
Larkspur	
Perennials	
Babies Breath	
Yarrow - Rose, Golden, Woolly	
Lamb's Ears	
Pearly White Everlasting	

These plants can be air dried by hanging them upside down in bunches. Put together small bundles of six to ten stems. Too big a bunch may mold, or the flowers might crush each other. The leaves of most flowers do not respond well to air drying and should be removed. I secure bunches with rubber bands because they accommodate shrinkage as the stems dehydrate.

Air dry flowers in a warm, dry, dark and well-ventilated area. I hang my flower bunches from hooks in the back of a loft where they dry in a few days to three weeks, depending on the weather and the type of plant. Garages, attics, or even unused rooms can be utilized for drying.

Many everlastings will dry almost completely while still on the plant, but the best quality is obtained if the flowers are picked before they are fully open. Some flowers, most notably strawflowers, have spindly or weak stems. Replace their stems with a hooked wire at the time of picking. Remember that the more quickly you dry flowers after harvest, the better you will preserve their color and shape.

Silica Gel

Flowers can also be preserved with silica gel. This sand-like material absorbs moisture from the flowers, but leaves the petals intact and the colors strong.

Put an inch of silica in an airtight container. Remove most of the stem and foliage from flower blossoms and place the blossom heads in the crystals. Gently pour more silica on the blooms until they are completely covered. Seal your container and leave it undisturbed for about a week. Pour off the drying agent and check their heads. If they are not dry, repeat the above steps and let the flowers dry an additional two days. When done, attach florists wire if you need a stem.

This drying procedure is the method of choice for delicate or long-petaled flowers such as pansies, zinnias and garden roses. Silica gel is available at most craft stores and can be re-used many times.

Every flower is a soul blooming in Nature

151

Some flowers don't air dry well: they shrink, shrivel or just fade away. To preserve difficult dryers, I use the glycerin method.

Glycerin-treated flowers and leaves stay nice for a long time. The colors remain rich and vibrant and the foliage supple, reminding me of sunny afternoons in my gardens. Glycerin-treated flowers are easy to work into craft projects. As an added bonus, containers full of flowers and branches can be enjoyed even while the drying process is going on. Here's how you do it:

Purchase unscented glycerin from your local pharmacy or sources listed in the Ready Reference in this book. Mix two parts water to one part glycerin for large flower stems, a three-to-one ratio for delicate flowers. Pour four inches of this mixture into a plastic container and stand freshly cut flowers upright in it. Don't add additional water as the glycerin mixture disappears.

In a little over a week, the glycerin mixture will be absorbed, supplanting the plants' natural moisture. The flowers should be soft and natural looking. Bunch them together and hang upside down until the stems feel dry, following the guidelines for air dried flowers.

Leafy branches can be preserved with glycerin as well. Smash the bottom two inches of woody stem with a hammer, or use pruning shears to feather the bottom open for better liquid absorption. Remove all leaves from the bottom six inches of stem (leaves left below the waterline will rot and have to be discarded) and follow the same procedure given for preserving flowers.

Crafts

Herbal wreaths

Wreaths are the best-known herbal decoration. I've made many since

I started gardening. Some were wonderful, others rather ordinary. All were unique, differing in their size, shape and materials that I had on hand. Don't be discouraged if your first attempts fall short of the beauties pictured in Martha Stewart's magazine. Making showcase herbal wreaths takes practice. One must combine good drying techniques with flower arranging ability; a wreath's appeal, after all, depends on how you combine colors, textures and shapes.

Begin your project with a pre-formed frame. You can buy a straw wreath base, a frame made of flexible grapevines or a wire frame. I prefer straw bases; they are cheap and make the fullest finished wreath.

Before you get started assembling your wreath attach a hanger to the backside. A piece of wire wrapped around the frame works well.

Cover your wreath frame with gray Spanish moss, widely available at florist and craft stores. This first step prevents bare spots and gives the wreath an expensive, custom look.

Next, attach small bundles of 4-inch long dried herbs and flowers to the base with florist pins or hot glue (florist's wire if you are using a wire or branch frame). Although some folks use fresh herbs to make their wreaths, I've had better luck with dried material. Some of the pickings I utilize from my herb garden include:

      Chive flowers
      Bundles of oregano and thyme
           (especially their flowers)
      Stems of pebbly textured sage
      Silver-leafed artemesias
      Rosemary sprigs
      Sweet Annie
      Sorrel seed sprays
      Feverfew
      Tansy

Carefully overlap the stems of the first bundle with the foliage of the next, laying them all in the some direction. Make sure the middle

153

The trouble with gardening is that it does not remain an avocation. It beomes an obsession

Phyllis McGinley

Tip

To *blend your pot-pourri scent, cover it tightly and place it in an undisturbed warm, dark place for several weeks. The closed closet of a spare bedroom is ideal.*

and outside of the wreath are well covered to give a full, lush look. When you get clear around the wreath, tuck in the last few bunches under the first so that there isn't a big gap.

Variety is the key to creating a beautiful herbal wreath. Wreaths can be made in a color scheme but I often work material around the wreath in random fashion, mixing whatever I have available. Contrast the colors, textures and accents by placing smooth leaves next to silvers and so on. For more color combine herbs with dried everlasting flowers such as yarrow, cockscomb, strawflowers, statice and baby's breath. Seedpods are also interesting. I particularly like poppy and iris seed heads in my wreaths. Although culinary herbs are often included in wreath arrangements, don't expect to use them in cooking.

Dried herbal wreaths are initially fragrant, but over time they lose their aroma and their colors gradually fade. They are also champion dust catchers that are difficult, if not impossible, to clean.

These drawbacks aside, herbal wreaths make a long lasting, striking decoration for a front door or interior wall and are a nice, personal handcrafted gift to give.

Potpourri

One of the easiest herbal crafts is concocting potpourri. Piled into small bowls and jars, these artful blends bring the freshness of summer into your house and are as pretty as they are fragrant.

Potpourri is a combination of dried herb foliage and flowers for color, texture and fragrance; spices for extra zip; fixatives to hold the aroma; and essential oils for extra perfume. I like to use flowers and herbs that I have grown or gathered myself with only minor additions of purchased ingredients. Seedpods, pine cones, even sprigs of fir can be included, depending on you personal taste.

It is important to pick fresh plant materials when they are dry; mid morning is usually a good time. As soon as you've gathered your ingredients, strip the flower petals, leaves and pods from the stems and scatter them on newspapers spread out of direct sunlight to dry. Whole blossom heads of some flowers—if they are not too fat and succulent— may be used as well.

Drying times will vary depending on temperature and humidity. Turn or stir your materials occasionally to ensure even drying. Your material is sufficiently dry if it crunches when you rub it between your fingers. Complete drying is key to prevent spoilage and molding.

Fixative preserves the fragrance of your ingredients. The most common fixative is orris root, the rhizome of a specific kind of iris. It is available at craft and herb stores. Orris root isn't cheap but you don't need much: two ounces will fix as much as three or four gallons of potpourri.

Scented oils, often called essential oils, complement and intensify potpourri's natural fragrance. A half ounce bottle of oil is also enough for three or four gallons of potpourri. Craft shops, pharmacies and retail stores that sell candles often stock essential oils.

Spices are optional in potpourri. I find stick cinnamon, a few cloves or a handful of star anise adds a nice accent, especially in the Christmas blends I occasionally give as gifts. Use whole or chunk spices only; ground spices look like dirt in potpourri.

Potpourri is easily made at your kitchen table. Mix your dried ingredients in a large glass bowl or container. Add chopped orris root and a few drops of the scented oil of your choice. Store the mixture in airtight containers for a minimum of two weeks to a month to blend

The Lazy Gardener's Basic Blended Potpourri

3 quarts Mixed scented ingredients. Dried rose petals, lavender flowers and leaves, lemon thyme, rosemary and pineapple mint are among the many good choices.

1 quart Decorative ingredients. Dried whole cornflowers, yarrow, artemisia flowers and leaves, feverfew, etc.

6 Cinnamon sticks (optional)
1/4 cup Whole cloves (optional)
2 oz. Orris root, chopped
1/2 oz. Scented oil of choice, such as rose, cinnamon, lemon or wildflower

Mix and store following narrative directions.

and mellow your potpourri's fragrance.

Remove the amount you need and store the rest in anything with a seal (I use large salad dressing jars) in a cool, dark place. Potpourri loses its potency when exposed to air and eventually relinquishes its pleasant scent altogether. When the aroma begins to fade, refresh it with a few drops of essential oil or replace the mixture with fresh potpourri.

Potpourri produces a different fragrance every time you mix up a batch. There are elaborate, time consuming recipes for blending potpourris, but truthfully these don't appeal to my lazy streak. I don't worry about exact ingredient amounts. I use my nose as a guide and pay attention when I'm mixing to create visual appeal.

Container Gardens

Who says you need space to garden?

Container gardening is the solution for people with small or no gardening areas and a big desire to grow plants. Self-contained, versatile and portable, they can transform balconies, porches, decks and front steps into exuberant plant landscapes.

I personally love the creativity that container gardening offers. I try different plants and new combinations each season. By controlling moisture and exposure, plants that might otherwise struggle in my garden beds thrive in their pots, tubs and barrels.

Although just about anything with adequate drainage can be used, containers should be big enough to allow for sturdy root development of their chosen plants. Good choices are at least 12 inches wide and 12 inches deep. Smaller containers work but require constant watering in warm weather.

When planting in containers, use a commercial soil mix rather than plain old garden dirt. Prepared mixes stay looser, retain water better, and don't contain fungi that attack plants.

Space container plants closer than you would if you were planting in the ground. Close planting makes the container look nice and full immediately. I try to use enough plants to hide most of the soil surface and perhaps trail over the edges. To achieve a full, well-balanced shape,

He who plants a garden plants happiness

Tip

*Lighten large out-
door pots by placing
wood chips or styro-
foam packing mate-
rial in the bottom.
Don't use biodegrad-
able "peanuts." They
will disintegrate and
lower the level of
your plants.*

place low trailing plants at the outer edge, medium ones just inside and the tallest ones at the center.

Contrasting shapes, textures, foliage and colors enliven container plantings. There is an enormous range of plants that can be planted in containers. Besides the old standbys of petunias and geraniums, a gardener may try plants grown for their interesting foliage. The silvery cut leaves of dusty miller set off the bright colors of every flower, and variegated vinca vine is a fine trailer.

Although annual flowers are most often used in containers because of their long bloom period, perennial flowers are sometimes included. If you put perennials in your planters, be sure to plant them in the ground in a more permanent spot in the fall; they are not likely to survive winter in a pot, as the soil will freeze. I favor sedum for small containers. Sedums have thick, fleshy leaves, low water needs and long lasting blooms. They are perfect for shallow planters because they require little soil for their roots. I've grown sedums on driftwood in tiny bowl-like depressions and even in pretty seashells.

I consider container gardening high maintenance. Watering is crucial. A container planting has limited soil and root space, and can quickly dry out. I try to check my containers every day in hot weather, less often if the temperature is cool. I only place them in spots my hose will reach, a lesson learned after carrying too many heavy buckets of water.

Frequent waterings quickly wash out nutrients in the soil, so plan on feeding your container grown plants throughout the season. At planting time I sprinkle a slow release pelleted fertilizer into the soil and supplement it with several applications of water soluble Miracle Gro® during the growing season. Organic gardeners might use manure tea or fish emulsion to feed their plants.

When I water my container gardens I groom each pot, removing withered blossoms and brown leaves. I also look for insect infestations. These are important rituals because container plantings are usually set in prominent locations and therefore viewed up close.

Containers

Whiskey Barrels

Some of my prettiest and most successful planters are whiskey barrels that have been sawed in half. These large, rustic planters are a familiar sight around Jackson Hole, where they blend into the western decor. Lumber yards and discount houses commonly stock the reasonably priced barrels in the spring.

Whiskey barrels are designed to swell when they are filled with liquid at the distillery, ensuring a tight seal. They obviously weren't meant to leak. Gardeners that don't provide drainage will end up with a mucky, stagnant and downright swampy container of dirt that will soon suffocate and rot oxygen-deprived roots. I use an electric drill with a large bit to drill six half-inch holes in the bottom of the barrel, a task accompanied by the pungent smells of Jim Beam. Elevate your drilled barrel on blocks of wood or brick to give it room to drain and to keep the surface below it from rotting.

Whiskey barrels hold a lot of soil; a good soaking keeps it moist much longer than smaller planters do. On the down side, soil-filled whiskey barrels are extremely heavy. If you must move them, you'll either have to empty them or use a backhoe. I sometimes lighten them up by placing wood chips or overturned plastic nursery cans in the bottom of the planter before topping them with soil.

Because of their large size and depth, a large variety of plants thrive in whiskey barrels. I've filled them with all kinds of flowers and vines, grown herbs and veggies, and have even planted bushes in them. Spring bulbs are among the few plants that don't work: they freeze solid in the barrels at the first cold snap. If you want your barrels instantly filled with billowing flowers, buy a large hanging basket, gently lift out the contents, and plant them intact in your barrel.

Bloom where you are planted.

Tip

Elevating containers on plant stands or on small blocks deters plant rot by allowing the container to adequately drain. Elevating pots also helps protect your porch or deck from water stains. If you use plant saucers under your indoor plants, empty them after each watering.

There is a lot to be said, both for and against clay pots. Thick clay walls are somewhat insulating—protecting roots from rapid changes in temperature—and porous clay containers "breath" better than plastic ones. Fine roots that grow along pot walls can more easily absorb life-giving air.

On the flip side, plants in unglazed clay pots dry out more quickly in our arid climate than plantings in plastic, wood or cement containers, and must be watered frequently. For this reason I don't use them for sprouting seeds or for moisture-loving tropical plants such as ferns.

Clay pots can also develop a crusty white film on the outside, formed when dissolved mineral salts are wicked from the soil through the walls of the porous pot. If you don't care for this grungy look (I admit to liking it), these deposits can be scrubbed off.

Left outside in winter, clay pots sometimes crack. Wet soil may freeze and expand, splitting the pot, or water enters the porous clay, expands during freezing, and cracks the clay. When you clean your pots in the fall, knock out the soil and store the pots upside down. The drier the pot is in freezing weather, the longer you'll have it.

Though not lacking faults, clay pots have traditional appeal. I love their warm, earthy look on the shelves of my greenhouse, mottled with age and filled with old-fashioned geraniums.

Unusual Planters

Relic planters with historic interest have real character. Antique mining scales planted with wildflowers, an old wringer washing machine brimming with red petunias or a wooden dynamite crate full of bright of orange calendula can set your garden apart. Virtually any item can be used as a planter if it is durable and can hold soil.

Nifty planters often begin as garage sale deals and second hand steals.

A wooden nail keg, an old toolbox, a kid's Radio Flyer wagon, even vintage coffee cans be used for container gardening. How about an old mop bucket, a galvanized wash tub, a rusty oil can? I sometimes find it hard to believe, but my husband refers to these found treasures as junk…

Not I. Bargain basement containers can be long lasting and cost efficient. Use a metal or concrete drill bit to add drainage holes, and presto, you have an inexpensive garden planter.

I fill my unique containers with a commercial potting mix rather than garden dirt. The store bought mix retains sufficient water and doesn't contain fungi or diseases. I over plant assorted flowers because I like glorious, colorful concoctions. If you consider them an inevitable jungle, grow one type of plant in each container. Bright red geraniums growing exclusively in a colorful olive oil can, for example, would be striking.

Unusual planters aren't limited to flowers. Culinary herbs grown in flea market pots are a charming addition to your windowsill or kitchen.

Be bold. Be imaginative. There's a future-pot-to-be waiting for you. Despite what your husband thinks.

Hanging Baskets

Hanging baskets offer advantages of color and greenery in places that a gardener would otherwise find impossible to consider. Flowery baskets can be suspended from a porch beam, from the top of a wall, or even from the branches of a tree.

Because the mountain growing season can be appallingly brief, I prefer to purchase fully mature, greenhouse grown baskets. If you would rather make up your own baskets from small starts, be sure to use lightweight potting mixture. This type of planter can get very heavy when wet.

Hanging baskets are usually over planted to burst with colorful flowers and vines. This fullness, however, means the container will need to be watered more frequently throughout the growing season. In the heat

Flowers and plants are silent presences. They nourish every sense except the ear.

May Sarton

161

Tip

To prevent soil loss, line the bottom of your window boxes with newspaper. The paper allows water, but not dirt, to pass through the drainage holes.

~

of the summer, that can mean twice a day. I use a weak solution of Miracle Gro® every two weeks to keep my closely planted flowers well fed, and routinely pinch off spent flowers. The result is baskets that bloom prolifically all season.

Because I'm not the stay at home type (the rivers and mountains beckon me) I choose my containers and plants carefully. Fiber pots are porous and dry out faster than plastic pots, which are at the top of the list for ease of care. Containers with side holes for planting —creating the "ball of flowers" look—need frequent watering. Wire baskets lined with pale green sphagnum moss are gorgeous but, unfortunately, impractical in the windy, arid West. If wind is not a factor, they can be used with better result if internally lined with a perforated plastic sheet to curb moisture loss.

Plant varieties must also be selected carefully if you can't actively babysit your baskets. Petunias and trailing lobelias have a difficult time recovering if allowed to once dry out, and will look sickly the rest of the season; impatiens cannot tolerate even light frost. I recommend purchasing or planting ivy leafed geranium for your baskets. These trailing plants survive hot, desiccating winds and the occasional out of town trip.

For those folks willing to give hanging baskets the care they need (and I sometimes wish I was one of them), a mixture of annuals can be striking. Nasturtiums and asparagus fern, sweet alyssum, pansies, violas, and verbenas are among the low and trailing annual flowers and foliage successfully used in hanging baskets.

The key is to match your baskets to your lifestyle. Disappointments will be avoided and continuous effort will be rewarded.

Window Boxes

Window boxes dress up a house wonderfully, making even a plain house noteworthy. From the outside, these planters lend a friendly, inviting look. That they can be seen from inside is simply a bonus. Nothing says more clearly that a "gardener lives here" than colorful, thriving window boxes. Drawing warmth from the closeness of walls, plants in window boxes thrive in cooler climates if you follow the basic guidelines below.

→ Plant flowers in your window boxes close together to create a full look from the start. Keep in mind that dense plantings have enormous root competition. Window box plantings rarely stay in prime form throughout a long growing season, but will last through most of the shorter growing season typical of higher altitudes.

→ Promote full, luxuriant growth by pinching back young plants and pruning leggy stems.

→ Remove spent blossoms. This encourages plants to produce more flowers.

→ Feed regularly, either by working a time-release fertilizer into the soil mix at planting time or making occasional applications of liquid fertilizer.

→ Since window boxes are often exposed to full sun, drying winds and the reflected heat of the house, it is crucial to water daily. You may even want to douse them twice on the hottest days. Never allow these containers to dry out completely, as the soil will be difficult to re-moisten.

Window boxes can be changed each summer. Different color combinations can be tried and new plants can be used. Don't be afraid to experiment. Every spring, garden centers are well stocked with candidate plants in six packs and four-inch pots that succeed in window boxes.

When the world earies and society ceases to satisfy, there is always the garden.

Minnie Aumonier

Look for geraniums and marguerite daisies, upright plants that provide height for the back of your box. Diasica, dwarf marigolds and violas are excellent, bushy filler plants; sweet alyssum, lobelia, cascading petunias and nasturtiums are good trailers. Vinca is a great vine to use in window boxes. I always tuck some in near the front to spill over the edge.

Don't try to grow tulips, daffodils or crocus in window boxes. Spring bulbs freeze solid in cold climates. For the same reason, window boxes are usually planted exclusively with annuals (flowers that only last one season). If you decide to incorporate a few perennials into your containers this summer, remove them and plant them in the ground in the fall.

Although these little elevated gardens are measured in square inches rather than feet, they are hard to miss and fun to grow.

Kitchen Herbs

Kitchen herbs are well suited for growing in containers because a single plant of any herb is usually sufficient for a good cook's use.

Smaller herbs—thyme, chives, oregano, sage, chervil, rosemary and parsley—can be grown together in a large pot or barrel. In fact, the bigger the pot, the better it is for herb growing, since most herbs have vigorous root systems that benefit from extra room. Planted in small pots, many herbs quickly become root-bound. You can pack a lot of plants into a single, large container, especially important if you lack a bona fide garden area.

Pay attention to herb characteristics when group planting. Some of the most useful kitchen herbs are tall and ungainly (dill comes to mind). Although dill will generally grow shorter when confined to a pot, it should be planted in the middle of the container, while spreading herbs like oregano and thyme should be at the edges so they'll cascade over the lip.

All kitchen herbs are sun lovers, so a bright sunny spot to set your herb pots is important. A deck or patio often works well. A sunny spot near the kitchen door is ideal, so one can step outside and pick a sprig or a few leaves for cooking.

I use a general purpose planting mix for my herb containers, and water whenever the soil surface is dry. Good drainage is a must for growing herbs; they hate soggy roots.

Some kitchen herbs could even be included in hanging baskets: curly parsley and basil are pretty companions to many annual flowers.

Herbs are plants that are best appreciated up close. Growing kitchen herbs in containers allows us to become well acquainted with each and every plant. Their beauty goes beyond the visual. You will want to touch, to sniff and even nibble many of the culinary herbs every time you pass by their pots.

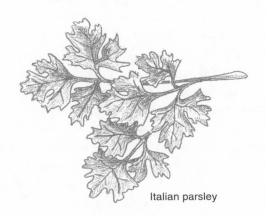

Italian parsley

You have to eat a lot of parsley to be an old sage.

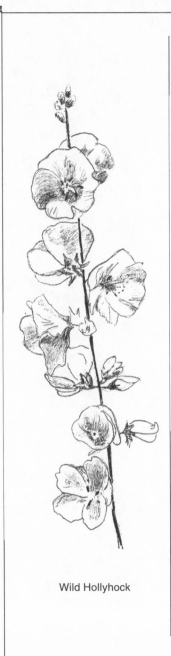

Wild Hollyhock

Speciality Gardens

Wildflower Garden

The thought of turning a part of your property into a wildflower meadow is appealing. Wildflowers offer a colorful exuberance, a lack of regimentation and a spontaneity that we who live in the mountains seek in our yards as well as our lifestyles.

Unfortunately, the trend in wildflower gardening has led gardeners to believe that all they need to do is toss out a handful of seeds, quit mowing, and watch their property be transformed into a beautiful mountain meadow rivaled only by those found in national parks.

This is a myth. Although a wildflower meadow looks carefree, successfully creating one is not an easy task. Wildflower meadows are one of the most demanding forms of gardening to undertake and do well.

Seed Selection

First, thought must be put into seed selection. There are dozens of wildflower mixtures on the market: dryland, wetland, southwestern, northern, etc. The best mixes contain a variety of annuals, biennials, perennials and possibly a small percentage of non-invasive filler grass. Many are packed with moisture absorbing material such as rice hulls or ground corncobs. An entirely pure mix is both hard to find and ridiculously expensive.

Study the contents before you buy wildflower seed. Of course you'll want cornflowers, California poppies, baby blue eyes and cosmos for quick, first year color. But aim to establish a meadow of long-lasting perennial flowers, not just annuals. Increase your chance of growing a successful wildflower garden by looking for mixes that contain a high percentage of flowers that grow wild in your area. (Be aware that white ox-eye daisies included in some mixes are regarded as noxious weeds all over the West and should be avoided.) It is not unusual for most mixes to contain the seeds of cultivated flowers as well as wildflowers.

Soil Preparation and Planting

After you have selected an appropriate and appealing mixture, do your plants the favor of preparing a good home for them before sowing. The site should be sunny, the soil loose and well drained. This can be accomplished by digging down a few inches and adding compost, peat, manure and other organic matter. Clean out existing grass and lightly cultivate your wild-to-be land, breaking up large soil clumps and removing rocks as you go. Shallow tilling is crucial, or you'll bring hundreds—maybe thousands—of dormant seeds to the surface.

Broadcast your seeds over your prepared site. Cover lightly with straw and push the seeds in firmly, then gently water. Don't fertilize. This rarely benefits wildflowers, and may direct the plants' energy to grow excessive foliage instead of flowering.

Care

Though your wildflower meadow won't need huge amounts of TLC, I recommend occasional watering and weeding. This means you will need to recognize the 'weedlings' from the seedlings. It would be awful

Cares melt when you kneel in your garden.

Tip

Wildflower names often end with "wort." Wort simply means "plant". It is derived from the Old English word "wyrt," meaning "root, herb or plant." Used in combination with another word, it may refer to an ancient plant use. For instance, lungwort was once used to treat respiratory disorders.

to pull out the bluebells and leave the bindweed.

The key to establishing a wildflower garden is hard work, a sunny summer and most of all a good deal of patience. Results will never be instant. The annual flowers often aren't in full bloom until August, and it may take two or more seasons before your wildflower garden stops looking like an abandoned lot. Remember that all good things come to those who wait.

And warn your neighbors.

Butterfly Garden

The right plants and conditions can make your garden inviting to a medley of pretty, fluttery butterflies. You won't have to fight your way through huge flocks of these winged insects to view your posies, but you will feel virtuous about helping a handful of these wonderful creatures. Habitat loss and indiscriminate insecticide spraying have caused butterfly populations to steadily decline.

Following these steps will coax these ephemeral beauties to reside in your garden, from egg to caterpillar, chrysalis to adult.

→ Select a warm, sheltered site. Butterflies are most active in bright sunlight out of the wind. It is easier for them to fly and feed in calm air. They rarely drink from any flower growing in the shade.

→ Plant groups of different nectar producing plants to entice a variety of butterflies. Mid and late summer blooming perennial flowers are preferred since that's when most butterflies are active. Include some continuously blooming annuals for a steady food source, and flat flowers, such as daisies, to provide landing places for butterflies to sip nectar. Yellow and red are favored colors, but most butterflies will move toward any bright color in bright sun. They prefer flowers with a distinct scent. Good butterfly flower choices include:

Perennials & Biennials
Shasta daisies
Hollyhocks
Bee balm
Daylilies
Black-eyed Susan
Dame's rocket
Asters
Purple coneflowers
Yarrow

Annuals
Cosmos
Zinnias
Nicotiana
Sweet alyssum
Sunflower
Nasturtium
Salvia
Verbena

Herbs
Dill, fennel, mint

→ Place light colored, flat stones in sunny spots around the garden for butterfly sunbathing. Butterflies are cold blooded and may often be found basking in the morning sun to warm their wings for flight.

→ Providing a shallow puddle or bowl of wet sand in the garden will also encourage butterflies to congregate. Did you know that they 'drink' at mud puddles to obtain needed mineral salts in their diet?

→ Include food for voracious caterpillars. An area left wild, with clover, thistles, milkweed, goldenrod, dogbane, nettles, and other native plants is ideal but hard to squeeze in a small lot. If you don't have room for a wild patch try incorporating some of the most desirable of these plants in your garden.

Creating a butterfly garden is a suspenseful form of art, akin to hosting a beautiful summer picnic and wondering if your guests will show

*And what's
a butterfly?
At best,
he's but a
caterpillar,
drest.*

*John
Gray
1727*

up. But when the day comes that you are working in your garden and a large tiger swallowtail settles on you as a resting spot, your endeavors are rewarded in a brief instant.

Hummingbird Garden

"Don't move," I whispered to my son. We stood motionless in my flower garden one sunny afternoon as we heard a buzzing, punctuated by high-pitched squeaks, headed our way. Within seconds a tiny brightly colored hummingbird flew around us, investigating Cooper's red baseball cap as it darted back and forth with incredible agility. Then—zoom—away it sped toward a stand of nearby petunias, satisfied we really weren't some strange new flower. Hummingbirds are always welcome guests in the garden. Although sugar water feeders appeal to a hummer's sweet tooth (or should I say tongue?) these quarter-ounce birds need better nourishment. After all, would you feed your kids only candy?

When planning a hummingbird garden, plant the type of flowers they like best. Red and orange-hued flowers lead the list, perhaps because these colors stand out sharply against a green background. Hummer fledglings soon associate red so strongly with food that throughout their lives every new source of that color is investigated, be it bandanas, roses or baseball caps.

The ideal hummingbird plant has large, solitary or loosely clustered blossoms that may droop. Hummers avoid double or many petaled blooms, as these seem to contain less nectar than single flowers, and the nectar is harder to obtain. Classic hummingbird flowers have trumpet-shaped blossoms that limit competition from insects. Ones that possess spurs (thin, hollow tubes projecting from the flower) are also favorites. Scent is unimportant, for these tiny birds depend on sight rather than smell.

Be sure to plant at least one or two flowers that bloom at different times of the season, so a food source is available spring through fall. If your yard is small or you only have a balcony, lure hummingbirds with well-placed, easily seen planters filled with preferred blossoms. Keep your plantings away from windows, which invite crashes.

Besides planting their favorite flowers, listed below are other things that you can do to make hummers welcome in your garden.

→ Provide water. Although nectar supplies most of their fluid, a strategically placed, shallow birdbath will give them a place to bathe.

→ Plant pussy willows in your hummingbird habitat. Hummers use the early season fuzz to build their nest.

→ Make sure that there are lots of perching areas for your hummers. A few dead limbs or trellises around their favorite flowers gives them a place to rest.

→ And, of course, hummers can be lured to feeders made especially for them. Fill these containers with a basic feeding formula of four parts water to one part white granulated sugar and hang in a shady, visible spot. You should soon be rewarded with a dazzling display of flight and color.

All hummingbirds have a high-energy lifestyle that requires lots of fuel. They are known to feed every 10 to 15 minutes from dawn to dusk, and may actually consume more than half their weight in food each day. A surprising portion of these little dynamos' diet consists of protein rich insects and spiders. Hummers gobble up aphids, gnats, thrips and tiny flies during their daily flights. For this reason, I consider hummingbirds' presence in my garden beneficial as well as beautiful. Pesticides present a grave danger to hummingbirds, and should be used with a light hand or not at all in garden areas they frequent. Indiscriminate use of most insecticides not only destroys insects—a potential food source

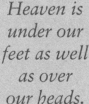

Heaven is under our feet as well as over our heads.

Henry Thoreau

for the birds—but coats the flowers themselves, which can sicken these exquisite creatures.

The Western US is especially rich with hummingbirds, with many of the numerous species widespread and commonly seen. But no matter where you live, a garden should be able to attract at least one species of hummingbirds to your yard. The beauty, boundless energy, bright colors and bold personalities of these miniature flying machines will delight all season.

Know Your Hummers

Once they begin to visit your garden, you will want to learn the names of these marvelous miniatures. The adult males are the flashiest dressers and are the easiest to identify; the immature birds and females don't sport showy colors. Here is a guide to hummingbirds a Rocky Mountain gardener is most likely to find flitting around the fuchsias.

Rufous hummingbirds

> Rusty red sides and a bright orange throat make them recognizable. They are the feistiest of all my garden hummers, and can be especially quarrelsome over food supply. These diminutive birds are belligerent and territorial, and will tirelessly defend a food source with a barrage of avian expletives and rambunctious flashing of wings. You may want to separate hummer plantings around the yard and garden to help keep the peace.

Calliope hummingbirds

> This smallest of North American birds prefers mountainous areas. When the light is right, you'll notice purple-red iridescent throat stripes.

Broad-tailed hummingbirds
> You will likely hear these guys before you see them. The male produces a constant, loud "zinging" with its wings. This species prefers high elevations and is found in the southern Rockies.

Black-chinned hummingbirds
> One of the most common visitors to flowers and feeders in western gardens. Look for a black throat bordered by violet.

Hummingbird Flowers

The following plants supply food for hummingbirds. Not all plants grow in all parts of the Rockies. Experiment and ask at your local nursery which ones are best for your area.

Perennials and Biennials	**Annuals**
Red Columbine	Four O'clocks
Bee Balm	Phlox
Any Of The Blooming Sages	Scarlet Larkspur
Scarlet Runner Beans	Morning Glory
Cardinal Flower	Snapdragons
Coral Bells	Nicotiana
Foxglove	Petunias
Hollyhocks	Nasturtiums
Lychnis	Red Salvia
Delphiniums	Fuchsias
Red Penstemmon	

Nature is loved by what is best in us.

Ralph Waldo Emerson

Rock Garden

While most Wyoming gardeners pull rocks out of their gardens, a special breed puts them back in. Rock gardeners collaborate with the stony fruits of geology to create charming environments for low-growing plants. The result can enliven level ground or effectively terrace a slope. True rock gardens occur only above treeline, where it is high, dry and cool. But with a bit of planning, you can imitate nature and build a rock garden in your yard.

Consider sunlight and topography when you make a rock garden. Rock gardens do best in sunny or lightly shady locations. Rocks indigenous to your area will look the most natural and be the least expensive to obtain. One kind of stone, rather than a collection, usually looks best. Stratified rocks have distinct layers and are easiest to arrange. Unstratified rocks, such as granite boulders, are handsome but difficult to combine gracefully.

Begin your garden by placing large rocks first, digging them in so they appear to be part of a bed, strata or layer. Try to keep the stone's most attractive side visible. It is generally easiest to place rocks at the front of your rock garden first and work up, shoveling enough soil around each large stone to secure it. Don't stand sharp pointed rocks upright or you'll get a "dragon's teeth" look.

When your large rocks are in place, haphazardly add smaller rocks to avoid an artificial look. You may want to let the soil and rocks settle for a few days and survey the results before planting. There should be obvious, inviting spaces to place your plants.

Plants

Rock garden plants are generally compact or dwarf perennials. Although I don't use strictly miniatures, I focus on small plants. Large flowered marigolds or huge delphiniums would look as natural in a rock garden as a poodle running with the Yellowstone wolf pack. Likewise, I don't plant in neat rows; instead, I strive for combinations that make plants and stones look as if they had been placed by nature.

Hardy species ideal for northern and high altitude gardeners include small bulbs, low growing, and spreading plants. Consider planting:

Mother Of Thyme	Snowdrops
Creeping Veronica	Crocus
Phlox	Winter Aconite
Sweet Woodruff	Grape Hyacinth
Yellow Alyssum	Armeria
Dwarf Columbine	Miniature Iris
Campanulas	Low-growing Pinks
Rock Cress	Sedum
Hen And Chicks	

Strategically select plants to enjoy color all season. Small blooming bulbs such as snowdrops and crocus brighten a rock garden in the spring; low-growing perennials bloom as summer progresses. I usually include plants that self-sow after flowering. Johnny jump-ups and California poppies for instance, pop up seasonally in all sorts of unexpected crannies, delightfully filling available niches.

Care and Maintenance

Like other types of gardens, rock gardens require care and maintenance. They are particularly susceptible to slugs and other garden pests that find shelter among the rocks, and should be checked regularly for predation. Other routine plant care includes:

→ Weeding. While small rock garden plants are typically adapted to withstand poor or little soil, weeds can crowd out even hardy plants

I have a rock garden. Last week, three of them died.

175

A good winter project, especially for kids, is to paint faces on clay pots. 6-8 inch pots look best. Fill the pots with potting soil and plant with oat or rye grass, available by the pound at the feed store. Placed on a sunny windowsill and kept moist, the green grass will give each face an amusing botanical hairdo.

growing in small areas. Pluck out the invaders if you want your garden to thrive.

→ Occasionally adding organic matter to give your plants a boost.

→ Cutting and dividing plants that have become root bound, leggy, or are squeezing out their flowering neighbors.

Stones are the bones of the earth. Don't overlook their beauty and function in your home landscape.

Children's Garden

Years ago when my son was small, I helped him make an insect collection. We captured beetles and grasshoppers and netted some pretty butterflies and moths. The insect that interested him most was the spittlebug we found hiding in a clump of clover in my herb garden.

Spittlebugs are small winged insects whose young surround themselves with globs of protective secreted foam (or spittle) while they suck nourishing juice from plants' stems and leaves. I told my son that this frothy mass was frog spit and he believed me.

In the years that followed our insect collecting excursions, I found the spittlebug's foamy hiding places many times on plants in my herb garden. This small distraction was only one of many. I still find myself side-tracked from a task by watching summer activity amongst my herbs. Aromatic herbs are a drawing card for birds and bees. Bees, hummingbirds and sphinx moths all love the red shaggy flowers of an herb plant called bee balm. Bees particularly love the tiny pink flowers of thyme; honey derived from thyme is said to be the finest in the world.

Here and there I spot ladybugs on the golden

176

tansy and sweet angelica and on the scented leaf geraniums I've potted and set on my steps. A century ago, when gardeners paid more attention to superstition, it was believed you would have good luck all day if a ladybug landed on you. I like that.

Swallowtail butterfly caterpillars, growing bigger and plumper seemingly every hour, munch down on my parsley and fennel plants. For some reason, these are the plants they prefer.

This summer I suggest you give your children the opportunity to grow things so that they'll come to know the simple pleasures and mysteries of a garden. Give them time to see butterflies and crab spiders, squeeze the fragrant herbs, and experience spittlebugs and frog spit. I hope that if you do, you'll be giving them an enthusiasm that will last a lifetime.

When a child is ready to try gardening depends on the child, but I've found most can be started quite early. With direction, even toddlers have fun. To make gardening with kids a good experience, I recommend the following:

→ Use fast germinating seeds. Kids need quick success to maintain interest. It is satisfying for them (and you!) to see radish and bean seeds pop up a few days after the seeds were planted. Consider planting seeds with differing germination periods on the same day so new seedlings routinely appear over the next few weeks and keep things exciting.

→ Use big seeds. It is hard for little fingers to scatter teensy-weensy seeds. Think squash, peas or chunks of seed potatoes.

→ Use kid-sized tools. Getting kids to dig is not a problem, but small hands need small tools. A few companies market true downsized children's equipment; these tend to be expensive and are not necessary. Simply use your smaller implements when working with kids.

It's not easy being green.

Kermit the frog

My own son loved a trowel with his name taped to it and a sawed off shovel.

→ Garden in the morning, when kids have the most energy. Working side by side in the morning can be fun; the same project in the afternoon might be miserable with a tired, whiny child.

→ Plant what your children like to eat. If the list is short add vegetables or flowers that are fun to grow. Produce that can be nibbled fresh is always a big hit with kids.

→ If there is room, let children have a small garden of their very own. Raised beds make good children's gardens because they have definite boundaries. Respect that this is their space and not yours, and be willing to tolerate a less than perfect garden. Crooked rows and weeds are really okay.

→ Let kids harvest the reward of their efforts, in spite of the frustrations this can bring. Juicy, ripe strawberries or peas won't all make it as far as the kitchen—but after all, aren't we *supposed* to be growing food to eat? Select a few flowers children can pick when they want to give you a bouquet. This is easier than screaming 'No, stop!" every time you visit the flower garden.

All of which brings me to my final recommendation: Enjoy yourself. Laugh when your child gleefully squirts you with the garden hose. Have fun looking at bugs together. Remember that gardening is caught, not taught, and not all children will be transformed into gardeners. You error if you involve a child in gardening and then make it a grim, "character building" responsibility.

For those who find gardening fascinating, it will become a lifelong joy. Make their first garden like their first love…never quite forgotten.

Color Theme Gardens

If you have enough room, it can be a kick to make a one-color garden. One-color gardens are great, endlessly amusing experiments. Plants that don't fit or satisfy are removed, replaced by ones you hope to like better. Surprisingly, one of the most interesting colors for such a garden is white.

Last summer I visited friend Melanie Hess' landscaping project. Melanie has large perennial flower borders that surround her house and enclose a small patch of mowed lawn. Within this profusion of vibrant color she planted a small internal garden of white flowering plants and plants with whitish foliage. I counted over 25 varieties in her small plot. Melanie loves to visit greenhouses in her spare time. Looking for the ultimate white plant apparently has been her quest for many gardening seasons.

Low growing plants edged the front of her white garden: tiny creeping baby's breath, white rock cress, creamy polygonum, silvery snow in summer, white creeping phlox. Medium sized plants came next: fuzzy lamb's ears, greenish edelweiss, white sweet William, pearly everlasting, pure white candytuft, two kinds of light grey dusty miller, white Jacob's ladder and white coral bells. Tall varieties filled in the back. Spires of white delphiniums and hollyhocks grew against a wood fence, kept company by scabiosa, pearl achillea, white coneflowers, peonies and lacy silver mound. And, of course, clumps of white Shasta daisies.

White gardens are sometimes called "moon gardens." When the light is fading and other more colorful plants look dull, the whites are at their best. They take on an added glow when there is no glaring sun to outshine them. If you work late and enjoy your garden mostly on nice summer evenings then the quiet beauty of an all white garden is for you.

Colors are the smiles of nature.

Leigh Hunt 1840

Tip

Most of us choose the plants we grow because we like their blossoms. There are, however, many plants grown primarily for their foliage. Some of the most outstanding are those with silver and gray leaves.

My gardening fancies change every season or so. Right now I'm crazy about silvers and grays. I find their lightness enlivens green gardens through spring, summer and fall. Silver and gray foliage also harmonizes the garden, making it possible to bring a variety of brilliantly colored flowers together. What makes leaves silver or soft gray? Most gray or silver plants get their pale coloring from a covering of diminutive hairs. This soft, felt-like down protects the plants from the moisture loss caused by sun and wind. Catalogues and garden centers carry a broad selection of plants with appealing silver and gray leaves. Below is a list of some I've successfully grown in the mountains.

Dusty miller

> This annual is a sure bet in container plantings. It creates a nice contrast to geraniums and other flowering bedding plants.

Silver brocade

> Silver brocade is a hardy perennial form of dusty miller. I've had good luck wintering it over in mountain climates. Its ground hugging stems bear deeply lobed leaves that look like they have been covered with white felt.

Snow in summer

> If you have a sunny spot and want to fill it in with light foliage, plant snow in summer. It thrives in rock gardens and has the added benefit of many little white blossoms in June.

White Nancy lamnium

Silvery leafed 'White Nancy' lamnium is a ground cover that can brighten semi-shady places. This low growing plant sports both beautiful flowers and foliage.

Silver mound artemesia

There must be room in every garden for lacy perennial silver mound artemesia. It's teensy weensy blooms matter not at all; foliage is what makes this plant a classic.

If you renovate your flowerbeds this season, consider adding some of these foliage plants. With the exception of the lamnium, give your silver and grays summer sunshine and they'll thrive. Silver and gray leaves amongst shades of green make a garden glow, even under overcast skies.

Tea Gardens

I've given up caffeine. I've found that it is nice to enter the day gently rather than be jolted into it. I'm now a big fan of herbal teas. Fruity, spicy and aromatic, they warm the body and soothe the spirit.

Although there are dozens of herbal teas on the supermarket shelves, consider growing your own "teacup garden." I find it a calming chore to tend any sort of herb garden, often lingering over the plants' delightful aromas, textures and flowers.

In the summer, sun-brewed teas are easy to make and taste great. Fill a gallon jar or jug (I use empty salad dressing jars begged from a local restaurant) with handfuls of well-washed herbs. Top off with water, cover with a plate or lid and place in strong sunshine for a day. Shake or stir when you pass by to help distribute the flavor. Strain the tea and add honey or sugar to taste. Pour over ice and

Where rosemary grows the missus is master.

181

garnish with a fresh herb sprig. If you prefer a hot cup of herb tea, pour boiling water over fresh herbs in a teapot and let steep for five minutes. Strain into cups.

An endless variety of tea blends can be created by mingling flavors and aromas, but don't overlook the wonderful flavor of a single, spicy herb. Peppermint by itself makes a lovely tea.

Herbs can be dried for brewing at a later time, but many are most flavorful when they are fresh. If you find your homemade teas have more aroma than taste, try adding dried citrus peel or dried apples, raspberries or rose hips. All complement the herbs.

Children especially enjoy making herbal tea. They have fun picking the herbs and like to watch the tea changing color as it warms up. It is a great project to do with their moms. And what better way it there to end a summer day than a tea party?

Herbs good for tea

anise • anise hyssop • bee balm • chamomile • lemon balm
cinnamon basil • lemon thyme • lemon verbena • orange mint
pineapple mint • peppermint • spearmint • rosemary

Lawn, Trees and Shrubs

Landscaping

L a w n s

Landscapes without lawns have become ecologically correct, especially in dry climates—but I'll be the first to admit that I'm attached to my grass. It provides a neat and trim, soothing green carpet for play and relaxation.

Lawns are both useful and aesthetic. They add value to real estate and symbolize safety, comfort and well-being. Perhaps it is because so much of the Western landscape is rugged and wild that a green mantle of grass is so psychologically satisfying. Moreover, we high altitude gardeners have time to pay attention to our lawn early season, when the ground is moist and the temperatures too cool to do much else.

I asked local experts to recommend a spring lawn care program. Here are their suggestions:

If the ground is compacted, aerate the soil. Most lawns are improved by aeration, particularly early season when the soil is warm enough for good root growth. Aeration perforates surface soil so air, water and fertilizer can penetrate it more readily and create favorable root conditions.

A power driven coring machine is the tool for the job. Coring machines cut out finger-sized sod plugs every 4-6 inches and deposits them on the surface to disintegrate. Local equipment rental companies rent corers, or a professional lawn service can aerate for you.

Patmore Green Ash

Annual aerating prevents the accumulation of "thatch," a tight mass of stems, plant runners, roots and leaves accumulated over a period of time—not just piled up grass clippings. If you lawn feels soft and spongy when you prod it with a finger and you don't reach soil, you can bet it has thatch. A little thatch is inevitable, but too much prevents water, fertilizer and air from reaching the grass's roots. A de-thatching rake or vertical mower (a power rake whose upright blades simultaneously yank and cut thatch) can be rented to remove thatch. Heavy raking, either by hand or machine, is best done before warm weather arrives. Power raking in the middle of the summer will damage the crowns.

After aerating and raking apply a spring fertilizer low in nitrogen but high in phosphorous and potassium, following directions on the bag. Phosphorous encourages healthy spring root development and potassium strengthens grass as it goes into the hot, dry summer months. Some lawn fertilizers also include iron, which quickly green up a lawn. Folks who really want a good-looking lawn fertilize once in mid-summer and again in the fall. Fall feeding is particularly beneficial because it encourages growth of grass rather than weeds.

If you have ugly bare spots in your lawn, turn the soil over the bare spot to a depth of four inches. (If the soil has been contaminated, replace it with fresh soil.) Rake the spot smooth and spread quality grass seed over it. Tamp lightly to firm down the seeds. Cover the spot with light mulch, such as straw or peat moss, and keep it watered until new grass is established.

If you have a weed problem—thistles, too much clover, prolific dandelions or black medic—apply a selective broadleaf weed spray around the end of May when the weeds are actively growing. If you don't get a chance to control the weeds in the spring, attack them in September when weeds draw sugars down into their roots. They will pull herbicides down as well.

Lawns need approximately one inch of water per week. When the weather gets hot deep root watering is the best approach. Instead of

Lawns, trees, flowers— they're all beautiful and I love them—so long as there's somebody else around to take care of them.

Bennett Cerif

watering everyday, water two or three days a week for longer periods of time.

Lawn grass should be mowed frequently to about two-inches high. Higher mowing is desirable during the warmest summer months because the shade of taller grass will keep the soil cooler and conserve water somewhat.

With sensible care, I believe that lawns can be ecologically sound. Besides, most of us aren't willing to give up the idea of a pretty emerald lawn surrounding our houses. Perhaps it is because so much of the landscape in the West is rugged and wild that a green mantle of grass is so psychologically satisfying—and well, just so wonderfully civilized.

Ground covers

Ground cover plants can be important in a home landscape. They free those who find lawn duty a chore and reduce the need to weed by forming a dense, fairly uniform canopy that inhibits weed growth. Many ground cover plants are water thrifty, cutting that chore as well. Ground cover plantings soften hard edges, such as the corner of a building or the front steps, and can direct foot traffic where needed.

Since good ground cover plants spread to fit the allotted space, they add pattern to the garden, aesthetically filling in chinks between stones in walks and patios. They also hold things together physically by binding the soil with a strong root structure. The latter quality makes them particularly useful on steep banks, where they help cut soil erosion.

You can select from a wide variety of ground cover plants. I prefer reliable perennials to annual plants, which must be replanted every spring and are therefore effective only part of the year.

Gardeners in cold winter areas should plant in spring, so the ground cover has an entire season to establish itself. Before you plant, prepare the area and soil as well as you would for any other "permanent" planting; ground covers are meant to be long term. Dig over the entire site and even out the surface with a rake. Although ground covers have a reputation for being tough, even they won't thrive in poor soil. Take the time to improve the area by digging in organic matter and broadcasting a well-balanced fertilizer at the rate recommended on the label.

Ground cover plants are usually sold in small pots, six-packs or gallon containers. The closer you space the plants, the faster they will fill in. If you are on a tight budget, decide on the distance and space them evenly. If you are setting ground cover plants out on a steep slope where erosion is likely to occur, arrange the plants in staggered rows and, if possible, make a small terrace for each plant.

Mulching between the young plants till they achieve good coverage will prevent them from drying out and keep weed seeds from germinating. Of course, ground covers need sufficient moisture to become established. Water plants thoroughly at planting time and keep them moist for the next few weeks.

If you don't let them dry out during the summer, chances are by fall you will enjoy the benefits and beauty of ground covers in areas around your yard.

To decide which ground covers work in your area, ask at your local nursery. Not all ground covers listed in books thrive in a mountain or northern climate. My picks are:

Sun	Shade
Creeping thyme	Ajuga
Sedums	Bishop's weed
Creeping juniper bushes	Lily of the valley
Creeping phlox	Vinca minor
Snow in summer	(periwinkle)
Creeping buttercup	Sweet woodruff
Creeping cinquefoil	

What was paradise but a garden, and a yard of trees and herbs.

William Lawson

Douglas Fir

Featured Ground Covers

Snow in summer

Perennial snow in summer is an especially tough plant. Technically know as *cerastium tomentosum*, snow in summer looks like its name. Tiny, fuzzy, silvery-gray leaves grow on creeping stems that quickly spread to form large, woolly mats. (In spots it likes, this plant may roam out of bounds.) Thick masses of snowy white flowers appear early summer.

This plant is an excellent choice for slopes where perennials are planted, as it helps stabilize the soil. It often decorates rock gardens, and can be planted in difficult dry areas where nothing else wants to grow.

I find snow in summer does best—with its mounds the most lush and billowy—when it is planted in an area that gets supplemental water. It tolerates almost any type of soil if the site is fast draining and in full sun.

In mid-summer, when the mats are done blooming and starting to look shabby, I give the plants a hard shearing. This grooming keeps the plants from seeding and rewards me with vigorous, new growth. With this little bit of extra effort, snow in summer looks good for the rest of the season.

I've noticed that after a few years the center of snow in summer plants often become brown and tired-looking. This indicates the plant needs to be divided. I simply chop the mat in sections with a sharp spade and replant the pieces. Winter may make snow in summer look shabby, but the plants rebound well in the spring. This is a perennial plant that I find very easy to grow.

If you are planning on making a new perennial flowerbed in your yard this spring, consider snow in summer as one of the tough and sturdy plants that will withstand severe winters and repeat year after year.

Bishop's Weed

It has been said that Bishop's weed should be only sold or traded with a warning attached. Why? Because it is one of the most aggressive plants you can grow. Once Bishop's weed gets a roothold, it sends runners in and around everything in its path. It can literally take over a flowerbed or rock garden, where it should never be planted.

On the plus side, its vigorous nature makes it a choice ground cover. It is often used to landscape shady areas, where it thrives.

Bishop's weed's variegated green and white leaves are easy to recognize. They die back in the fall and emerge each spring, quickly blanketing the ground. While Bishop's weed does blossom in mid-summer, the long stemmed heads of tiny white flowers are unimportant. Its thick mass of multi-hued leaves is what makes Bishop's weed useful.

I've never seen seeds for sale for this plant, although it does produce them. Gardeners typically purchase trays of greenhouse starts or create new plantings through division. Once Bishop's weed becomes established, there are always plenty of creeping underground roots to give away.

With sufficient water, Bishop's weed can be counted on to look after itself. If your aim is to fill a shady spot quickly with a pretty plant, it is the perfect candidate. Planted between the house and a concrete path, or contained by an underground barrier, Bishop's weed will grace your landscape for years.

Flowerbed Edging

If a flowerbed is bordered by lawn, edging should be put in place to stop grass from invading. A neat edging defines the bed and makes it all the prettier.

To forget how to dig the Earth and to tend the soil is to forget yourselves.

— *Mahatma Gandhi*

Anything impenetrable can be used to edge a bed, as long as it can be set deep enough into the ground to stymie invaders. One of my favorite decorative borders is old brick. I like them angled halfway into the ground. New bricks could certainly be used but lack the character used ones have acquired. For permanence, a sturdy steel edging is hard to beat. It's also a wonderful choice if curves are needed. Steel edging can usually be purchased at welding shops. Redwood and treated lumber (2 x 6 minimum size) is often used for straight edged borders, as are railroad ties. All are rot resistant wood that lasts many years.

I've had little success with polyethylene and other fast assembly plastic edging. Because these types of edgings have little support, bumping into them with a lawn mower or other equipment easily jostles the plastic out of the ground. Though cheap, their life span is short.

Smooth river rocks offer a nice means to edge a flowerbed. Grass can be kept at bay by tucking low-growing, compact plants such as alyssum, aubrietia and sedum between them, and the polished stones possess an inherent beauty.

Installing a good edging to finish off a flowerbed will make a difference for many seasons, not only in appearance but also in the amount of time spent keeping the grass and weeds out.

Planting Under Trees

If you live in a house that is a few decades old, your lot probably has at least one mature tree. Or perhaps you live in the woods and have wild trees that the builder spared. In either case you know—or will discover—that it is a challenge to get anything to grow near the base of a large, established tree. Roots riddle the soil, and since the tree has used up most of the nutrients, the earth beneath it is typically dry, shallow and somewhat infertile.

If you are determined to garden under a tree, start by improving these less than promising growing conditions. Spread a layer of fresh soil over the area you want to plant. If the tree is a conifer, rake up fallen needles before you begin. Keep your soil application under a foot deep and stay away from the trunk.

When you complete planting your shade-tolerant selection, applying organic mulch such as shredded leaves, straw or compost around your new bed will supply nutrients and help keep the soil moist. You may want to fertilize as well. Mature trees don't need much fertilizer, but the plants under them do. Use time-release pellets when you plant, or spray with a diluted solution (I like Miracle Gro®) several times a summer.

Water frequently. A tree takes more than its share of limited water, leaving plants underneath it thirsty, and tree branches may prevent the ground below from getting a good soak even in rainy weather.

Finally, don't get your hopes up too high. Planting under an old tree is tough. I've seen many tattered shrubs, sparse grass and weedy, struggling plants just barely hanging on. Your best chance of success may be selecting shade-loving ground covers such as Bishop's weed or sweet woodruff.

Low raised beds away from the trunk or a nice arrangement of container plantings are alternatives that may be rewarded with greater success.

Fire zones

It seems that every summer there is a warning of "high fire danger." The temperatures have been high, the weather dry. For those of us who live in wooded, mountainous and fire-prone areas, it's worrisome.

While forest fires ultimately may be inevitable in much of the Rocky Mountains, prudent planning can reduce potential damage to personal property. Well-planned landscaping is an important strategy in meeting fire-prevention goals for wild land homeowners.

Teton County, Wyoming, Fire Marshal Rusty Palmer recommends creating a defensive space, or green zone, of at least 30 feet around

I talk to trees. I whisper them good fortune. I know they hurt when they're assaulted and I mourn for them when that happens.

Bert Raynes

Tip

Avoid using lawn fertilizer containing herbicides near trees. The trees may aborb the herbicide and die.

homes built in forested areas. This safety zone reduces the amount of fuel immediately surrounding a building, providing a firebreak that will slow a fire and give firefighters a better chance to move in.

A green zone can be lawn grass, border plantings, flowers and vegetables or a variety of plants that are kept well watered during the hot, dry summer. Some plants are actually less flammable than others. Well-watered deciduous plants are somewhat fire resistant, while all needle-leafed trees and shrubs are dangerously flammable, even when watered regularly.

During periods of extreme fire danger, it is important to mow grass short. At my house in Wyoming, wild native grasses comprise my green space on two sides of my house. These grasses can easily grow to be a couple of feet tall. I use a hand-held weed eater to keep them low and safe during peak fire danger months.

If you are really serious about protecting your house from wildland fires, consider pruning the lower branches off old, tall trees. Remove dead branches that hang over the roof or that are near a chimney. Beyond 100 feet from any structure, it may be of some help to clear out dead wood and thin out some of the oldest trees.

I live in the woods and I know. When the radio announces "extreme fire danger today," I sleep better if I have firescaped my property. You will, too.

Serviceberry

Trees, Shrubs & Bushes

Trees

There is no planting job more virtuous than that of planting a tree. Trees are more than just something to sit under on a hot summer day. They are necessary for a healthful, quality life on Earth. Without trees our beloved planet would be bald, scoured by winds sweeping unfettered over the surface. Most songbirds would disappear and the environment would heat up to an unbearable temperature. The atmosphere would be a haze of dust and pollutants. Trees help purify the air by taking out carbon dioxide and giving off oxygen. They can cut noise pollution by 75%. And on top of all that, they are unparalleled soil builders.

If you need more reasons for planting trees, any real estate professional will tell you that a well planted, healthy tree adds dollars to the resale value of your home.

Have I said enough? Are you ready to plant a tree? I thought so. It is important to plan before you plant. Trees should be planted where you will benefit from them the most. Evergreens on north and west sides of a cabin will block winter winds and reduce heating bills. Deciduous trees on the south side will shade a home in the summer and let in warm sunlight in winter.

Select trees for the long term: once a tree has grown to its mature height, it will probably be there for a lifetime. When people buy trees,

A man does not plant a tree for himself, he plants it for posterity.

Alexander Smith

193

Balled and burlapped
tree

many make the mistake of not taking into account how big trees and shrubs will get. Those little sticks of golden willows that you loaded, pots and all, into the backseat of your car at the nursery can grow 50 feet tall and almost as wide.

Unless you want—and can afford—an instant landscape, don't waste your money on trees over 10 feet tall. Smaller trees are easier to work with and quicker to establish themselves. Trees and shrubs that are containerized or root-ball wrapped can be planted anytime during the growing season. In a cold climate, I prefer to plant in the spring so the plants have the benefit of warm soil to spread out their roots and all summer to build up reserves to make it through the winter.

Balled and Burlapped trees

Trees are sold three ways: bare-root, planted in fiber, or with their root ball covered with burlap and tied with string to base of the trunk. This is called a balled and burlapped, or B&B, tree.

If you select B&B stock from a local nursery, exercise care when moving it to the planting site. Handle the tree by the root ball, never by the trunk. This will avoid breaking the fine feeder roots within the dirt ball. Lower your B&B tree carefully out of the truck or trailer, often a two-person task. Dropping it with a thud is a sure way to break or crack roots.

Thoroughly water B & B trees—it is difficult to get a dry root ball completely wet after it is in the ground—then dig your planting holes.

Preparing the Planting Hole and Planting

Tree and shrub roots spread horizontally more than they go down. Holes should be at least one foot wider that the diameter of the root ball but not much deeper, so it grows at the same above ground height as when you purchased it. I poke holes in the sides of the hole with a digging fork to loosen the soil and give the roots a place to go.

Surprisingly, it is not advisable to add compost or fertilizer to the dirt when you refill the planting hole. If you make the planting hole too attractive then the roots might not want to budge from all that luxury: they will grow as if they are still in a pot.

Place your tree in the freshly dug hole, disturbing only those roots that may have started to grow in a circle. These you can loosen with your hands or a garden fork. Set it at the right depth and backfill the hole, packing in the soil to eliminate air pockets. Soak the ground deeply. This may settle the ground somewhat, so you will have to add more dirt. You can make a little moat of soil around the planting hole if you want to help channel water to those newly planted roots.

Once trees and shrubs have been planted in the proper locations, basic care will help them thrive. I fertilize once a year and make sure they are watered well on a regular basis. During a tree's first and second year of growth it needs thorough soakings to help establish a good root system. After that I still water slowly and deeply during extended dry spells to keep my lovely trees and shrubs healthy and happy.

Topping Trees

When I mentioned "tree topping" to local tree surgeon Rolland Kuhr he became noticeably upset. Words like "mutilation," "senseless destruction," and "permanently desecrated" flew out of his mouth. Apparently, this guy is a passionate tree lover. What raised his ire? I decided to look into the matter.

My investigation unearthed an informative bulletin published by the tree-friendly National Arbor Day Foundation that described the consequences of tree topping, plus its alternatives.

But first things first. What is topping? This common procedure involves squarely cutting off a portion of the tree's crown, or top. Trees are topped because they grow into utility wires, interfere with the view

They kill good trees to put out bad newspapers.

James Watt

195

Tip

If you plant a tree near a power pole, make sure its mature height does not exceed 25 feet. Tree branches striking lines are a major cause of power outages.

Aspen leaf

or solar collectors or simply outgrow the area where they were planted. Many people believe topping is good for trees because there is often an obvious flush of new growth.

The National Arbor Day Foundation's bulletin, however, outlined the pitfalls of topping. The cut stub may have a difficult time forming a callus, leaving the tree stressed and highly vulnerable to insect invasion and fungi that cause decay. Topping may also remove so much of the crown that the tree's food-making ability is temporarily cut off.

Kuhr recommends a kinder solution called "drop crotch" pruning. This method of pruning reduces tree height without weakening the tree or creating an eyesore. It combines thinning the crown with cutting lateral branches at an angle; the lower lateral branch takes over as the tree's leader.

Before you do anything drastic to those lovely old trees on your property, consider consulting the experts. Your trees will thank you for it.

Tree Diseases

Cytospora canker

If you have aspens in your yard there is a good chance they have a fungal disease called cytospora canker. Cytospora attacks trees by damaging the cambium, the life-supporting inner bark that allows nutrients to flow from leaves to roots. The common name for this tree crud is "branch die back," because infected twigs are quickly girdled by the fungus and killed. Cytospora first appears as sickly patches of gray and orange underneath the bark. As the disease progresses, the tree may ooze an orangish-red liquid.

Cytospora canker is an airborne disease. The fungi's spores are dispersed by wind, birds and rain splash, and may lie in a dormant state on many surfaces. When a tree becomes stressed and weakened, the fungus effectively infects its host.

Cytospora canker is common in western Wyoming and may affect cottonwoods, birches, crabapples, willows, aspens and spruce trees as well. It can be found in native tree stands as well as in nursery stock.

There is no single method for controlling this fungal affliction. One should, of course, avoid introduction by carefully checking nursery trees for any signs of disease. In addition to dead twigs and bark discoloration, in the fall cytospora produces fruiting spores on orange tendrils that may be as much as an inch long.

If you remove dead and diseased branches, infected trees often survive. Pruners must be sterilized in a bleach solution after each cut to avoid spreading the fungus. Skip applying the black gooey tree wound dressing that is on the market: it has little value other than aesthetic.

Just like a person, a healthy tree combats disease minute by minute. Minimize affliction susceptibility by keeping your trees well watered and fertilized.

Spruce tree galls

A tiny insect with a big name—the Cooley spruce gall adelgid—has the power to deform the mighty spruce tree.

Female adelgids winter at the base of spruce buds, emerging early spring to lay eggs near branch tips. When the eggs hatch two weeks later, the nymphs crawl to expanding, new-growth buds and begin to feed. It is then that these unique little critters create a snug home for themselves. Their saliva, which is injected during feeding, contains an enzyme toxin. This toxin induces galls that gradually cover the insects, protecting them from pesticides, predators and bad weather. The nymphs turn into winged adults mid-August, leaving the galls behind as they complete their life cycle. The abandoned galls dry out, turning into unsightly, reddish brown nodules that resemble pendant cones.

Cooley spruce gall adelgids won't kill a tree, but they do affect new growth. The main reason for control is appearance. If your Colorado blue spruce or Engelmann Spruce have galls, you may want to clean

A tree may in summer wear A nest of robins in her hair.

Joyce Kilmer

Trees help purify the air by taking in carbon dioxide and giving off oxygen. We need at least three trees for each person on Earth to keep our atmosphere healthy. We should plant 10 trees for every 100 cars and 100 trees for every truck. It takes 100,000 trees to offset the effects on one jet on a cross-country trip. Whew!...We'd better get busy.

them up. One method of control is simply to clip off the galls in early spring and summer when they are still green and growing.

The alternative is to spray your trees. I consulted with licensed sprayer Rolland Kuhr (I personally wouldn't touch those strong chemicals) about the how and when of spraying spruce trees. He applies the chemicals carbaryl or dursban in early spring and again, if needed, in late September for fairly complete control.

Aspen Inkspots

Many aspen are afflicted with "inkspot" during wet mountain springs. This airborne fungus is normally present in my valley, but really seems to thrive in extended wet periods. Leaves blacken and fold up, waiting, I suppose, for better weather.

Although the fungus doesn't kill healthy trees, some folks choose to treat affected foliage. A general fungicide spray containing daconil is effective. Follow the directions on the product you choose.

Trees to plant

While the eastern US is a botanical wonderland for the landscaper, the dry, arid West is much more limited and challenging. Trees that are predictably successful can be counted on one hand. The following are used most often by professional Wyoming landscapers.

Blue Spruce

Grows to 60-75 feet. Good specimen tree with broad, pyramidal shape. Colorado blue spruce is prized for its Christmas tree shape and steely blue color. The bluest trees often command top dollar. Blueness is genetically determined, and color varies greatly. Don't be fooled into thinking that blue colors come with age: it doesn't. Pick a spruce you like and that matches your expectations, because what you take home won't change.

198

Quaking Aspen

Attractive white trunk; brilliant amber foliage in autumn. Spreads underground via suckering to form small groves. Typically attains height of 20-50 feet, and a trunk diameter of 1-3 feet.

Patmore Green Ash

Typically attains heights of 40-50 feet. This broad-crowned, very hardy tree is often used in city parks, as it offers shade and requires minimal care. Its fall foliage is a dull yellow.

Canadian Red Cherry

Canadian red cherry is a small ornamental tree with striking maroon leaves and white spring flowers. Though it only attains a height of 12 feet, it is a tough tree that can withstand extreme weather.

Lodgepole Pine

At full height, this straight pine looks like a telephone pole with a Christmas tree on top of it. It typically grows to a yard height of 50 feet, but can grow to be 70-80 feet tall. In my valley, many are dug by permit from surrounding Forest Service land and sold by local nurseries. Lodgepole look best when planted in stands.

Although lodgepole and other pines are technically coniferous evergreens, that doesn't mean they never lose their needles. Pines drop and replace about a fifth of their needles every autumn (some don't fall off until spring). Needles last approximately five years. Those that you see turning brown and dropping have reached maturity.

The young pine knows the secrets of the ground. The old pine knows the stars.

Golden Willow

At maturity goldens obtain heights and widths of 50 feet. This prodigious tree is a poor choice for small yards, as its vigorous root system can compromise sewer and septic tanks. It is among the easiest of trees to cultivate: merely cutting branches and leaving them in a pail of water for a few weeks will render ready-to-plant saplings. If you plant them in a sunny spot and water well, a rooted whip can become a big bushy tree in just a few years. Be sure to plant your willows so they will not rob your neighbors' sunlight at maturity.

Pussy Willows

On a recent sunny spring day I made pilgrimage to my secret spot to check out the willow bushes. When the willow's buds begin to look swollen, I will snip a bundle of branches to coax into "bloom" in my warm house. Although true pussy willows (Salix discolor) *are not often found in my valley, mountain willow bushes have delightful, pearly gray catkins that can be forced early spring.*

Select branches with plenty of flower buds, which are plumper than the slender pointed leaf buds. Use sharp shears to make the cut and place the sticks in a container of lukewarm water. If the buds are very tight, keep the cuttings in a cool place away from direct light until they swell a little bit more. When the buds reach full bloom, the catkins will be plump and woolly and laden with bright yellow pollen.

Goldens harbor a natural rooting hormone that can be used to root other kinds of plants. To make this simple rooting stimulant, add chopped pieces of willow branch to a pot of boiling water. Remove from heat and let steep until the water cools. Discard the sticks and store the liquid in the refrigerator to use as needed.

Featured Trees

Crabapple Trees

Despite their cranky name, crabapples are the most beautiful of all fruit trees. Few trees match their spectacular spring show, when emerging leaves disappear in clouds of white, pink or red blossoms. The fragrance of prolific blooms permeates the warm spring air, quickly fading our long Rocky Mountain winters to a dim memory.

This springtime flower display is the reason many gardeners include crabapple trees in their landscapes. Fruit size distinguishes crabapple trees from their "eating apple" cousins, since both belong to the genus *Malus*. Trees bearing fruits larger than two-inches in diameter are classified as apple trees, while those bearing smaller fruits are crabapples. Crabapple species range from eight foot, multi-stemmed bushes to spreading, 30-foot shade trees. In form they may be round, oval, upright, horizontal or even weeping. Leaf color varies from rosy red to soft green. The fruit color is also variable, with shades of red, orange, yellow green and purple.

Crabapples grow well in cold climates (as low as Zone 2). These hardy trees rouse from their dormant state at spring temperatures under 45 degrees Fahrenheit. Old-fashioned "Dolgo" and "Hopa" are particularly noted for their durability in harsh climates, as are "Chestnut," "Radiant" and "Selkirk."

Urbanites whose neighbors object to messy apples on their sidewalks and driveways may want to try one of the newer hybrids that

Knowing trees, I understand the meaning of patience.

Hal Borland

201

Tip

Mice and other small rodents can severely damage or kill young trees by girdling the bark near their base. Protect new trees over the winter by removing tall grass around the trunk. This prevents nesting. Wrap hardware cloth around the base to prevent nibbling.

retain their fruit, such as "Red Jewel." Fruits that linger on the tree throughout the winter not only create an interesting spot in a snowy yard but also furnish food for songbirds. Be aware, however, that these beautiful hybrids tend to be less hardy.

While it is possible to buy dormant bare root trees to set out early spring, I prefer to plant established container-grown stock purchased from local nurseries. Because weather in the mountains can be painfully unpredictable, potted trees can be held and planted anytime during the season, even into autumn. Fall soil still retains heat from the summer, and holds moisture throughout the winter. Newly planted trees should be watered regularly (but not kept constantly wet) until the roots become established, usually through two growing seasons.

Crabapple trees grow in a wide range of soils, though alkaline soil may slow growth by tying up trace minerals. Sites that receive full sun yield the sweetest fruit and lessen the potential for disease. Apple scab, cedar-apple rust, fire blight and powdery mildew can appear in a wet, rainy spring. Luckily, the dry summer, high elevation climate of the Rocky Mountains spare them the common weather-related diseases their East and Midwest counterparts endure.

Although mountain crabapples suffer fewer diseases, wild critters are often a concern. Moose and deer browse on branches. If damage is frequent or severe, you may need to fence them out. Voles gnaw on young bark under the snow in late winter and sapsuckers can do extensive trunk damage be drilling rows of sap wells. I love wildlife but sure hate to see it nibbling on my trees. Although nothing is 100 percent effective, you can deter wildlife by hanging aluminum pie pans in the branches. Critters are wary of the shiny items flapping in the breeze. You could also try hanging mesh bags filled with a strong scented deodorant soap such as Irish Spring™. The soap's odor masks the scent of the tree, "hiding" it from animals.

Crabapples benefit from light pruning every couple of years, preferably in early spring before growth begins. Thinning allows better airflow and sunlight to the tree's interior. This discourages fungal disease, reduces wind resistance that can cause breakage, promotes abundant flowering and maintains an attractive form. Remove branches that overlap, rub or cross. Prune water sprouts (vertical branches in the middle of the canopy) as well. Cut back drooping branches on older trees to prevent them from excessively shading lower foliage.

Crabapples often produce shoots, called suckers, from their roots. Grafted trees are especially prone to suckering if the top grows more slowly than the rootstock. Trim suckers at ground level every year after the trees spring growth spurt. If a tree has been neglected for years or even decades, spread out its required pruning to remove no more than one-third at one time. Otherwise, the tree will respond by producing a mighty crop of water sprouts.

In general, crabapples are underused in the West. Whenever I need a housewarming or wedding gift for friends, I choose a flowering crab. I can't think of a better present, for the dazzling spring blossoms and hardy nature of crabapples make these little trees sure to please.

Although crabapples are generally too sour to eat out of hand, they make delicious jelly. They are naturally loaded with pectin; there is no need to add a commercial one. The mouth-watering end product may be rich ruby red, deep pink or even amber, depending on the variety.

Crabapple Jelly

From the Teton County, Wyoming, Extension Office

    3 pounds of fruit
    3 cups water
    4 cups sugar

Sterilize five pint jars by washing them in hot, soapy water and rinsing them well. After shaking off as much water as you can, dry them in a 325-degree oven for at least 10 minutes.

Wash crabapples. Cut out blemishes and remove stem and blossom

*Bind the
aspen ne'er
to quiver
Then bind
love to
last
forever*

*Francis
Palgrave
1875*

Tip

Last spring I "forced" a bouquet of crabapple branches, bringing spring into my kitchen day earlier than the calendar did. I used sharp shears to cut branches laden with buds, and placed them in tepid water. In a matter of days the warmth of my house prompted the boughs to bloom, delighting me in no small way.

Crabapple bloom

ends. Don't pare or core. Cut apples into small pieces and place in a large pot. Add water, cover the pot and bring to a full boil on high heat. Reduce heat and simmer 25 minutes until fruit is soft.

Squeeze pulp mixture through a moistened jelly bag, or a colander lined with a towel. Measure four cups of the resulting juice into a large enamel kettle; add water if you have less than four cups to reach that measure. Add sugar, stirring to dissolve. Boil over high heat until jelly sheets off the edge of a clean spoon, about 15 minutes. Remove from heat. Skim off foam and pour into sterilized pint jars, leaving a minimum quarter-inch space. Cap with lids and bands. Place jars in a boiling water bath for five minutes. Remove jars and cool.

A nice variation of this jelly is Crabapple Plum jelly. Follow the directions above, except use three cups of strained crabapple juice instead of four, and add a cup of plum juice.

Reduced-Sugar Blackberry /Crabapple Jam
Recipe by Kate Pugh

Note: The set of this spread is softer than conventional jam as it has less sugar. It must be kept refrigerated, but will keep up to one month. Use a set of metric measures (these are often printed on glass measuring cups based on the English measuring system we use.)

500 g Blackberries

300 g Crabapples

200 ml water

350 g sugar

2 tbs. Lemon juice

Sterilize jars, following the instructions given in the first recipe, for approximately three cups of jam. When you are finished, put a saucer in your refrigerator to chill.

Grate the crabapples, discarding the cores, or cut out the cores and finely chop the fruit in a processor. Place the berries, apples and water in a saucepan and bring to a full boil. Reduce heat and simmer five minutes, stirring occasionally. Add sugar and lemon juice, stirring until sugar is dissolved, then increase heat and return to a boil. Boil rapidly for seven minutes. Remove from heat and test for set. Put a teaspoonful onto the chilled saucer and return the saucer to the refrigerator for two minutes. At the end of that time, this is what the jam will be like when it is cooled. If it's too thin, clean your saucer and put it back in the refrigerator and boil the jam for another two minutes. Test again. When happy with set, ladle the jam into sterilized jars and put on lids. Place jars in a boiling water bath for five minutes. Remove jars and cool.

Shrubs & Bushes

We often put more thought and money into choosing trees, but shrubs can play an equally important role in home landscaping. They can tie your house to the rest of the its surroundings and can make a property look well-tended and cared for. While large trees can frame a house, shrubs can accent windows and doorways or hide unsightly, aboveground foundation walls. Shrubs can also screen unpleasant views, serve as windbreaks and form hedges that define property lines.

Unlike trees, shrubs grow quickly. Many mature within five years and are, in general, long-lived. Follow the planting hole instructions and care guidelines outlined for trees when you plant your shrubs.

Garden centers and nurseries carry a wide range of reasonably priced shrubs—so many, in fact, that it can be difficult to make a decision about which one to buy. Some have beautiful blossoms, some colorful berries. Some feature vivid autumn color or interesting winter bark. The following list includes varieties I have found do well in northern, high altitude climates. Keep in mind that a small shrub *will* grow. Find out the size of the shrub at maturity before you buy it.

Won't you come into my garden? I'd like my roses to see you.

Richard Sheridan

Bush Cinquefoil

Grows to a height of 2-4 feet. Blooms all summer until frost in shades of yellow and white. Cinquefoils are best planted in groups. Cut them back whenever they start to look stringy to keep their shape compact.

Cotoneaster

Grows to a height of 8-10 feet. Very cold hardy. Features small pinkish flowers, dark glossy berries, and red autumn foliage.

Lilacs

Attains height of up to 15 feet. Lilacs need full sun for good bloom. They grow slowly in a cold climate. Color ranges from white to lavender to dark purple.

Honeysuckle

Honeysuckle grows 8-10 feet tall. Many varieties are available; 24 species of this plant are native to the US. All have small flowers and red berries. Honeysuckle fruit is eaten by birds and chipmunks. Honeysuckle is sometimes used to screen an object or view.

Dwarf Mugo Pines

Grows 2-3 feet tall. Dark green mugo pines are native to Switzerland, so they feel right at home in mountain climates and are very cold hardy. Their branches are a deer magnet in the winter months.

Siberian Pea Shrub

Grows 8-12 feet tall. This shrub produces yellow spring flowers, often used as hedges or wind breaks. It is very fast growing, making it a good choice for new yards.

Blue Arctic Willow
>
> Grows 8-feet wide and up to 8-feet tall. This attractive shrub has narrow, blue-green leaves. Like all willows, it requires lots of water and benefits from annual pruning.

Chokecherry and Serviceberry
>
> These grow wild in Wyoming, but can be purchased and planted throughout the Rockies and northern locations. Both have clusters of white blossoms followed by edible berries. Chokecherries grow up to 20-feet tall at maturity. Seviceberries are smaller at 3-10 feet tall.

Tam Juniper
>
> Grows 2-3 feet tall. These low-growing, spreading evergreens are not my favorites because they can get beat up by winter snow and ice accumulation. I include them because so many folks use them as foundation plantings.

Red Twig Dogwood
>
> Grows 5-12 feet tall. Native to Wyoming, characteristics of this shrub include small white blossoms and fruit, maroon fall foliage and colored bark. It thrives in wet places, such as proximity to a pond or creek, and in partial shade.

Honeysuckle Aphids

Though honeysuckle aphids were not found in the US until 1980, they have become a huge problem on non-native honeysuckle bushes. Bushes infested with aphids develop stunted, folded leaves and disfigured ugly branch ends. If left unchecked, several years of infestation will severely stunt the bush.

Tiny honeysuckle aphids torture their namesake by sucking life-

Gardeners, I think, dream bigger dreams than emperors.

Mary Cantwell

giving plant juice all summer long, particularly attacking succulent new tip growth. Come autumn, infested terminals turn brown quicker than normal foliage and the damage becomes apparent.

To control these pests, spray with a systemic insecticide such as Orthene® two or three times a season beginning early June. Repeated sprayings are required because, like other aphids, this species can reproduce without mating. Unmated females give live birth to hundreds of young every seven to 14 days. That's a lot of aphids to contain.

The end of summer doesn't signal the end of control measures. Incredibly, honeysuckle aphids can survive –50 degree weather by holing up in witches' brooms, an abnormal ball of small twigs and branches. It is critical to clip the clusters off, bag them and throw them away. Raking up leaves and debris beneath the bush helps as well.

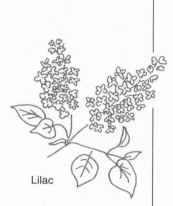

Lilac

Featured Shrubs & Bushes

Lilacs

One can never have too many lilacs. Southeastern European immigrants brought native lilac starts with them across the Atlantic, unwilling to part with the legendary fragrance of these exquisitely colored, lavish blooms. Century-old bushes still bloom near springs on long-deserted homesteads, testimonials to their hardiness and the pioneers who carried these plants from the old country to the new.

As their popularity and longevity suggest, lilacs are cold hardy to Zone 3 and easy to grow. Good soil, drainage and sunlight insure optimum performance; planted in poor soil and partial shade lilacs will bloom, but sparsely. Lilacs prefer alkaline soil, prevalent in the West. Adequate air circulation discourages powdery mildew.

As long as lilacs are planted properly (not too deeply) and receive adequate care (watered regularly to keep moist), potted or balled-and-burlapped plants can be set out anytime during the growing season. Although digging up and replanting the outside shoots can propagate lilacs I recommend buying nursery-grown stock. In a high elevation, northern climate, lilacs grow painfully slow because of the short and often cool summers.

Lilacs are versatile landscape additions. They may be placed singly as specimen plants, grouped to form backdrops, ordered into hedges or incorporated into beds. While most lilacs will bloom sparingly the second or third year after planting, these long-lived plants take up to five years to become fully established and produce true-to-type tresses.

The old fashioned *Syringa vulgaris* is the most widely planted lilac, but the interested buyer may come across other useful hybrids. Ask your nurseryman about some of the Canadian cultivars that have proven to be extremely hardy and vigorous.

If you have an old, scraggly lilac—one that blossoms only at the top and has lost its elegant form in a tangle of unattractive shoots—you can rejuvenate it, but you must be bold. Immediately after flowering (so as not to remove next year's buds) grab your pruning saw and loppers. Remove dead, diseased or crossed stems at ground level. Cut about a third of the old growth to the ground as well. Prune away most of the suckers (the stray shoots that spring directly from the root structure) under the soil level. Removing spent flower clusters is not necessary, though many experts encourage the practice.

Lilacs have charmed gardeners, poets and almost everyone else for centuries with their nostalgic beauty and haunting fragrance. A lilac in full bloom is something to behold. It quickens the memory and reminds us of grandmothers and bygone days.

Shrub Roses

Every mountain gardener probably wishes he could grow roses. Roses have a sensual appeal that makes them the world's best-known and most popular plant. Unfortunately, the beautiful hybrids that make romantic Valentine's Day bouquets are tough to grow in high elevation or northern climates. With a short growing season and sub-zero winter tempera

Deep in their roots, all flowers keep the light.

—

Theodore Roetke

Rose Hips

When the last rose of summer has faded and gone, rose bushes are colored with an abundant crop of bright red fruit. These pulpy seed pods are called rose "hips." Most varieties of roses have hips the size of a pea or marble. Rugosa roses have the largest fruit, some attaining the size of a quarter.

Rose hips are rich in vitamin C and contain smaller amounts of calcium, phosphorus and iron. I sometimes munch on fresh rose hips as I work in my yard. They have a tart, apple-like taste. Many enjoy rose hip tea. To make, steep chopped berries in boiled water for three to five minutes or until the desired strength is reached, or mix fresh, diced hips with your favorite tea blend. A single cup of rose hip tea contains as much vitamin C as six oranges.

Rose hips can be preserved, with some nutritional loss, by drying them in an airy place away from direct sun. The process typically takes a week to 10 days. An easier method of preservation is to freeze them in bags or glass jars and thaw as needed.

This wintertime fruit—a popular food source for game and song birds, squirrels, rabbits, bears, moose and deer—offers both good health and landscape beauty in traditionally drab months. Research reveals roses grown in the North produce hips with the highest quantity of vitamin C. Perhaps this is one of nature's compensations for severe winters.

tures, it is difficult for many of the fancy roses to survive more than a single season.

Climate-challenged gardeners can, however, grow shrub roses. Wilder and more rugged in appearance than hybrids, these extremely winter hardy plants can survive the worst of winter weather. Shrub roses are grown on their own roots rather than from grafts that create hybrids such as fancy tea roses. Even if an unusually cold winter kills the top, shrub rose roots resprout. Varieties that do well up to 8,000 feet include:

Austrian Copper
    Bright orange, single petaled
    blossoms
Harrison's Yellow
    A spectacular mid-summer
    show of yellow blooms
Theresa Bugnet
    Fragrant, double pink rose
Red Leaf Rose
    Dark leaf, small pink flowers
Woods Rose
    Pale pink, fragrant flower.
    Avoid planting this mountain
    native in a flowerbed because
    of its prolific suckering.

Mountain nurseries usually carry a supply of most of these bushes. It is also easy to propagate a new bush from established shrub roses. Sever a shoot (shrub roses seem to always have some) with a spade. If your selected shoot has a well-developed root system, move it immediately to a new location; if not, select a new shoot. Transplant in a hole deep enough to completely cover the roots and apply a small amount of fertilizer to give it a boost. Keep your transplant well watered to ease its period of adjustment.

If you've picked a good shoot, in a few years your scruffy little start will reward you with a cloud of exuberant blossoms.

Mugo Pines

Mugos are handsome, ornamental bushes stocked at nurseries, typically as mere babies in one-gallon pots. They look like neat, muffin-like shrubs when planted, and can go unpruned for two to three years to reach their desired size. Planted on a berm or at the edge of a yard they can be left as unpruned, handsome little trees their entire lives. But they lose their appeal when the shrub-now-tree crowds the tulips, blocks the picture window and generally muddles the landscape.

Mugo pines begin their new growth cycle each spring by sending out new, scaly shoots called candles. Needles eventually sprout from the scales as the candles grow into branches. It is these easily recognizable shoots that should be pruned to control the size and shape of a mugo pine.

The only tool necessary to prune a mugo is a sharp pair of hand clippers; nothing big or electrical is needed. Snip the new candles off at an angle at the next whorl of branchlets. It is important not to make the cut in mid-stem, or new growth will begin there.

Mugo pines are a very hardy tree, either pruned or unpruned. The most important point to remember when purchasing a mugo is that if you buy it because it was short and cute, keep it pruned or you'll end up with out-of-kilter landscaping in prominent places in your yard.

We come from the Earth. We return to the Earth. And in-between, we garden.

211

Fruits & Vines

Raspberries

Raspberries, not apples, are the fruit of temptation. Picture a hot summer day when you reach into a tangle of thorny brambles to pick that one perfect berry. A light touch is necessary or it will burst at your fingertips—leaving only a red stain—and you'll likely be scratched for your effort. But oh, it is worth it!

Raspberries are garden ambrosia. It is not surprising that I get asked lots of questions about their cultivation every year. Mountain gardeners will be heartened to know that it is not difficult to grow and maintain a patch of these succulent bramble fruits. If you are planting a new bed of raspberries, select a sunny site that can be utilized for a number of years; well managed, perennial raspberries can last a decade.

Next, thoroughly prepare the ground. Create a rich loamy soil by working in plenty of organic matter. Don't neglect this step if you want a thriving patch.

Time to plant. Good varietal choices for the home garden include "Indian Summer" and "Redwing," both of which have fewer thorns than berry bushes of yesteryear; "Canby" is a thornless raspberry for gardeners who can't stand being pricked. Redwing is my personal favorite; the taste is unbeatable. "Honey Queen" is a tasty yellow variety that I just can't bring myself to grow. To me raspberries are red and I won't have them any other way.

If you have room, plant two or three varieties. Berry starts should be planted at the same level as they are growing in their pots and spaced three feet apart. Lightly tamp down the soil and thoroughly water. Maintaining moist soil and keeping competition from weeds and grasses to a minimum will boost berry production. Keep in mind that although bushes grow quickly, it takes two or three years for a bush to yield a full crop.

Once your plants begin fruiting, they need annual pruning. I could expound on first year primocanes and second year floricanes, but simply put the pruning requirements are as follows: Each spring, cut out the old, woody canes that fruited last season and leave the fresh-looking canes that will bear fruit this summer. Several solid canes will produce better and be easier to harvest than a jungle of brambles.

After pruning, I recommend applying a balanced fertilizer that includes iron. Raspberries are susceptible to chlorosis, a disease caused by iron deficiency. Other threats to your raspberry patch may include hungry bears and children of all ages. In my yard, moose and porcupines do most of the pruning, much to my dismay.

But there's always some left for me—and they taste better than any I've bought in the supermarket. Success is sweet.

Strawberries

Strawberries are one of the most popular small fruits for home gardeners. To me few berries are as delectable as fully ripe strawberries, to say nothing of the glorious concoction our mothers made with them. Juicy, fresh picked morsels sliced over a sweetened biscuit and topped with a mound of luscious whipped cream. Strawberry shortcake. Yummmmm.

Strawberries thrive in cool, dry climates where long winters curb diseases that plague them in other areas. Care should be taken, however, to select varieties that are hardy to high elevation, northern regions. "Ogallala" and "Fort Laramie" plants both do well in a

A woman and a melon are hard to know.

213

Tip

Cut the leaves off rhubarb stalks as you harvest them. Rhubarb's edible foliage can be spread around garden plants to act as a layer of mulch that conserves water.

cool climate. Though considered everbearers, the short growing season allows them to produce just one heavy crop in mid-summer. (Elsewhere, everbearers produce an early and late summer crop.)

Choose the site for your strawberry bed with the sun in mind. At least eight hours of full sun a day is best, so a southern exposure is ideal. Strawberries prefer a soil that is not too alkaline; a pH between five and six yields the best results. Create well-drained, fertile soil by digging in manure, compost and peat. Set the plants so the base of the crown is right at ground level.

Strawberries, like all fruit plants need generous quantities of water to produce plump, juicy fruits. And although it seems a shame to do so, it's beneficial to pinch blossoms off as they come out the first year. (I have to admit to having never done this. Who can be so virtuous as to wait a whole year for a taste of homegrown strawberries?)

A strawberry bed eventually declines. While longevity varies, plants become woody and less fruitful after four or five years. When this happens, the bed needs to be renovated with new stock or planted with runners from existing plants. Timing for this task is important, as plants need good root growth to make it through the winter. Fall transplants may not have time to develop. I suggest renovating your bed in the spring to give plants more weeks to develop. Luckily, spring is the time most of us are at peak energy and enthusiasm for taking on major gardening projects.

Growing fruit seems somehow superior to growing, say, cabbages or onions. Considering the ease of strawberry culture in cool climates, a gardener is almost foolish to not grow a patch. After all, there may be a summer of too much lettuce or too many green beans, but it is inconceivable there could ever be too many strawberries.

Rhubarb

The theory that the urge to harvest is linked to ancient survival instincts falls apart when it comes to rhubarb: I know folks who would rather die than eat the stuff. My husband is one of them. This is regrettable, because rhubarb thrives in areas that brave frigid winters. Its bright red nubs poke out of the ground as soon as the snow melts, fulfilling my winter-deprived need to gather.

Rhubarb is propagated from a fleshy root division begged from a friend, or from rootstock purchased at a nursery. Make sure each root piece has a good, strong eye. Plant three or four inches deep in fertile soil amended with lots of organic matter. This big-leafed plant prefers full sun. Water regularly. Give the plants two growing seasons before harvesting their red stalks; rhubarb is long-lived if you tuck it in the right spot and let it establish a good root system.

I think many people dislike rhubarb because their mothers forced them to eat it as a stringy, stewed sauce when they were kids. A pity. Rhubarb makes a great pie or cobbler, and is a wonderful addition to berry jams. To me, though, the best way to eat rhubarb is uncooked, straight off the plant when I'm working in the garden. When I bite down on a tart, juicy red stem I know spring has arrived.

Hop Vines

Hops are one of the few vines that grow well in mountain climates. This herbaceous, non-woody vine sports three or five-lobed leaves. My vines seem to grow 6-7 inches a day in July, vigorously climbing the stair railing and spilling onto the deck. Before the days of indoor plumbing, our grannies planted this fast-growing vine to discreetly cover the outhouse. Nowadays they make a good screen wherever they are planted.

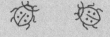

Ladybug Ladybug

In the Middle Ages, English farmers used ladybugs to control pests in their hops fields. The rhyme, " Ladybug, ladybug, fly away home, your house is on fire, your children will burn," expressed concern the farmers had for this tiny insect when they burned their hops in autumn.

Hop Vine

To start hop vines, ask a friend for a shovel full of their ropy, underground hop rhizomes, or obtain rootstock from a plant nursery. Hops should be transplanted in early spring before much growth occurs. Plant the rhizomes 2-inches below the soil surface and water regularly until good, above ground growth appears. Once established, this robust vine will live for decades with little or no care.

Hops grow at a Jack-and-the-Beanstalk pace until they flower in August. Hundreds of pale-green, papery flowers bloom in cone-shaped catkins that shake in the slightest breeze. Ripe, dried catkins are the "fruit" that gives beer and malt liquor their distinctive flavor.

When nightly frosts become a regular occurrence, I unwind and cut down my hop vines. Hops are herbaceous, or non-woody, vines. This means that although they are root hardy to minus temperatures, hops die back to the ground each autumn and send up new shoots each spring.

In no time at all, the hops will be heading towards the sky.

A Gardener's
Ready
Reference

Fun Places to Visit

Botanic Gardens, Arboretums
& Nature Centers
Compiled by the Editor

It is not surprising that gardeners are drawn to botanic gardens and arboretums, where professionally designed displays of fantastic plants and trees await. Aficionados of both will want to bookmark Botanique before their next travel excursion. This comprehensive Web site lists over 1,700 gardens, arboreta and nature preserves in the US and Canada, organized by state or province. It also includes a calendar of gardening events across North America, and a directory of botanical resources. Botanique's URL is www.boranique.com. A sampling of interesting gardens and arboreta found in the Western U.S. and Canada is presented below.

Western U.S.

Albuquerque Biological Park
2601 Central Avenue NW
Albuquerque, N.M. 87104
Phone: 505-764-6200 • Fax: 505-764-6281
www.cabq.gov/biopark

This large complex includes a botanic garden, aquarium, zoo and aquatic park: There's definitely something for everyone. The Rio Grande Botanic Garden's glass conservatory showcases desert and Mediterranean pavilions. Outdoor displays include herb, rose, Old World design and children fantasy gardens. Over 11,000 plants are collectively exhibited at the gardens. The aquarium is home to a 285,000-gallon shark tank; the zoo sports more than 1,000 animals. The facility is open 362 days a year. It is closed on Thanksgiving, Christmas and New Year's Days. Numerous shops and restaurants are on the grounds. There is an admission charge.

218

Arboretum at Flagstaff
3.8 South Woody Mountain Road
PO Box 670
Flagstaff, AZ. 86002
Phone: 602-774-1442

Open May through September, this 200-acre arboretum includes more than 10 acres of specialty gardens. Landscape plantings, wildflower meadows, herb and vegetable, children's and shade gardens are featured. A nature trail, visitor's center and horticulture center showcasing a solar greenhouse are also on the grounds. There is an admission fee; children under 18 are free.

Arizona-Sonora Desert Museum
2021 N.Kinney Road
Tucson, AZ. 85743
Phone: 602-883-1380

Open year-round, this combination 12-acre botanical garden, museum and zoo features more than 1,300 plants and some 300 animal species in natural settings. A mile of path connects the cactus garden, hummingbird enclosure and desert garden. The latter is sponsored by *Sunset Magazine*. Guided tours are available May through January. There is an admission charge.

Betty Ford Alpine Gardens
183 Gore Creek Drive
Vail, CO. 81657

Phone: 970-476-0103 • Fax: 970-476-1685
www.vailalpinegarden.org

Perched at an altitude of 8,200 feet, Betty Ford Alpine Gardens constitutes one of the highest alpine gardens in the US. Four separate gardens showcase a collection of plants found at high elevations: The Alpine Display Garden, Mountain Perennial Garden, Mountain Meditation Garden and Alpine Rock Garden. There is an admission charge.

Bloedel Reserve
7571 NE Dolphin Dr.
Bainbridge Island, WA. 98110-1097
Phone: 206-842-7631 • Fax: 206-842-8970

Bloedel Reserve was established in 1988. Japanese, moss and reflection gardens grace its 150-acre grounds, as does an historic 1931 French chateau that serves as the facility's visitor's center. The reserve is presently open by appointment only, Wednesday through Sunday. There is an admission charge.

Chatfield Arboretum
8500 Deer Creek Canyon Road
Littleton, CO. 80123
Phone: 303-973-3705 • Fax: 303-973-1979
www. botanicgardens.org/chatfld.htm

Managed by Denver Botanic Gardens, this 700-acre arboretum features flower gardens, nature trails, wildlife and a restored 19th century farmstead listed on the National Register of Historic Places. A one-room schoolhouse dating back to the 1870s serves as the facility's visitor center. The arboretum is open year-round. There is a small admission fee. Guided tours are available by reservation only.

Cheyenne Botanic Gardens
710 S. Lions Park Drive
Cheyenne, WY. 82001
Phone: 307-637-6458

Cheyenne Botanic Gardens is located in a 6,800-foot, three-section greenhouse within Lions Park. Senior, youth and handicapped volunteers provide 90 percent of the facility's labor, a unique program that has been recognized by Presidents Reagan, Bush and Clinton. The conservatory is 100 percent solar heated. It includes tropical, herb, vegetable and flower gardens. The outside grounds include six acres of perennial, annual, wildflower, rose, cactus and peace gardens. There is no admission charge, but donations are appreciated.

Denver Botanic Gardens
1005 York Street
Denver, CO. 80206-3766
Phone: 303-331-4000 • Fax: 303-370-8004
www. botanicgardens.org

Established in 1952, this 22-acre facility is one of the largest botanical gardens in the US, and a recognized leader in Rocky Mountain horticulture. A large conservatory and greenhouse are surrounded by numerous outside gardens, including rose, herb, Japanese, and rock alpine cultivated areas. Lilacs, daylilies and alpine plants are among the gardens specialty collections. A restaurant, gift shop and visitor's center grace the grounds. Parking is free, but there is an admission charge. The facility is open year-round.

Fairmount Cemetery
430 S. Quebec Street
Denver, CO. 80231
Phone: 303-399-0692

The grounds of Fairmount Cemetery comprise the largest arboretum in Colorado. Its 260-acres were planted over a century ago with 200 kinds of trees. Today only 50 species remain, but they are among the biggest representatives of their kind in the state. The grounds are also home to 100 old rose bushes, which are now being propagated. Fairmount Cemetery is open daily from sunrise to sunset.

Idaho Botanical Garden
2355 Old Penitentiary Road
PO Box 2140
Boise, ID. 83712
Phone: 208-343-8649

The Idaho Botanical Garden is located within the sandstone complex of Idaho's former state penitentiary. Its 50 acres includes a children's garden, nature trail and meditation garden. The grounds are noted for their iris, roses and peonies. There is an admission charge; children under six are free. The garden is open April 15 through October 15.

International Peace Gardens
1000 South 900 West
Salt Lake City, UT. 84105
Phone: 801-974-2411

Open May through September. Eight acres in Jordan Park are planted in 25 different gardens, representing countries worldwide. In late August, representatives from included countries sell food and crafts from their homeland at the annual Peace Garden Festival. There is no admission fee.

Japanese Garden at Washington Park
611 SW Kingston Avenue
Portland, OR. 97208
Phone: 503-223-1321 • Fax: 503-223-4070

Located on a hillside overlooking the city's skyline, the Japanese Garden of Portland is hailed as the most authentic Japanese garden outside of Japan. Five gardens grace the five-and-a-half-acre grounds: a Tea Garden, Sand and Stone Garden, Strolling Pond Garden, Flat Garden and Natural Garden. The grounds are open year-round, with the exception of Thanksgiving, Christmas and New Year's Days. Parking is free; there is an admission fee.

Ohme Gardens
3327 Ohme Road
Wenatchee, WA. 98801
Phone: 509-662-5785

Established in 1929, this nine-acre alpine garden is situated on a bluff overlooking the Wenatchee Valley, Cascade Mountains and Columbia River. The benches and paths are cut from rough native stone, and the grounds include an historic lodge. Ground covers, phlox and creeping thyme are among the garden's specialties. It is open from Memorial to Labor Day; there is an admission charge.

Owen Rose Garden
300 N. Jefferson
Eugene, OR. 97402
Phone: 503-687-5333

The world's largest cherry tree and over 400 varieties of roses are the attraction of this public garden. Established in 1951, it's eight-acres include a picnic area and restrooms. Guided tours are available; June is the recommended month to visit. There is no admission charge.

Red Butte Garden and Arboretum
18A de Trobriand St.
Salt Lake City, UT. 84113
Phone: 801-581-4747
www.utah.edu/redbutte

Red Butte Gardens and Arboretum are

open year-round. The 30-acre garden is surrounded by natural areas containing four miles
of mountain trails. A children's garden, oak
tunnel and wildflower meadow are among the
grounds attractions. There is an admission fee.
Entrance is free the first Monday of every
month, April through October.

Rhododendron Species Botanical Garden
2525 South 336th St.
Box 3798
Federal Way, WA. 98063-3798
Phone: 206-838-4646 • Fax: 206-661-9377
www. olympus.net/gardens/rsgshow.htm
    Nestled on 24-acres between Seattle and
Tacoma is one of the largest species collections
of rhododendrons in the world. This botanical
garden is home to over 2,000 varieties of
rhododendrons—including azaleas—beautifully displayed in natural settings. Carniverous
plants, hardy ferns and primula species are also
among the garden's specialty collections. RSBG
is open year-round. It is closed on Thursdays
and Fridays as well as Thanksgiving, Christmas and New Year's Days. Guided tours are
available; there is an admission charge.

Sundance Farms
3303 West 2400 South
Charleston, UT. 84032
Phone: 435-654-2721 • Fax: 435-654-4026
Email: sundancefarms@shadowlink.net

Sundance Farms was started in 1988 by
Robert Redford to produce vegetables, flowers
and herbs for his nearby resort. June through
September, visitors may stroll through the organic gardens and visit the historic botanical
drying barns. A garden gift shop and handmade
soap studio are on the premises. There is no
admission fee. Guided tours for a minimum of
five people are available by reservation year-
round.

University of Idaho Arboretum and
Botanical Garden
205 CEB
University of Idaho
Moscow, ID. 83844-3226
Phone: 208-885-6250
    The 63-acre arboretum and garden, located
on the university's campus includes important
collections of maples, lilacs, crabapples and
Idaho conifers. It is open daily and has no ad-
mission charge.

Utah State University Botanical Garden
1817 North Main Street
Farmington, UT 84025
Phone: 801-451-3204
    Founded in 1954, this botanical garden fea-
tures a greenhouse, weather station, and outdoor rose, herb and children's gardens on its
seven-acre grounds. Guided tours are available.
Parking is free and there is no admission charge.

Canada

Butchart Gardens
www. butchartgardens.com

The 50 acres that comprise Butchart Gardens were formerly an abandoned quarry on the estate of Mr. and Mrs. R. P. Butchart. In an effort to beautify the area, the gardens were begun in 1904. Today they are a world-renowned expanse of luscious color. Admission prices vary with the amount of bloom on the grounds; peak season is roughly mid-April through October. Facilities include three restaurants, a seed and gift store and a plant identification center. Group tours are available.

Devonian Botanic Garden
University of Alberta
Edmonton, Alberta
Canada T6G 2E1
Phone: 780-987-3054 • Fax: 780-987-3054
www. botanique.com/tours/cantour/alberta

Established in 1959, Devonian Botanic Garden is the northernmost botanic garden in Canada. It is recognized for its collections of cold hardy and alpine plants. Alpine, herb, peony, iris, native plant and Japanese gardens extend over 80 acres through a rolling landscape of pines and wetlands. The grounds are surrounded by an additional 110 acres of natural areas. Facilities include a pavilion, gift shop and café. Pre-booked guided tours are avail-

able. Devonian Botanic Garden is open year-round; there is an admission charge.

Minter Gardens
Business Address: 10015 Young Street North
Chilliwack, B.C.
Canada V2P 4V4
Phone: 604-792-6612 • Fax: 604-792-8893
www. minter.org

Located in the scenic Fraser River Valley near Harrison Hot Springs Resort, Minter Gardens house 11 theme gardens on its 27 acres. Waterfalls, ponds, a living maze and topiaries are featured among the different gardens, which are connected by meandering pathways. A small gift and plant shop is located on the grounds; Minter's operates extensive retail garden centers in nearby Chilliwack and Sardis. The gardens are presently open April through October. There is an admission fee.

University of British Columbia
Botanical Garden
6804 SW Marine Drive
Vancouver, B.C.
Canada V6T 1Z4
Phone: 604-822-9666
www.hedgerows.com/UBCBotGdn

More than 10,000 varieties of shrubs, flowers and trees grow on the University of British Columbia Botanical Garden's 70 acres. Asian, perennial, alpine, food, winter, arbor and native gardens comprise the grounds. Particularly noteworthy is the Nitobe Memorial Garden, a traditional Japanese tea and strolling garden. Pre-arranged private group tours are available; general tours are offered to the public twice a week from March through October. Admission to the year-round gardens, located on the UBC campus, is free during the winter season.

Victoria Butterfly Gardens
Box 1461
1461 Benvenuto Avenue
Brentwood Bay, B.C.
Canada V8M 1R3

Located near the entrance to Butchart Gardens, Victoria Butterfly Gardens is an indoor, tropical facility completed in 1994 to house and breed moths and butterflies from all over the world. Visitors are treated to 700-1,000 butterflies and moths flying free among beautiful host plants, including hibiscus, bougainvillea, and bird of paradise. Among the 35 varieties of butterflies and moths are the Red Periot, Giant Owl, Blue Morpho, Giant Swallowtail and the Atlas Moth, the largest moth in the world. A nature shop featuring educational gifts and a restaurant are on the grounds. The facility is open daily March through October.

Farmers' Markets

Part theater, part street fair and a produce shopper's dream, farmers' markets are increasing in popularity nationwide. The US Dept. of Agriculture's National Farmers Market Directory listed over 2,400 farmers' markets in 1996, over 600 more than 1994, and the upward trend appears to be continuing.

These colorful, friendly markets are delightful places to shop. Held in parking lots, downtown squares and county parks, the personality of individual farmers' markets varies widely. Some allow crafts and homebaked goods to be sold; others offer strictly produce. My farmers' market purchases have included jars of golden honey, farm eggs, perennial plants, preserves, pottery, peacock feathers and homeground flours as well as a wide and wonderful assortment of produce. It's downright inspirational!

Farmers' markets abound in every state, providing folks the opportunity to enjoy fresh-picked, homegrown food. Call local Chamber of Commerce offices to visit a farmer's market this summer. Or, check the state-by-state listings posted on the USDA's Web site at www.ams.gov/farmermarkets. Be forewarned that farmers' markets come and go. The ones that follow are well established.

Utah

Downtown Alliance Farmers' Market
Pioneer Park • Salt Lake City, UT
    Held late August through October on
    Saturday morning

Montana

Gallatin Farmers' Market
Bogart Park Pavillion
South Church Avenue • Bozeman, MT.
    Held July through mid-September on Sat-
    urday morning.

Sweet Pea Festival
Lindley Park • Bozeman, MT.
    Held the first full weekend of August. This
    famed sweet pea growers' competition fea-
    tures plays, food booths, a parade, and a
    craft area for kids.

Billings Farmers Market
Downtown on Broadway • Billings, MT.
    Held July through mid-September on Sat-
    urday.

Helena Farmers' Market
Memorial Park • Helena, MT.
    Held mid-July through September on Sat-
    urday.

Idaho

Growers Market of Idaho Falls
501 West Broadway • Idaho Falls, ID.
    Held July through September on Saturday
    morning.

Downtown Boise Farmers' Market
8th and Main Street • Boise, ID.
    Held July through September on Wednes-
    day.

Boise Farmers Market
Franklin & Curtis Roads
and 4106 Sand Creek • Boise, ID.
    Held July through September on Saturday
    and Thursday

Twin Falls Farmers Market
K-Mart Parking Lot • Twin Falls, ID.
    Held August through September on Tues-
    day and Saturday.

Wyoming

Casper Farmers' Market
Central Wyoming Fairgrounds
Fairgrounds Road
Casper, Wyoming
    Held mid-August through September on
    Saturday morning.

Colorado

Boulder County Farmers' Market
13th Street between Arapahoe & Canyon
Boulder, CO.
 Held April through November on Saturday and May through October on Wednesday

Washington

Olympia Farmers Market
Market Pavillion • Olympia, WA.

Held Thursday throufh Sunday, April through October. Held Saturday and Sunday November and December.

Vancouver Farmers' Market
5th and Broadway
Vancouver, WA.
 Held April through October on Saturday.

Pike Place Market
85 Pike Street
Seattle, WA.
 Open daily, year-round.

Bulb Farms

Washington Bulb Company
15867 Beaver Marsh Road
Mount Vernon, WA. 98273
1-866-4Tulips (1-866-488-5477)
email: info@tulips.com • www.tulip.com
 Founded by Dutch immigrants William and Helen Roozen in 1947, Washington Bulb Co. is the largest tulip, daffodil and iris grower in the United States. Roozengaarde is the company's two and one-half acre display gardens open to the public. It is open year-round. Call or email for peak bloom information.

Lefeber Bulb Co. &
The Museum of Tulip History
Mount Vernon, WA. 98273

1-800-725-7251
 Also founded by Dutch immigrants, Skagit County's oldest flower bulb farm features 75 varieties of tulip and 40 varieties of daffodils, a display garden, flower shop, picnic area, and a museum of the history of bulb growing in northwest Washington.

Skagit Valley Bulb Farm & Tulip Town
Mount Vernon, WA. 98273
(360) 424-8152 • email:liltulip@fidalgo.net
www.tuliptown.net
 Tulip Town, a collection of artisans, musicians and Skagit Valley businesses, is enjoyed by visitors to this bulb farm. Admission benefits the Children's Hospital of Seattle.

Annual Events

Sweet Pea Festival
Lindley Park • Bozeman, MT.
Held the first full weekend in August

This famed sweet pea grower's competition features Shakespearean plays, a parade, food booths, a juried art fair, dancing, storytelling and a craft area for kids. For information, call the Bozeman Chamber of Commerce at 1-406-586-8286.

Crested Butte Wildflower Festival
Crested Butte, Colorado

For a week in July (dates change, but the festival is typically held at the beginning or middle of the month), this festival features wildflower walks and hikes, photography workshops, classes, tour and slide shows in a beautiful mountain setting. For information, call the Wildflower Festival Office at 1-970-349-2571.

Skagit Valley Tulip Festival
LaConner, Washington

Held in early April, 11 greenhouses and nurseries participate in this well-known festival that includes displays and tours, flower shops, an antique show, sporting events, food booths and music events. For information, call the Skagit Valley Tulip Festival Office at 1-360-428-5959, or visit www.tulipfestival.org.

Vancouver Dahlia Society Annual Show
Van Dusen Botanical Garden
\5251 Oak St. • Vancouver, BC

The top growers from Vancouver Island, the mainland and Washington State compete for "Best of Show" honors in this annual show, which typically displays over 2,000 colorful entries. For further information, email: williamcbeer@telu.net, or contact Betty Girard of the Vancouver Dahlia Society at 604-584-5124.

Oregon Camelia Society Annual Show
Japanese Garden • Portland, Oregon

2001 marks the 69th year of this show, sponsored by the American Camelia Society. For further information, visit ACS' Web site at www.camellias-acs.com, or contact Grace Bayley at 1-503-646-4726.

Mail Order Suppliers

Plant and Seed Catalogues

There are good nurseries and garden centers within driving distance of my house. I buy most of what I need from them, as I want to support small local businesses. However, it is not always possible to find everything I want and need in Jackson Hole, so I rely on trusted mail order companies every year to supply additional items.

Many of these catalogues are free, others may be available for a small fee. Contact the companies to find out how to obtain a copy of their catalog, or ask a gardening friend if she or he has one that you can borrow.

Bluestone Perennials
7211 Middle Ridge Road
Madison, Ohio 44057-3096
Phone: 800-852-5243 • Fax: 440-428-7198
www.bluestoneperennials.com
email: bluestone@bluestoneperennials.com

Bluestone Perennials grows over 1,000 varieties of plants in its three-acres of greenhouses. The company ships over three million plants each spring, and guarantees what it sells. Its well-organized Web site allows you to shop on-line by plant zone, flower color, height, soil conditions, blooming season, etc., helping you select items that will work in your garden.

The Cook's Garden
PO Box 5010
Hodges,SC 29653-5010
Phone: 800-457-9703 • Fax: 1-800-457-9705
www.cooksgarden.com

The Cook's Garden offers organic seeds and supplies for the kitchen gardeners. On-line ordering and print catalogue available.

Evergreen Y. H. Enterprises
Box 17538 • Anaheim, Ca. 92817-7538

Phone/Fax: 714-637-5769
www.evergreenseeds.com
email:eeseeds@aol.com

Evergreen stocks over 200 varieties of Oriental vegetable seeds, most imported, plus a large assortment of Chinese, Taiwanese, Japanese, Thai, Korean and Vietnamese cookbooks.

Burpee
Warminster, PA. 18974
Phone: 800-888-1447 • Fax: 800-487-5530
www. burpee.com

Burpee's was begun by W. Atlee Burpee in 1876. This well-established, reputable company sells a wide selection of flowers, vegetables, herbs, fruits and berries, ground covers, vines and shrubs. It guarantees your plants will arrive in ideal condition for transplanting, or you'll get your money back or replacement plant. Gardening supplies and tools are also stocked by this gardening mail order giant. You may pursue their offerings on-line or request a copy of their catalogue.

Garden City Seeds
778 hwy 93 N
Hamilton, MT 59840
Phone 406-961-4837 • Fax: 406-961-4877
email:seeds@montana.com
www.gardencityseeds.com

Garden City Seeds carries vegetable and flower seed adapted to tough growing conditions, plus a complete line of organically approved fertilizers and pest control products. On-line ordering available.

Good Scents
1308 N. Meridian Road
Meridian, Idaho 83642
Phone: 208-887-1784

Good Scents grows over 400 varieties of potted herbs. All of its plants are propagated by seed, division or cuttings. None are wild harvested, as many wild medicinal herb varieties are endangered. The nursery has particularly nice selections of lavender, rosemary and scented geraniums. A full plant list with descriptions can be obtained by sending $1 to the address above.

High Altitude Gardens
PO Box 1048
Hailey, Id. 83333-1048
Phone: 208-788-4363 (catalog requests)
Fax: 208-788-3452
www.highaltitudegardens.com

High Altitude Gardens specializes in seed varieties from around the world adapted to grow at the company's 6,000-foot mountain location. Over 400 tested varieties are available for sale. High Altitude Gardens founded the International Seed Saving Institute, a non-profit organization dedicated to seed saving. On-line ordering and print catalogue available.

High Country Gardens
2902 Rufina Street
Santa Fe, NM 87505
Phone: 800-925-9387 • Fax: 800-925-0097
www.highcountrygardens.com

High Country Gardens is the mail order arm of Santa Fe Greenhouses. The plants featured in the catalogue are selected for their cold hardiness, easy-to-grow nature, and adaptability to the arid climate of the West. Unless otherwise indicated, plants are frost hardened and ready to plant upon arrival. On-line ordering and print catalogue available.

Johnny's Selected Seeds
Foss Hill Road
Albion Maine 04910
Phone: 207-437-4301 (orders) • 207-437-4357 (customer service)
Fax: 800-437-4290
email:johnnys@johnnyseeds.com
www.johnnyseeds.com

Established in 1973, Johnny's operates its own certified seed trial and research farm to grow and evaluate seed. It sells flower, vegetable, medical and culinary herb seeds. On-line ordering and print catalogue available.

Lingle's Herbs
2055 N. Lomina Avenue
Long Beach, California 90815
Phone: 800-708-0633 • Fax: 562-598-3376

email: Info@linglesherb.com
www.linglesherbs.com

Lingle's informative, on-line catalogue features over 150 plants. The family-owned nursery's plants are organically grown outside instead of greenhoused, factors which the company says "makes for the hardiest, healthiest and safest herbs. When you receive your plants, just put them right in the garden or on a windowsill, with none of the inconvenience of gradually exposing them to real sunlight or hardening off." The company, like all those featured here, guarantees safe delivery.

Mountain Valley Growers
38325 Pepperweed Road
Squaw Valley, California 93675
Phone: 559-338-2775 • Fax: 559-338-0075
email: mvg@spiralcomm.net
www.mountainvalleygrowers.com

In business for 15 years, Mountain Valley Growers is the largest certified organic mail order plant nursery in the United States. The company's plant list numbers over 400 varieties, but they will contract grow anything. You can order a free catalogue from them or save a tree and view their entire catalog on-line.

Nichol's Garden Nursery
1190 North Pacific Highway
Albany Oregon 97321-4580
Phone: 541-928-9280

email: nichols@gardennursery.com

Nichol's carries a large assortment of European and Oriental vegetables and traditional and hybrid flowers, but has primarily earned recognition from it's large selection of more than 200 herb seeds and plants.

Pinetree Garden Seeds
Box 300 • New Gloucester, ME 04260
Phone: 207-926-3400 • Fax: 1-888-52-Seeds
www.superseeds.com

Pinetree offers economical selections of gardening vegetable and herb seeds. In addition to the usual suspects, they feature Oriental, Italian, and Latin American vegetables. Onion sets, seed potatoes, mushrooms and asparagus roots are available. Pinetree also sells soap making supplies, spices, kitchen gadgets, gardening tools, books, and bird, bat and butterfly products. Paper and on-line catalogue.

Seeds of Change
PO Box 15700
Santa Fe, NM. 87506-5700
Phone: 888-762-7333 • Fax: 888-329-4762
email: gardener@seedsofchange.com
www.seedsofchange.com

Seeds of Change' motto is "Goodness from the Ground Up." The farm sells organic seeds grown on its certified organic research farm and by a network of other certified organic family farmers. Flower, herb, and vegetable seeds—

produced without pesticides, herbicides or fungicide—are offered. The company also sells a good selection of sturdy tools, seed starting items, greenhouse equipment, composting items, and a library of useful books. As an added bonus, mail order shoppers can order a selection of the company's organic food products. These include speciality pasta sauces, salad dressings, salsas, rice and grain blends and soup mixes.

Richters Herbs
357 Hwy. 47
Goodwood, Ontario LOC1AO, Canada
Phone: 905-640-6677 • Fax: 905-640-6641
email: info@richters.com
www.richters.com

Richters is one of the largest herb nurseries in North America, offering over 800 varieties of culinary, medicinal and aromatic herbs. Plants, seeds, dried herbs, books and videos are included in the company's offerings. You can browse its on-line catalogue or request that a catalogue be mailed to you.

Ronninger's Seed & Potato Co.
PO Box 307
Ellensburg, WA 98926
Phone: 509-925-6025 • Fax: 800-964-9210
email: potatoes @irish-eyes.com
www.irish-eyes.com

Ronninger's offers the largest selection of

potatoes, garlic, shallots and onions in the US to home gardeners, market growers and garden centers. Their informative catalogue is packed with information and cultivation tips.

Shepherd's Garden Seeds
30 Irene Street
Torrington, CT 06790-6658
Phone: 800-444-6910 • Fax: 860-626-0865
www.shepherdseeds.com

Known for its great selection of European vegetables and herb seeds, Shepherd's also sells flower and fruit seeds, gardening tools and supplies. Renee Shepherd's *Recipes from a Kitchen Garden* is a best seller. Browse through their on-line catalogue or request a printed copy.

The Thyme Garden Herb Company
20546 Alsea Highway
Alsea, Oregon 97324
Phone: 541-487-8671
www.thymegarden.com

This family owned and operated nursery organically grows over 700 varieties of herb plants. It ships well established herbs in 4" pots. Shipping is a bit more expensive, but the company notes that the larger size increases the survival rate of sending plants through the mail. Thyme Garden's 72-page catalog is sort on pictures but long on useful information. It features herb seeds and plants, dried herbs, seasoning and tea blends. To obtain a copy, send a $2 check or money order to the address above.

Gardening Supply Catalogues
Compiled by the Editor

Where can you find the perfect sundial? A gross of ladybugs? A decorative arch or gate? If your local garden center or nursery doesn't have what you're looking for, one of many mail order garden supply or related companies will. The basic list below will get you started. A comprehensive listing—though now somewhat dated—can be found in Barbara Barton's classic *Gardening by Mail*, published by Houghton Mifflin in 1994. At the time of publication, Barton listed virtually every plant and seed catalogue, garden supply company, professional horticulture or gardening association and botanical reference library in existence. It's worth a look.

Alsto's
Box 1267 • Galesburg, IL. 61402-1267
Phone: 800-621-8258 • Fax: 309-343-5785
www.alsto.com

Alsto's carries a nice selection of yard and garden products, including planters, composters, trellises and arbors, tools, sprinklers and gardening apparel. On-line ordering and print catalogue available.

Duncraft, Inc.
102 Fisherville Road
Concord, N.H. 03303-2086
Phone: 800-593-5656 • Fax: 603-226-3735
email:info@duncraft.com
www.duncraft.com

Duncraft is for the birds. They stock bird houses, bird feeders, bird seed , and bird baths. Anything made for our feathered friends can be found at Duncraft. On-line ordering and print catalogue available.

Gardener's Eden
Box 7307 • San Francisco, CA. 94120-7307
Phone: 800-822-9600 • Fax: 415-421-5453

Gardener's Eden sells upper end garden furniture, ornaments and tools. Formerly a division of Williams-Sonoma, the mail order company was recently purchased by Brookstone, which sells hard-to-find tools and gardening supplies, so their offerings may change in the future. Print catalogue.

Gardener's Supply Company
128 Intervale Road
Burlington,VT. 05401
Phone: 800-863-1700 • Fax: 800-551-6712
email:info@gardeners.com
www.gardenerssupply.com

Wide selection of gardening items, including tools,irrigation equipment, greenhouses, fertilizers, pest control, garden furniture, books and decorative statuary, trellises and planters. On-line ordering and print catalogue available.

Indoor Gardening Supplies
Box 527 • Dexter, MI. 48130
Phone: 800-823-5740 (orders only)
Fax: 734-426-7803
www.IndoorGardenSupplies.com

Great source for lights, carts, trays, frames, seed starter kits, meters and timers—basically everything indoor gardeners need to grow plants. On-line ordering and print catalog available.

Kinsman Company
Box 357
Old Firehouse-River Road
Point Pleasant, PA 18950-0357
Phone: 800-733-4146 • Fax: 215-297-0450
www.kinsmangarden.com

Kinsman carries many harder-to-find items, including English window hayracks, topiary forms, patio planters, strawberry jars and living wreath forms. Markers, labels, ornaments, supplies, tools and videos fill their 96-page catalog. On-line ordering also available.

Kitchen Krafts
PO Box 442 • Waukon, IA. 52172-0442
Phone: 800-776-0575 • Fax: 800-850-3093 or 319-535-8001
www.kitchenkrafts.com

Kitchen Krafts offers a broad selection of canning supplies and equipment for food preservation, including water bath and pressure canners, food dehydrators, vacuum sealers, jars and bottles and decorative labels. On-line ordering and print catalogue available.

Landscape USA
PO Box 5382 • Salem, OR. 97304
Phone: 800-966-1033 • Fax: 503-378-1926
www.landscapeusa.com

Landscape USA is one of the leading on-line resources for landscapers, irrigators and gardeners. Plants and seeds, tools, organic amendments, cold frames and greenhouses, bird feeders, statuary and ornaments and garden gifts are part of its large inventory.

Mellingers
2310 West South Range Road
North Lima, OH. 44452
Phone: 800-321-7444 • Fax: 330-549-3176
email:mellgarden@aol.com

www.mellingers.com

In business for over 70 years, Mellingers is now on-line. (Print catalogue available, too.) This comprehensive gardening source sells plants and seeds, trees and shrubs, books, planters, fungicides and insecticides, organic controls, tools and equipment, greenhouses, and just about everything else.

Peaceful Valley Farm Supply
Box 2209
Grass Valley, CA. 95945
Phone: 888-784-1722 • Fax: 530-272-4794
www.groworganic.com

Over 2,000 gardening and farm items, including tools, irrigation supplies, fertilizers, composting equipment, growing and propagation supplies and seed and cover crops. Economical prices. On-line ordering and print catalogue available.

Unique Insect Control
5504 Sperry Drive
Citrus Heights,CA 95621
Phone: 916-961-7945 • Fax: 916-967-7082
email: ladybugs@a-1unique.com
www.a-1unique.com
Unique Insect control is the primary and largest supplier of ladybugs in the US. They also sell other beneficial insects, including lacewings, praying mantis and fly parasites.

Wood Classics
PO Box 291 • Gardiner, NY 12525
Phone: 914-255-7871 • Fax: 914-255-7881
www.woodclassics.com

Wood Classics specializes in fine, handcrafted teak indoor and outdoor garden furniture. It is not inexpensive, but more economical pre-cut kits are also available. Planters, rockers, steamer chairs and loungers, trellises, benches, Adirondack chairs, swings and umbrellas are among the items it manufactures. On-line ordering and print catalogue available.

Herbal and Flower Craft Suppliers
compiled by the editor

San Francisco Herb Company
250 14th Street
San Francisco, CA 94103
Phone: 1-800-227-4530
www.sfherb.com

San Francisco Herb Company sells potpourri ingredients, essential and fragrance oils an potpourri containers. Its Web site features potpourri recipes and directions for herbal wreaths and swags. On-line ordering available. Printable order sheet may be downloaded from Web site. Volume discounts offered.

Craftswholesale.com
1243 Marvin Road NE, Ste. B
Lorey, WA 98516
www.craftswholesale.com

This large on-line business began as a single craft store in Olympia, Washington in 1969. The business now encompasses numerous stores in Washington and its on-line outlet, which stocks over 18,000 items. Here you'll find silica gel and glycerin; wood, wire and grapevine wreath forms; all kinds of base mosses; ribbon, etc. for crafting with your everlastings.

Floral Home
www.floralhome.com

This wholesale on-line company sells bulk herbs and botanicals and a nice selection of beautiful bottles and jars for herbal lotions, vinegars and potpourri.

Soap Crafters
2944 Southwest Temple
Salt Lake City, Utah 84115
www.soapcrafters.com
1-801-484-5121

If you are interested in making herbal bath and body products, this is a great on-line site. Soap Crafters sells molds, fragrances, packaging supplies and instruction books.

Gardening Resources

Informative Web Sites
Compiled by the Editor

The listings that follow feature helpful reference sites offered by horticultural professionals. Because Internet sites change frequently, it is not intended to be all-inclusive, but to serve as a starting point for further information on a wide spectrum of gardening topics. And, of course, to have fun!

www.gardenweb.com
Large site contains a useful glossary of over 2,000 botanical terms; directories of garden-related organizations and businesses; and "The Garden Exchange," where gardeners can post requests for seeds and plants. Presently the top gardening site on both Yahoo and Lycos.

http://garden-gate.prairienet.org
Garden Gate is a selected collection of links to horticulture Internet sites around the world. Particularly useful is their "Teaching Garden," described as "enough glossaries, FAQ's, special topic WWW pages, collections and plant lists to keep the info-junkies among us busy for quite

a while." (And they aren't kidding.) Site also features on-line ordering of a large selection of garden products.

www.gardennet.com
GardenNet is a clearinghouse for gardening publications, wholesale suppliers, public gardens, on-line garden shopping, and catalogue requests for mail order companies. The site also features an extensive information directory for types of gardens, plants and gardening equipment.

www.vg.com
Virtual Garden presently boosts the Web's

largest gardening library as well as forums, tips, a zone finder, yellow pages and an event calendar. It also includes "dig the net," a search engine for gardeners that list pertinent sites.

www.garden.org

Sponsored by the National Gardening Association, this site features a plant name finder, dictionary, articles, industry research, and a national calender of events, among other categories.

www.backyard gardener.com

Billing itself as "your backyard information source," this well-organized site offers clear, helpful information on alpine gardens to vegetable gardens and everything else in-between. A garden forum, classified ads, plant finder and catalogue listings round out the site.

www.twoorganics.com

This is the URL for Terra Viva, perhaps the best site on the Web dedicated to organic gardening. It includes organic growing advice and tips, FAQs, information on organic fertilizers and natural pest controls, featured products and a monthly newsletter.

www.herbnet.com

Comprehensive site for those seeking information on herbs, herb products and remedies. Contains list of associations, articles, uni-versity classes and seminars, herb shops and mail order companies.

www.hortmag.com

Horticulture is the oldest gardening magazine in the country. Articles from this venerable resource are now on-line. In addition to an article archive, the site features excerpts and reviews of new gardening books, a chat archive of past expert discussions, plant and zone finders, and a gardener's "A to Z" resource section of reference links. As a special bonus, *Horticulture* has also included information on its garden tours and trips to Italy, France, England and Ireland. Beware: you may skip the tomatoes in favor or touring Tuscany.

www.gardenguides.com

Billing itself as "a growing guide for gardeners," Garden Guides features easy-to-understand, useful profiles on a large selection of flowers, vegetables and herbs; gardening articles; tips and techniques; and links to other gardening sites.

www. botanical.com

Site features text of *A Modern Herbal* , a comprehensive reference work first published in 1931. The interesting folklore of over 800 herbs and plants are detailed in this hypertext version. Site also includes an index of herbal recipes and poisonous plants.

Recommended Gardening Magazines

There are many gardening and gardening-related periodicals on the market. The ones I consistently find the most useful are:

Country Living Gardener
PO Box 1748 • Sandusky, OH 44871-1748

Fine Gardening
PO Box 5506 • Newton, CT 06470-5506

Horticulture
PO Box 51455 • Boulder, CO 80323-1455

National Gardening
PO Box 52874
Boulder, CO 80322-2874

Organic Gardening
Rodale Press, Inc.
33 E. Minor St.
Emmaus, PA 18098

Recommended Gardening Books

Bradley, Fern Marshall and Barbara Ellis, ed. *Rodale's All-New Encyclopedia of Organic Gardening*. Emmaus, Pennsylvania: Rodale Press, 1992.

Bremness, Lesley. *The Complete Book of Herbs*. New York, New York: Viking Studio Books, 1988.

Cunningham, Sally. *Great Garden Companions*. Emmaus, Pennsylvania: Rodale Press, 1998.

Hiller, Malcolm. *The Book of Container Gardening*. New York, New York: Simon and Schuster, 1991.

McClure, Susan. *Easy Care Perennial Gardens*. Emmaus, Pennsylvania: Rodale Press, 1997.

Michalak, Pat and Cass Peterson. *Rodale's Successful Organic Gardening: Vegetables*. Pownal, Vermont: Storey Communications, 1996.

Sears, Elayne. *Step-by-Step Gardening Techniques*. Pownal, Vermont: Storey Communications, 1996.

Stone, Pat. *Easy Gardening 101*. Pownel, Vermont: Storey Communications, 1996.

Selected Bibliography

Bowell, Michael. "The Art of Container Gardening." *Fine Gardening,* March/April 1992, pp. 31-34.

Buchanan, Rita. "Spring Flowering Bulbs." *Gardener,* Sept./Oct. 1997, pp. 89-95.

Buchanan, Rita. "Dividing Perennials." *Country Living Gardener,* March/April 1996, pp. 83-90.

Craighton, LuAnn. "Butterfly Gardening." *Fine Gardening,* May/June 1992.

Davis, Rosalie. "Flowers for Cutting." *Horticulture,* January 1990, pp. 67-75.

DiSabato-Aust, Tracy. "Deadheading and Cutting Back." *Fine Gardening,* March/April 1992, pp. 44-47.

Galitzki, Dora. "Fertilizer 101." *Martha Stewart Living,* March 1999, pp. 106-110.

Gruenberg, Louise. "Resplendent Potpourri." *The Herb Companion,* Dec./Jan. 1997, pp. 28-31.

McClure, Susan. *The Herb Gardener: A Guide for All Seasons.* Pownal, Vermont: Storey Communications, 1996.

Mastalerz, John. "A Mulch Primer." *Fine Gardening,* Jan./Feb. 1993, pp. 42-45.

Nardozzi, Charlie. "Landscape Fabrics." *National Gardening,* March/April 1992, pp. 31-34.

Rogan, Helen. "Starting Seeds." *Martha Stewart Living,* March 1999, pp. 100-104.

Sears, Elayne. *Step-by-Step Gardening Techniques.* Pownal, Vermont: Storey Communications, 1996

Stone, Pat. *Real Gardeners' True Confessions.* Pownal, Vermont: Storey Communications, 1996

Waters, Marjorie. "Down in the Dirt with Kids." *Horticulture,* March 1993, pp.18-22.

Index

H

hair, human 55
hanging baskets 161
hardening off 4, 39, 74
hardy geraniums 95
hay 44
heirloom seeds 4
Helena Farmers' Market 225
heliopsis 92
heliotrope, purple 83
helipterum 150
hen and chicks 99, 175
herb gardens 136
herbicide, pre-emergent 46
herbs, comfrey 149; culinary 141; dividing
    138; lovage 148; site selection 136;
    starting from seed 137
hollyhocks 87, 169, 173
honesty plant 86
honeysuckle 206; aphids 207
hop vines 215
horseradish 119-120, 145
hoses 7; soaker 42
houndstongue 49
hummingbird, gardens 170, 171; Broad-
    tailed 173; Black-chinned 173; Calliope
    172; Rufous 172
humus 4
hyacinth bulbs 108
hybrid 4

I

Idaho Botanical Garden 220
insecticidal soap 60
International Peace Gardens 221

Irish Spring 55, 202
ivy leafed geranium 162

J

Japanese Garden at Washington Park 221
Johnny jump-ups 175
Johnson's Blue 95
journaling 13

K

kitchen herbs 164, 234
kohlrabi 127

L

ladybugs 61, 215
lamb's ears 100, 137, 150
landscape architect 12
landscape fabric 45
landscaping 184
larkspur 115, 150; scarlet 173
Latin names 5
latitude 2
lavender 150
lawns 184; fall fertilizing 68
leafy spurge 48
Lefeber Bulb Co. & The Museum of Tulip
    History 226
lemon balm 182
lemon thyme 182
lemon verbena 182
lettuce 123; crisphead 123; bibb 124; Boston
    124; butter-head 124; Iceberg 123 loose-
    leaf 124; rocket 125; romaine 124;
    roquette 125
light requirements 8, 33

lilacs 206, 208
lily of the valley 187
lobelia 77, 164
lodgepole pine 199
lovage 148
love-in-a-mist 83, 115
lupine 94
lychnis 94, 173

M

mail order plants 30
Maltese Cross 94
manure 24; tea 25
marigolds 75, 77, 115; dwarf 164
mason sand 128
mice 44
microclimates 32
miniature iris 175
minor bulbs 110
mint 120, 142, 169
Minter Gardens 223
moose 53, 202
morning glory 173
Mother of thyme 175
movement 54
mugo pines 211; dwarf 206
mulch 44
musk thistle 49

N

nasturtiums 162, 164, 169, 173
naturalizing 109
newspaper, as mulch 45
newspaper pots 37
nicotiana 80, 169, 173
nirembergia 82

nitrogen 26, 44
noxious weeds 47

O

Ohme Gardens 221
Olympia Farmers Market 226
onions 120
open pollinated 4
orange mint 182
oregano 143, 150, 164
Oregon Camelia Society Annual Show 227
organic matter 22
Oriental poppies 89, 93, 102
ornamental kale 132
orris root 155
Orthene 208
overhangs 11
oversowing 35
overwintered plants 71
Owen Rose Garden 221
ox-eye daisy 51

P

painted daisy 96
pansy 75, 76, 115, 162
parsley 142, 164
partial shade 8
pasteurized soil mix 38
Patmore Green Ash 199
pearly white Everlasting 150
peas 119
peat moss 23, 24
peat pots, as seed starting containers 36
pencil gardening 13
peonies 115; staking 91
perennials 4, 69, 88

periwinkle 187
perlite 38
pesto 143
petunias 75, 76, 164, 173
phenology 2
phlox 173
phosphorus 26
Pike Place Market 226
pineapple mint 182
pinks 76, 175
planters, unusual 160
plants 29
pocket gophers 105
polystyrene plug trays 36
poppy seeds 103
potassium 26, 128
potatoes, All Red 129; German Butterball
    129; hilling,130; Peruvian Purple 129;
    planting 130; scab 130; speciality 129;
    Yukon Gold potatoes 129
potpourri 154
power veggies 134
pre-emergents 46
pruning 196, 202
pruning shears 8
purple coneflowers 169
pussy willows 200

Q

quaking aspen 199

R

raised bed 118
rake 7
raspberries 212; Canby 212; Honey Queen
    212; Indian Summer 212; Redwing 212

Red Butte Garden and Arboretum 221
Red Leaf Rose 210
red orach 126
red penstemmon 173
Red Twig Dogwood 207
residence proximity 10
Rhododendron Species Botanical Garden
    222
rhubarb 119, 215
Richters Herbs 140, 231
Rio Grande Botanic Garden 218
rock cress 175
rock gardens 174
root bound 39
rootstock, iris 103
rose campion 87
rose hips 210
rosemary 137, 143, 164, 182

S

Safer's soap 60
sage 143, 164
salt 11; as slug control 58
salvia 169; red 173
sapiglossis 82
sawdust 22, 44
scabiosa 82, 115
scarlet runner beans 173
scent, as wildlife control 55
sedum 175, 187; Autumn Joy 90
seed, selecting 31; starting 35
seedling s 29, 37, 134
serviceberry 207
shovel 7
shrub roses 209; Theresa Bugnet 210;

trowel 7
tuber 103
tulips 107, 110, 115, 164
Twin Falls Farmers Market 225

U

Uinta ground squirrel 53
Unique Insect Control 234
University of British Columbia Botanical
    Garden 223
University of Idaho Arboretum and Botanical
    Garden 222
unusual Planters 160
Utah State University Botanical Garden 222

V

Vancouver Dahlia Society Annual Show 227
Vancouver Farmers' Market 226
vegetable gardens 117; watering 122
verbena 162, 169
vermiculite 38
veronica (speedwell) 95
Victoria Butterfly Gardens 224
vinca 164; minor 187
violas 164
vitamin C 128, 134
voles 44, 105, 202

W

Washington Bulb Company 104, 226
watering 41; container gardens 158; veg-
    etables 122
weeds, control 43; noxious 47
wheelbarrow 7
whiskey barrels 159
white gardens 179

White Nancy lamnium 181
wildflower gardens 166
wildflower seeds 166-167
wildlife control measures 54
wildlife problems 52
wildlife signals 15
window boxes 162
winter aconite 175
winterizing 67
wire stem 38
wood ash 23, 25
wood chips 44
woolly thyme 137
worms 63
wormwood 150
wreaths, herbal 152

X

xeranthenum 150

Y

yarrow 115, 150; 154
yellow alyssum 175

Z

zinnias 115, 169
zone ratings 32

There can be no other occupation like gardening in which, if you were to creep up behind someone at their work, you would find them smiling.

—

Mirabel Osler